Russian Religious Philosophy

1989-1990 Lectures

by

Fr. Aleksandr Men'

Translated by Fr. S. Janos

Russian Religious Philosophy

frsj Publications
Fr. Stephen J. Janos
P.O. Box 210
Mohrsville, PA 19541

Contents

Dedicated to the 25th Year Memory of

Fr. Aleksandr Men'

† 9 September 1990

The Predecessors of Vladimir Solov'ev

It will be 90 years soon, since the death of the great Russian philosopher, Vladimir Sergeevich Solov'ev. And at the beginning of this year I conducted a television interview from the room, where he reposed. He died on the estate of Prince Sergei Trubetskoy, likewise a remarkable philosopher and publicist, a rector of the Moscow University, and a close friend of Vladimir Solov'ev. At present this room has been remade into a billiard-parlour, and prior to this I went there on the sly, in order to serve a panikhida memorial service at the place of death of a great thinker. During the time of the television interview we floated the question, whether the room might be transformed into a memorial place. And you know, actually, that "Uzkoe" belongs to the Academy of Science, the rest home of the Academy of Science is situated there, and thus also upon this organisation depends the deciding of the question of a memorial room. Back in the decade of the 1920's was decided the question, to whom would be put memorials at Moscow and Leningrad, and on this list of philosophers was put the name Solov'ev, true, and then they crossed him out.

It is difficult to say, who Solov'ev was. He was a philosopher, but along with this he was a theologian, a sociologist, a critic, political. A person indeed universal! And in this regard he is actually similar to Pushkin. It is as though there happened some sort of a creative explosion within him.

But just as Pushkin appeared not by chance, not from out of nowhere, so too Solov'ev had a great preliminary history. And just as Pushkin was preceded by Archpriest Avvakum, Sumarokov, Fonvizin, Derzhavin, Lomonosov, so too Solov'ev was preceded by the growth of the philosophic and religious ideas of the XVIII-XIX Centuries. He summed up much of what was found there, and probed into what was revealed. But insofar as quite much has been written about this period, I shall speak but briefly.

Vladimir Solov'ev set in place the foundations for the unique, and I would say, unrepeatable Russian religious philosophy of the XX Century, which in itself includes such names, as Sergei Bulgakov, Nikolai Berdyaev,

Semeon Frank, Pavel Florensky, Nikolai Lossky and indeed very many others. I repeat -- a veritable explosion! And again -- such an entire Pleiade, an enormous current, which was cut short by the stormy events of war and revolution. The greater part of the members of this movement wound up abroad. And again at present their names return to us anew. But what however does Russian philosophy itself represent, why til now does it evoke wonder? And why is it necessary for us to know it, or at least, have some sort of idea about it?

Let us consider three elements: those who preceeded Solov'ev, Solov'ev himself, and those, who are derived from him, like the wellsprings of a river. Today I concentrate on the predecessors of Solov'ev. I have to ask your pardon for my being brief, because cramming a thousand years of the history of thought into a small space is difficult enough.

Already way back during its first stages the old Kievan Rus' culture had its writers, its preachers and thinkers appear, making the first attempts to ponder the verymost complex problems of existence.

In the XI Century Metropolitan Ilarion posits quite sharp theological questions, in particular, the question as regards law and grace. This is a very important question. All the religions of antiquity were somehow or other were grounded upon law. The law -- is something we have a grasp of: a system, a structure, wherein this is prohibited, this is allowed. When we begin to teach children, we say to them: this must not be done, and then too this must be done. And therefore law as a form of religious life is inevitable at the beginning of the developement of a culture. But there comes a moment, when another world opens up. Law permits and it forbids. But in grace is revealed the wellspring of a new power. Here already there is no prohibition, which would land the human will in chains or set up barriers for it, here instead is an immanent an inner power, which impels it to creativity, to good, to beauty, to self-renunciation. Here is that antithesis between law and grace, which Solov'ev later so brilliantly revealed in his book, "The Spiritual Foundations of Life", -- and a mere 70 years after the Baptism of Rus', way back still in the XI Century, Metropolitan Ilarion was pondering over it in his "Discourse on Law and Grace". This cannot be called a book, this is a "discourse", a small essay, as we might term it. He writes, that this is addressed not to ignorant people, but to people, who understand the point of the question, to educated people. Already back then he had a serious audience, with whom he could speak about such complex things.

But after this, Russian religious thought was expressed primarily along a moral direction, through brilliant preachings, modeled upon Byzantine works, the sermons, say, of Smolyatich or Kirill of Surozh. And questions herein were put forth, very important for human life, concerning -- what is good and what is evil. Questions, which are always essential.

Likely perhaps, you remember the Tarkovsky film, "Andrei Rublev". Faced with all these tragedies of Russian life, both the simple peasant, and the prince, were compelled to ponder -- what is the purpose of man, where is the truth, and where the lie, towards what ought we to look for. And when we imagine, that they were dealing too lightly with these questions, we are then mistaken. They understood all this no worse than us, actually even better, since our age has arrived at the foolish notion (foolish in the bad sense of the word) -- that morality and ethical norms -- are not something traditional, but rather something that people have merely fabricated, they merely agreed upon an arrangement, that this is good, and that this is not good. But amidst such a relativism of morality, things quickly start going to pieces, and suddenly it shows, that the whole of society has stood upon this foundation, and without it things get topsy-turvy, and collapse.

All of us today are witnesses of this terrible process. But people in the Middle Ages (or as they say nowadays, the "obscure Dark Ages"), they indeed did understand, that when man transgresses against the commandments of God, he is not simply breaking some sort of concordat or agreement, he instead is violating the moral world-order, the objective moral world-order, and as they tended to say in the old days, he "kicks against the pricks".

I want to turn your attention to this, that these commandments are given us namely because they call for the best, that is in man. They foresee the possibility of other dark elements arising within people. We indeed have no commandments to "eat", or "drink", or "walk", since these things are natural for us. But how to conduct oneself, so as to spread the good, so as to avoid vileness -- is not something necessarily innate within man.

The history of the XX Century, during which moral values were demolished, has shown, to what depths of beastliness men can sink, when they are contemptuous of the principal commands of God. But way back when already the old Russian thinkers were speaking about this selfsame command. None of them were mere theoretical men, and if we look at their biographies, at their lives, we shall then see, that they were struggling for real, in real life, within history, within the context of history, for the realisation of these moral principles.

The great historian Kliuchevsky called the Monk Sergei [of Radonezh] the "graced nourisher of the spirit of the people". And in actual fact, the people were situated many a decade already under the heel of a foreign conqueror, and they certainly did receive painful blows too in the moral sphere; there was a period of decline, but the Monk Sergei by his effort, by his example, by his spirit (and indeed spirit -- this is what is spread forth!) contributed to the renewal. The renewal occurred later in the activities of many of his students and in the creativity of one of the greatest of iconographers, Andrei Rublev, whom the Monk Sergei surely knew; for in any case, the "Holy Trinity" icon is dedicated to him.

Later on begins the period of the Moscow tsardom. Altogether a sorry state of affairs: fighting against the Asiatic onslaught, the incursions of Asiatic despotism, the Moscow realm itself to a certain degree adopted the methods and principles of an Asiatic despotism. And here against this despotism there rise up figures of a spiritual enlightenment. Metropolitan Philip (XVI Cent.) -- is a man, whose history would make any people proud. Some of you, surely, have seen the film, "Ivan the Terrible" by Eisenstein, the second part, where Metropolitan Philip was presented as a conniving man of ambition, who wanted to get a grip of power over the soul of the tsar. This is a fiction, inaccurate and improper! Philip was a monk and had never wanted to occupy the primal-hierarch's cathedra-seat at Moscow; he became metropolitan (head of the Russian Church) only on the condition, that he would receive the right to intercede for those suffering repression, the honourary right to "bespeak a grievance". And Philip did not meddle in affairs of state, but he unrelentingly rebuked the tsar, face to face and publicly. He considered this as his duty and he distinctly knew, how all this might end (it should need no explaining to you, what sort of an atmosphere prevailed at the time and throughout all the Moscow realm). Metropolitan Philip died a martyr: he was deposed, arrested, imprisoned in a monastery, where he was later suffocated by Maliuta Skuratov. And his death was not by accident.

Ivan the Terrible went to Novgorod, in order to crush the final outpost, as I term it, of Russian democracy. The historian Georgii Petrovich Fedotov emphasised, that the despotism, as embodied in Ivan the Terrible, was by no means the sole tradition in ancient Russian history. Novgorod in the northern region had within it the inceptions of a people's sovereignty, and moreover, quite developed. And therefore it was not by accident that the army of Ivan the Terrible went to Novgorod, as against an enemy, in order to wipe it off the face of the earth. Even the Novgorod bell, summoning gatherings of the people -- to the Veche, the People's assembly, was taken away! Along the way Maliuta Skuratov headed off to the monastery, wherein Metropolitan Philip was, and he besought of him a blessing for this campaign. The saint refused and was strangled by this executioner of Ivan the Terrible.

In this same era, during the times of Ivan the Terrible, within our Trinity Lavra-monastery was imprisoned Maksim the Greek, one of the most consequential theologians of the XVI Century, -- a translator, a philologist, polemicist, writer, one who had received an humanistic education, who had lived in Italy, in the monastery of Saint Mark, one who had heard the preachings of the noted Florentine leader -- the monk Girolamo Savonarola. He had journeyed to Rus' to make corrections in books and he got drawn into the struggle of two church factional parties.

These two parties had likewise a direct influence on the formative process of Russian religious thought. The adherents of the one party were called Josephites (after Iosif Volotsky). The Josephites pushed for the social effectiveness of the church, for its close connection with the state, for its free rein to make use of methods of repression -- the methods of crushing dissent. Against these views stood the "Non-Possessors" (termed thus, since they were against monastery landholdings), and at their head stood Saint Nil Sorsky: they expressed quite precisely the view, that the execution of dissenters is improper. And between these two currents there arises conflict. Maksim the Greek comes out on the side of the Non-Possessors. He is brought to trial, where he is under suspicion of heresy, and handed over to the torture-chambers. There are various proceedings, slanderous accusations -- and then he dies at the Lavra of Sergiev Posad, where at present his tomb is situated.

Maksim the Greek brought to Rus' primal elements for an understanding of Holy Scripture. For Christian religious thought this is very important, since up til now people often, in opening the Bible, begin reading it simply as an ordinary book, and they think, that all the world consists in what they see on the surface. But contrary to such a perspective, Saint Maksim showed how semantically complex is the structure of the Bible, how multi-faceted, which thus demands various approaches to it.

Any deeply profound work is semantically complex, but the Bible -- is particularly so.

In the XVII Century begins the encounter of Russia with the West. But just as in our own day, the encounters often occur not upon scientific a plane, at this first level there do not emerge the lofty values of Western culture, but rather moreso elementary lifestyle aspects and technical matters. This enabled an expansion of mercantile trade, and political alliances. However, Russian and Western spiritual elites remained in a serious mutual estrangement (except for unique figures, such as Naschokin).

Tsar Peter I forces a break-through -- roughly, shattering old traditions, bearing enormous harm to the culture. But then nonetheless, a new era of the culture is created, and we have no right to be indifferent and scornful towards it. Because, if there had not been this Peterburg period of the Russian empire, we would not have had either Lomonosov, or Pushkin, or Dostoevsky, or Tolstoy, or Blok.

During the XVIII Century the problem of faith and knowledge comes to face Russian thinkers. Back during the XVII Century there had occurred an explosion of science. The XVII Century -- this was the century of the creation of classical physics, the mechanical aspects, and it became imperative for philosophy to find a synthesis between scientific discoveries and the spiritual perspective. This synthesis was not only possible, but also organically it entered into the thinking of the founders of classical physics. And particularly for Galileo there was no sort of problem in this, as to how Scripture correlates with astronomy and mathematics. He straight out said, literally: "The Bible teaches us, how to get to Heaven, and not about how the heavens turn". Which is to say, he separated the purely scientific and rational problems from the spiritual ones. And Kepler thought precisely the same. He said, that seeking in the Bible to establish the facts of the knowledge of nature, -- is simply a misuse of the Holy Book, which was written for altogether different purposes. This same problem however became all the more acute in the XVIII Century, when scepticism and mechanistic materialism began intensively to develope, the materialism of Diderot, Holbach, Voltaire particularly, although he was not a materialist in the strict sense of the word.

All this arrived in Russia. But not only this. Lomonosov found in Western Europe not only scepticism, he found also suchlike people, who had been able to combine knowledge and faith into a single synthesis, in the philosopher [Christian] Wolff especially. Lomonosov wrote, that the Creator gave man two books: in one of them He manifested His wisdom, and this book -- is nature, whereas in the second one He revealed His will, and this Book -- is the Bible. Further on he wrote: "Unbalanced gets judged the scholar, who recourses to the Psalter to discern the laws of the world". And in actual fact, to man has been given reason, and man ought to strive at comprehending the world edifice, but Revelation is oriented rather towards such dimensions of being, which are inaccessible to purely rational analysis. The struggle between reason and the intuitive, between reason and faith -- is abnormal a phenomenon. This is a conflict, destructive of the integral wholeness of man! And this is because man was created with dual an aspect. Man was created as a being, who lives by both the heart, and by the mind. Get rid of either of these, -- and the image of man becomes distorted. The task is one of harmonisation: in human physiology they have established, that by these two ways of cognition there is a governing of life by two hemispheres, and when the coordinative balance between their activities is broken, there occur distortions to the human psychical state. "The dreaming of reason begets monsters", the dreaming of the heart -- likewise, and in even more frightful forms.

The unity of the will, of reason, of the senses in man -- this is the ideal, and not only in everyday life, this is the ideal also in cognition and in science. And Lomonosov was striving towards this, while constantly deflecting attacks by the pseudo-theological, who reproached him for trying to penetrate into the secrets of nature. Lomonosov in irony wrote: "What sense is there for the erudite to have questions, as to how is this or some other formation arranged or how does this or some other process occur, and merely to answer: "God created it thus -- and that is all there is to it". For him it was clear, that God had created it thus, but indeed he wanted to know, how this was arranged, how He had created it. And Lomonosov reckoned himself fully justified to actively move forward in his knowledge, as far as reason might allow. And the more he penetrated into the secrets of matter, the more he understood about them, the more he then came closer to ponderings about the Creator and Fashioner. You all surely remember his learning-selection of verse, "An evening pondering on the grandeur of God amidst an occurrence of the auroral great northern lights". In this verse Lomonosov advances several hypotheses as to what the northern lights are, and what in general occurs from the coelestial bodies. He says, that the holy fathers of old, Basil the Great and others, had written about the logical reason, which is lodged within nature (or as we might now say -- codified within nature), and he comes to this conclusion: indeed how much more would they have had the right to speak thus, if they had been endowed with our instruments, our theories, our methods! In continuing with the thought of Lomonosov, I would say, that from the XVIII Century the world has advanced still further, and the universe which we now conceive of, has become extremely more complex, and consequently, quite moreso demands investigation. The more complex it has become in our eyes, all the more mysteried becomes its primal foundations.

At the same time as Lomonosov there lived another thinker, a remarkable man (likewise very alone), a God-wanderer -- Grigorii Savvich Skovoroda, an Ukrainian seer. (Incidentally, Vladimir Sergeevich Solov'ev -- was one of his descendants.) At his tomb is written: "The world chased me, but did not catch me". The monks both wanted to entice him, and at the Academy they pulled at him, but he was a free-spirited man, he withdrew from everywhere, he wandered about with his knapsack and books, and he wrote his paltry rhymes, his deliberations, his ponderings. Skovoroda arrived at thoughts, which had not concerned Lomonosov. For Lomonosov precise and clear thinking, with rational comprehension sufficed, in order to grasp the ultimate reality. But Skovoroda sensed, that this was insufficient, that there was needed something other (he did not use the word "intuition"), that there was necessary a different, -- a deep and spiritual approach, that the reality of God is revealed as it were by other paths. Skovoroda detected and exposed those people, like Emel'yan Yaroslavsky (already closer to our time)[1], who took from the Bible only the externals and then exclaimed: what an empty waste of time! Yet all this was foreseen, and was predicted by Grigorii Savvich Skovoroda.

The XIX Century begins. A malign crisis shakes Russian civilisation, or more accurately expressed, the elite of the civilisation, the predecessors of the Russian intelligentsia (back then, these were basically people from the aristocratic segment). They begin to feel, that the official state Church, which under Peter I had been enslaved, which had been engrafted onto the state mechanism, does not satisfy them. Why? Because the love of freedom had already set deep roots among the people, and this

---

[1] translator note: Emel'yan Yaroslavsky (1878-1943), Communist revolutionary and leader of the militant anti-religious league.

love of freedom became embodied within the spirit of thinking people. Novokov, Radischev (end XVIII Cent.) already had been smitten over the sufferings of mankind. And beyond the normal churchly paths they began to search in philosophy, and the mystics: they seek for them in occultism, in theosophy, in Masonism, in the cult of folly... These were intense searchings. You remember, there is the scene in "War and Peace", when Pierre Bezukhov enters into the masonic lodge. This was not merely a chance matter inserted by Tolstoy -- Pierre was one of many, who searched paths non-churchly. This sort of people -- is it possible to understand them? It is indeed possible, since the church as an institution had gotten bogged down in a very grave state of affairs, entangled from all sides by the aims of the government departments. And this mistrust for it became an enormous tragedy, it introduced a splintering wedge between the churchly tradition and the incipient intelligentsia.

During the early XIX Century there begins the search for contact with the philosophic currents of the West. Who was it, that influenced the Russian philosophy of the XIX Century? First of all, -- Schelling. Over the course of an entire century his influence was enormous -- both directly, and indirectly. Peter Yakovlevich Chaadaev personally knew Schelling, Tiutchev was friends with Schelling, Vladimir Solov'ev based himself upon Schelling, and from Schelling, possibly, Bulgakov took his start.

There was also another influence -- the influence of Hegel, -- and perhaps less positively so (in part, because they assimilated Hegel in very distorted a form -- though also, because no one ever understood him, and even Hegel himself said: "Only my one student has understood me, and that one incorrectly so!"). When they said to Hegel: "There are facts, which contradict your theories", he replied: "then all too bad for the facts". He was unique a man, unique a thinker, and his influence upon Russian thought was, regretably, moreso on the negative side. They tended to find in him things, it seems, that were not in him. Belinsky was very fascinated with Hegel, yet without having read a single line (indeed both because Hegel had not been translated into the Russian language in the last century, and because Belinsky did not know the German language).

In the first half of the XIX Century there arose two currents, the representatives of which are customarily termed Slavophils and Westernisers. And here indeed we can already say, that genuine religious thought begins a process of self-consciousness. The early Slavophils (Khomyakov, Kireevsky) came out in opposition to the trends in rationalism and they speak about the mystical roots of philosophy. They consider, amidst this, that such an approach of truth -- is something intuitive, profound, non-rational -- and is possible only within the Slavic culture. They created a special philosophy of the Slavic people, searching back into its antiquity. Khomyakov attempted to sketch out a philosophy of history upon this basis, but he did not complete his work. The Westernisers, on the contrary, rightly reckoning that Russia -- is part of Europe, tend in fact to disdain everything in their past and they instead orientate themself upon progress, enlightenment, science, technology. Belinsky, who was a typical Westerniser, as they report, trudged his way outside into the square (which we now call the Komsomolsk) and there he gazed upon "the great work of the age" that they had built there, -- the Nikolaev (present-day Leningrad) train station. In this edifice he felt, so to speak, was the breath of the coming industrial age, and he, poor fellow, reveled in the spectacle.

The Westernisers were under the seductive influence of the utopias of progress. Among them was Hertsen, a romantic and utopian, who became deeply disillusioned in his own utopia. He got no farther than scepticism and Feuerbach. But at some particular moment he realised, that within this utopia a free person would suffocate, that social progress -- this is a Moloch, which devours its children, and an end to this occurrence is not to be seen. And at last he finally states: and why is it stupid to believe in God? Why instead necessary to believe in man? Why necessary to believe in progress? And he, this great utopian and romantic, thus suffered a severe moral shock. He was a man of brilliant philosophic talent, but a philosophical system he did not create, he assembled fragmented materialistic doctrines, and ultimately that was that.

In whom had these two paths remained still conjoined? In Peter Yakovlevich Chaadaev, -- one of the greatest thinkers in Russia in the first half of the XIX Century. When he wrote his book, "Philosophic Letters", the first article (the first chapter, the first letter) was published in a journal. You know, surely, what a scandal this caused: the journal was shut down, the editor fired, and Chaadaev himself declared a madman, though he did not get dragged off to an insane asylum. And why was this reaction? Because with this chapter he had wanted to awaken the awareness of his readers! He wrote bitter, severe words about the stagnation, which had overtaken society.

Chaadaev was a great patriot. He did not feel, that the West is absolute an ideal, but he also did not feel, as did certain of the Slavophils, that it is necessary to return back to the pre-Petrine era. Chaadaev stood as it were for the principle of balance, of harmony: he said, that the land, situated between Asia and Western Europe, between East and West, is capable of uniting the two perspectives, and not only the perspectives, but also the realisation of the ideal upon earth. To his book he wrote an epigraph from the "Our Father" prayer: Thy Kingdom come, Thy Will be done on earth, as it is in heaven. He felt, that the Christian ideal is not something abstract, not beyond the grave, not up in the clouds, but the rather is earthly: Christ brought it to earth, so that people should make it happen! And Chaadaev asserted, that this is possible only through the uniting into a single current the Western activeness and the Eastern depth of contemplation. And he suggested, that this synthesis is possible especially in his own country. In Russia his book was not published. It came out abroad, but it was only two years ago that it was published in full. From 1830 to 1987 there has elapsed so very, very many years. But now, when one gets to read this book, one is astonished at the depth of insight of this thinker. One of his basic, very profound ideas consists in this, that any civilisation, if it wants to be healthy and growing, is necessarily bound to have a spiritual and religious foundation -- that inner impulse, which tends to guide it. A civilisation, built only upon worldly and material conditions, tends inevitably to go into decline and decay. And these words got proven correct, I think, with each generation -- both in ours, and all over the world.

Chaadaev is one of the most direct predecessors of Solov'ev. He lived in Moscow, at Basmann, and he died, surrounded with the aura of being a madman, an eccentric, a regular at the English Club (the Museum of Revolution is there now). He was, as you know, a friend of Pushkin, and he much wanted to attract Aleksandr Sergeevich to questions of historiosophy, to German philosophy, to the religious philosophy of Schelling.

And further on there occurs a new split. Slavophilism loses its religious grounding and passes over into its worldly phase. Danilevsky and others -- there is here only the mundane national and historiosophic approach. The Westernisers shed their romanticism and change into preachers of social utopias. Here we have Dobroliubov, Chernyshevsky, and Pisarev. Certain of them begin to be activists: Nechaev, Bakunin.

Bakunin -- was a materialist, an atheist. His is a philosophy of destruction. But all the same he is drawn to freedom. It must be said, that this sowing of the anarchistic model into Russian philosophy was something serious, and not only among such unbalanced people like Bakunin (a man passionate, with very tragic a fate), but also people profound, of rank, such as Peter Kropotkin, who adopted this "truth". And from where did they get it? From the Slavophils! Khomyakov said, that every state governance -- is evil, and every ruling power -- is based upon coercive violence. Khomyakov taught, that the tsar's power of authority receives its sanction from the people. And this was indeed an untraditional point of view. Khomyakov wrote, that in actual fact at the basis of Christianity -- is freedom, and the in-common oneness of people, which is the Church -- is Sobornost' and spiritual an unity. Certainly, this was the ideal. And certainly, this was not the earthly and empirical reality. And it is not surprising, that Khomyakov had to have his books published in the "foreign-press" -- in Russia the censor would have prohibited their publication. Nevertheless, the ideas about freedom, about the dignity of value of the person, about Sobornost', about the possibility of the realisation upon earth of the Christian ideal -- all these ideas remained alive and tended still to find their followers.

Moreover, many of the Russian utopianists had come from families of the clergy, from the seminaries. Having lost their faith under the influence of a vulgar and primitive materialism (on the type of Buechner, of Moleschott) and parroting the words of Bazarov: "Nature is not a church, but rather a workshop, and man is a worker in it", they contained an enormous moral pathos. And surely, many of you have read Nabokov's "The Gift" ["Dar"]. This is a book, which includes in it a satirical biography of Chernyshevsky. And when one reads it, a bit nasty towards Nikolai Gavrilovich, it is because Nabokov -- is a man, bereft of spirituality, though also possessed of great talent, and is very shallow in comparison with the hapless Chernyshevsky, who was given to having various fantastic ideas, and holding onto them with great heroism.

All these contradictions created also the prerequisite settings for the emergence of Vladimir Solov'ev as a philosopher. Into his philosophy were mixed in the idea of synthesis from Chaadaev, and the emancipatory idea from Chernyshevsky, and the conviction that socialism in some varied forms is possible (this Solov'ev likewise took from them), and an absolute opposition to the materialistic doctrine (this he took from the Slavophils and from all the original Christian philosophic tradition), and the idea about the especial role of Russia, situated at the intersection of the Western and Eastern worlds, and the thought concerning the possibility or impossibility to strive towards this, -- that the Christian ideal be not merely abstract, a diversion, but rather that it might be vitally alive, a life-creating force.

This pathos, inherent within Vladimir Solov'ev, had been engendered throughout the course of the whole developement of Russian religious thought, and it took on flesh at that moment, when in 1874 in the auditorium of the Moscow University a long-haired young man defended his master's dissertation in philosophy. It had the title, "The Crisis of Western Philosophy", with the sub-heading, "Against Positivism" (i.e. basically against materialism). Solov'ev faced a literal swarm of opponents, they were all materialist-positivists, but he bested them all brilliantly! And they were compelled, having been impressed with the energy and clarity of thought of the young dissertation defender, to grant him status and offer him the possibility to occupy a professional chair at Moscow University. Thus began the activity of Vladimir Solov'ev. And thus opens a completely new stage within the history of Russian religious thought.

8 October 1989

Vladimir Sergeevich Solov'ev

Almost 90 years have passed since the day Solov'ev (1853-1900) died, and it is also 70 years since we had the last printing of his works. His theoretical works were published during the time of the First World War, and that was it! Then in 1921, with but meagre a circulation, there came out verses. Later on, the verses emerged moreso in the years following -- during the "time of stagnation". And only at present has there appeared a two-volume set. Moreover, I fear that hardly even five percent of those present here have been successful in getting this two-volume set...

I repeat once more: Vladimir Solov'ev had predecessors, who looked into the various sides and problems of human life. And Solov'ev was one, who like Lomonosov, tended to combine within himself all of this. He was an excellent poet, he was a remarkable translator. He was a man, who elucidated the problems of knowledge, he wrote about nature, about love, about social and political problems. He was a sharp and feckless literary critic, publicist, societal activist, churchly writer. He was a commentator on the Bible, a translator of Plato and Biblical Old Testament texts. He was an author of books, which can be considered an authentic introduction into the Christian life. In particular, I have in mind his book, "The Spiritual Foundations of Life" -- concise, clear, polished, precise, it reveals as it were the quintessence of whole books about the basic principles of Christianity. And at the same time, he -- was an activist, he -- was a forerunner of the Ecumenical Movement devoted to the bringing together of Churches.

He was a man of extraordinary seriousness, and at the same time, he loved joking, he wrote parodies, punning words, satirical verses. He left after him twelve sizeable volumes on various works plus four volumes of correspondence. And up to the present all sorts of more things are being discovered, which were not included in the collected works. And this man died at a mere forty-seven years of age (he was 10 years older, than Pushkin). Moreover, he began his activity at quite young an age, challenging the whole cultural and philosophic tradition.

15

Vladimir Sergeevich was born into the family of a noted historian. I presume, that the name of Sergei Solov'ev is familiar to all of you. He lies buried at the Novodevichi Cemetery, and on his tomb are inscribed the words of the Apostle about how he had run his course, finished his effort, and preserved his faith, and had now a crown prepared for him. Sergei Solov'ev was a man, totally immersed in his work. Strictly speaking, nothing was more important to him in life than his grandiose work: giving university lectures and the writing of that immense multi-faceted book, which received the title, "History of Russia" (we had a reprint of it not so long ago). The Solov'ev family was very talented, and with interesting roots. On his mother's side, Vladimir Solov'ev derived in part from Polish ancestry, partly from Ukrainian, and involved kinship also with the noted Ukrainian wanderer, the seer Grigorii Savvich Skovoroda (XVIII Cent.). And his father was a priest-son, hence a descendant of clergy lineage. The grandfather of Vladimir Solov'ev, Mikhail, served as a parish priest, and the future philosopher revered faithfully his memory.

Vladimir Solov'ev underwent the crisis of atheism, the crisis of God-struggle. Once even as a mere boy, he threw his icon out the window. (You have to understand, though, how the times were different back then!)

Vladimir Solov'ev was born in the year 1853. His youthful thought, his early maturity occurred during the era of the sixties, the era of Chernyshevsky, Dobroliubov, the fascination with Pisarev. An instance is known of, when the young Vladimir Solov'ev at the dinner-table declared to his father that he had read Feuerbach's book, "The Essence of Christianity", and stating that "he sure tears apart and makes an end to Christianity!" But his father avoided arguing with his son, and simply said: "there are things one tugs one's ear at". And why did he do this? Right off he decided, that the boy would reach it all by himself. And he perceived, that soon this lanky long-haired youth, with his dark locks of hair down to his shoulders (he wore his hair long as a sign of protest, revolutionary-like) would turn to the study of philosophy. The sharp mind appeared in him early. As proved by the brilliant dissertation he wrote, when he was but little more than twenty years old.

Solov'ev goes on to study the philosophy of Spinoza, of Schopenhauer, of the foremost thinkers of Europe. And very quickly he forms his own particular conception of the developement of philosophic thought. First of all, he discards materialism... But I said "discards" -- and this is imprecise an expression. Actually, Vladimir Solov'ev from the time of his youth til the final years of his life followed a principle, once spoken by the philosopher and mathematician Leibnitz. Leibnitz said: "A man is always incorrect, when he goes negative, especially so the philosopher; and any doctrine, any teaching becomes weakest particularly in this, in that it be negative". This was a chief principle in the life and thinking of Solov'ev.

Upon whatever he turned his mental attention: upon socialism or a teaching about revolution, upon the developement of the Old Believers or the fate of Russia, -- Solov'ev always took from it something of value, he understood, that there is nothing under the light of day merely useless and fruitless, his thinking worked along the lines of what he himself called "all-unity". This word is rich in meaning, but for us in the given instance it might signify the splendid mental ability of Solov'ev to construct and synthesise. And yes indeed, he certainly did polemicise much, he came out much with articles and even whole books against his intellectual opponents. But not a single one of his opponents, whom he smote, did he leave merely for dead -- he always took from him something, which he regarded valuable. And in suchlike a manner, very quickly he constructed a synthesis of thought. His was an open mindset. And this impressed the university professors.

During this period, in the 70's of the XIX Century, positivism was the ruling trend. This is a teaching, similar and close to materialism, though not entirely identical with it. It was a teaching, that the ultimate truths, the final mysteries (the mystery of God, of immortality, the soul) are unknowable for man, that man knows only nature, and nature -- is the natural reality graspable by us, and the developement of thought and philosophy consists ultimately, -- in the developement of science, in the knowledge of the natural realm. Everything prior to this, positivism considered outmoded (just as, we might say, outmoded for modern technology are the old-fashioned instruments of production, the tools for work). And here, having completed university study, the young Solov'ev hurls a challenge to the professors. At first he occupied himself at university with the naturalist trend; nature-knowledge interested him, but as a thinker (already he had matured as a thinker) what attracted him was the major mysteries of the world, and nature-knowledge was only one of the bricks of the enormous edifice, which he constructed.

He gets his teaching chair. The darkly dovelike gaze, the thick black brows, the gauntly drawn face, the long locks of hair as I have already said falling to his shoulders, an almost icon-like face, thin as with an awkward youth, producing a puzzling and strange impression! And during those years, when he was teaching, he journeyed also to us at Sergiev Posad, and there he gave some lectures on theology and philosophy (freely attended). And even there, where people with long hair were nothing out of the ordinary, he produced a somewhat mysterious impression. For a certain while he was here in this city, he lived with us at the Lavra, and there he found it pleasant. The theologians and monks loved him, and later even the students, when he had attained reknown, and half seriously half ironically he would distribute in small bottles the water, in which he had washed his hands, and said: this is "Vladimir Solov'ev water".

With what was Solov'ev involved in his dissertation? It was sub-titled "Against the Postivists" ("The Crisis of Western Philosophy" -- was the title of this book). And suchlike was the power of his thought (but, as mustneeds be said, there was also the objectivity of the philosophers, of the then university professors, back at the beginning of the 1870's), so that despite his critique of their position and despite that they were in opposition to him (they did not hold it against him on either account), his status was instead awarded him, and the majority of his intellectual and philosophical opponents tended to admire his thinking, his methodology, his clear and crystalline language.

In two words, about what was this book? In it Solov'ev explained, why Western philosophy had arrived at a crisis towards the end of the XIX Century: because it had adopted in the capacity of instrument of knowing -- only reason, hence all more and more bestowing upon cognition quite one-sided a character. Solov'ev initially points out, how in the Middle Ages reason becomes freed from theology, freed from the Church. It then becomes autonomous, independent, and later comes to occupy all more and more a place and finally hits the limits, attainable by it. And then disintegration ensues. In this youthful book, in which there is already the presentiment of a new spiritual synthesis, Solov'ev shows how, in the philosophy of Schopenhauer and other philosophers, attracted to the holy books of the East, the dry rationalism seeks to transcend itself. He predicted all this.

In his doctoral dissertation, which he entitled as "Critique of Abstract Principles", Solov'ev has in view this synthesis. What is all-unity? All-unity -- this is spirit, which connects the elements of nature, connects the spiritual realms, connects society, us -- with the supreme sole Principle.

And when people take into account one part whatever of the all-unity, of the organic and then isolate it, there then occurs what he termed an "abstract principle". And therefore cognition based upon reason, having become abstract, sundered and cut off from being, in the final end suffers defeat. Empirical science, which ceases to take into account the inward and spiritual experience, and having then only the deductions of an abstract metaphysics, likewise in the final end tends to hit an impasse, a blind alley. And Solov'ev critiques all the fundamental "abstract principles", which thus comprises the content of his doctoral dissertation.

This was indeed nowise simple a man. From his early years (he was not yet in age ten), there began for him a peculiar and mystical (or, if you prefer, occult) experience. He began to perceive the feminine in aspect somewhat the existence of a cosmic character. He experienced the encounter with it as an encounter with the Soul of the World. Vladimir Solov'ev largely never did believe, that the world-edifice -- is a mere mechanism, a mere aggregate of things. He had seen the Soul of the World! The first time was in childhood, in the church of the Moscow University. The second time he intentionally began to seek it, he implored that it should appear. And this happened during the time of a mission abroad, when he visited Western Europe after defending his dissertation. Solov'ev was living in London, he was working at the reknown British Museum, studying old texts of old mystical teachings (Jacob Boehme and others). And during a time of very intense work in the library he suddenly caught sight of a face, the cosmic feminine face itself, that same which had appeared to him in the university church, when he was but 8 years old. This was unique indeed an experience. Solov'ev attempted to describe it in his poem, "Three Meetings". The poem was penned with irony, with self-irony, since he was a man sensitive, chaste and delicate. In spite of all his sharp wit, despite it seemed that he was as it were hemmed in by a sort of chain-mail armour, -- in actual fact his soul was a wanderer, and it sensed itself quite chilly in a cold world. And when he spoke about what was most dear for him, he intentionally spoke about this with irony.

Well, and so what happened with him? Vladimir Solov'ev decided, that it was in Egypt, in that ancient cradle of mysteries, of the great religions, of gnostic theosophy, that he would see all that comprises the Soul of the World. And so here one time in Cairo he sets out from the hotel and wanders off along a barren stony desert area, in his top-hat and European attire, he wanders about aimlessly, and falls into the hands of

Bedouins. He himself has no idea, where it is that he had gone. He fell asleep on the cold ground, and when he awoke, refreshed, suddenly he saw (at that moment, which they tend to call a semi-awake condition, when a person is midway between sleep and alertness), suddenly he glimpsed -- another world, something altogether different. And how as it were that the world-edifice surrounding him suddenly shone in a new light. Here is what he wrote in one of his poems: "Dear friend, see thou not, that all the visible for us -- is but a reflection, but a shadow of the unglimpsed by eyes". And this was a primal inward experience of his.

Back then, in Egypt, he was already consciously a Christian. Moreover, in these youthful years of his there arises a bold and quite calculated decision: to create a system, in which the eternal truth of Christianity would be expounded upon in the language of contemporary philosophy and science. Is such a thing indeed possible? He saw this as a possibility within the context of his own methodology. Solov'ev began writing a book, "The Philosophic Principles of Integral Knowledge"; in it he overlooks neither science, nor technology, nor economics, nor metaphysics, nor theology -- all this is arranged into an enormous synthetic whole. On the elementary level -- are various sciences of knowledge: the economic sciences, the natural sciences, then abstract knowledge -- metaphysics, and finally, mystical knowledge. All this gets interwoven together, just as it is in man himself! Within man lives aspects of tangible things, the corporeal, the biological, in him lives abstract thought, and also in him lives something other, something deep, intuitive, which begets the power, known as faith. And faith is the capacity of man to assimilate the Divine Revelation.

At first Solov'ev was thinking to write an history of religion, which would point out the place of Christianity in the religious world-order of things. He spoke about this to his fiancee. But this plan did not come to fruition.

What was the chief thing in his later efforts? In 1881 Solov'ev became an independent writer and philosopher. Here he was, heir of a scholar, son of the reknown Solov'ev; he had his master's and then his doctoral degrees, -- why not stay lecturing philosophy at the university? But also indeed he was a Christian, and a political and social thinker! When Alexander II was killed, Solov'ev writes tsar Alexander III a letter and comes out with a speech, in which he says, that the tsar as a Christian ought to reprieve from death sentence those guilty of the tsaricide, of those people, who had murdered Alexander II. Speaking as a Christian namely, and nowise denying the crime committed. He said, that to answer murder by murdering -- is no deciding of the question for a Christian. And needless to say, that the expressing of this created around Solov'ev an unhealthy aura, causing him to leave the university. And from that time, from 1881 til 1900 when he died, Solov'ev leads a way of life, somewhat similar perhaps, to the form of life led by his distant ancestor, Grigorii Savvich Skovoroda. How strangely he lived! I am amazed only, that he did not die sooner. He had no fixed domicile, he sustained himself on whatever befell, lived out of hotels, led a nomadic life from city to city, from land to land. And how could he write so much? This remains a mystery even now. He wrote so extensively, sometimes on mere scraps of paper. He had many friends, in particular, he was on good terms with the family of the deceased poet, Aleksei Konstantinovich Tolstoy. In this family he met a woman, whom he loved over the course of many years. But she was married, and when her husband died, something in their relations chilled, and Solov'ev thus also remained alone.

He led an ascetic, spartan way of life. But in this there was nothing artificial, nothing contrived, on the contrary, he loved good company, and he loved, when this company had the wine flowing. Obviously, he did not approve of drunkenness, but for intellectual people, he said, to raise their spirits with a glass of wine -- this is not the only benefit, and here he would always hearken back to the example of the heroes of the Platonic Dialogues, especially the "Symposium" of Plato. And this man -- he had neither house nor home -- all the money, which he earned, he gave away to whomever he chanced upon, he walked about in clothing sometimes with a strange shoulder knapsack... He was often mistaken for a bishop, or for a priest, and one time a little boy in the hotel even exclaimed: "Here comes God", -- Solov'ev went about in an old fur coat, he had already a long beard, long hair. He was near-sighted, his eyes tended to gaze into the distance. An icon-like face. A man of mystery!

There is a very keen description of him by Andrei Bely, the poet, who in childhood had seen him. His contemporaries have left a mass of recollections about him: about his eyes, which varied in their colour, and about his laugh, which to someone seemed Homeric and joyful, but to another something demonic, and concerning the contradictions in his life, and about his love for quibbling words.

And this enigmatic, this strange and homeless man writes a book, which he entitled "The Great Controversy and Christian Politics". He says, that the West for a long time already has been in dispute with the East. Simply speaking, the Eastern consciousness is this, that -- "man -- is as nothing, and God -- is everything!" The inhuman dreadsome God! And in the West -- -- is godless man; spiritually with emphasis upon the human "I". But Christianity, the Gospel, is, according to Solov'ev, a synthesis of East and West. "And the light, issuing forth from the East, doth reconcile West with East", he wrote in one of his poems. Perviewing the panorama of the history of the Church, brilliantly analysing its struggle with heresies, he begins pondering the problem, which later becomes the content of his life: why ultimately is it that the antagonism won out! Why, when Christianity with the Gospel had united the East with the West, why then they again split apart, and this time already it is under the aegis of Christian signs: what happened with the Christian East and the Christian West?

Later on Solov'ev writes a book, "The Spiritual Foundations of Life", about which I have already told you. He writes about faith, about love, about fasting -- three elements. And how does he write? Clearly, simply, in language which was not overly clerical, nor archaic, cluttered with "churchly" quotations, -- in that same language, in which he had written his crystal clear philosophic books, his journal articles. Many of his contemporaries said, how some people (and not a few) began their acquaintance with the traditions and the writings of the Holy Fathers, particularly from the book of Vladimir Solov'ev, "The Spiritual Foundations of Life".

At Peterburg he gives his lectures on God-manhood. God-manhood -- is moreover one thought innate to him. For materialism, for positivism, the history of the world and nature -- are all matters earthly, and human. And for those, who deny the significance of the earthly, for spiritualism, for the extremes of spirituality -- this is all an insignificant nothing. Christianity does not spurn matter and the flesh, does not spurn nature, it sanctifies them, since all this -- is the creation of God and God was incarnated in flesh in the world. And once He was incarnated in the world, it means that all the entirety of the process of the world-edifice -- is a process Divine-Human, in which the God-Man participates.

But Solov'ev peers on into mysteries deeper: man suffers from his own contradictions, he lives abnormal a life, these days we all tend to admit this. What occurred, what happened with man? And he answers: it is

22

a fallen world. The connective bonds of love, of mutual understanding, of brotherhood -- have been lost. Even connections with the material world have been lost. Everything has fallen apart, has gone to pieces. The Creator -- is the source of oneness and unity, of fullness in harmony, of the fullness and triumph of the conception of unity and oneness. This is the picture of things, created by God outside of time. And what however is it, in opposition to this? What sends the world spinning somewhere right down into the pit? Freedom, -- answers Solov'ev.

But how can there be this freedom, apart from and beyond man? Solov'ev says, that nature has a single soul. His experience of an encounter with the World Soul led him to thoughts about the spiritification of the cosmos, about the spiritification of all the world-edifice. He seeks for and he finds a name for this Principle: its name -- is Sophia (the Greek word for wisdom). Divine wisdom is already spoken of in the Bible. Divine wisdom -- in our modern terminology is the information, which God has lodged innately within nature. And for Solov'ev this is the certain spiritual focal point of the world, wherein is embedded freedom. And the world has fallen, under the effect of this freedom, has fallen away from its harmonious condition.

The consequent history of the world (suchlike as at present) -- is a return to eternal harmony, to the eternal Divine symphony, the opposite of dissonance, of disintegration. Every aspect of hatred, every manner of force, which separates, seeking to destroy thought, feelings, the body, nature, -- is a principle in opposition to God. Today, in an era of ecological crisis, of national and geopolitical conflicts, Solov'ev's emphatic thought, -- that the Divine unites, and everything which disunites, is satanic -- is to an utmost degree apparent.

And naturally, after this he ponders a problem, about which I have already made mention: the problem concerning the unity of Christians. At first glance, this problem seems simple. For those of you, for whom it is not clear, I will offer an elementary example. Let us say, there is some man who is dying. His children love him dearly and are making their final farewell with him, in tears. And they say to him: "Father, what is thine last wish? Anything, whatever thou say, we will do". This is naturally and legitimately proper in this situation. And he then says: "Children, I have for you but one request: that you live in unity amongst yourself, that you not wrong one another, that there be not rifts between each other. All so that you preserve and hold together our family". The father dies, and the children all begin quarreling. Why do they hate one another? Why do they even want to know one another? They tend to find objective reasons, perhaps, and quite serious ones at that. And after a while one of them suddenly remembers, that their father had commanded indeed otherwise. And then the children see, that they have done him wrong, they have transgressed his final wishes, the biddings of his will. And similarly the pre-death final wishes of Christ for us, as Christians, is well known. Each of us in the Bible can read these words, which Our Lord Jesus Christ was praying before His Death: "Let them all be one, as Thou, Father, art in Me, and I in Thee, so that they thus be one in Us", as the Father and the Son are unified as one, -- thus that they all should be unified as one. Herein is the thought of Christ, His Last Testament as it were, His final wishes. The commands of His Testament have been broken, as is quite evident. And broken for all sort of objective reasons. Everyone has a share in the guilt, each in his own way. And perhaps, some are more guilty in certain aspects, while others are more guilty in other aspects. People in the West tend to say, that the East is more guilty in its arrogance, while people in the East tend to say, that the West is more guilty in its lust for power, and so on. But that this Testament of Christ, this Covenant, has been broken -- this is already all too evident.

And here Solov'ev was thus pondering and thinking about a way for the surmounting of Christian divisions. But to start with, he puts to us, as Christians, a very important question: what exactly is our Christian faith? Is it -- an ideology? An abstract philosophy? Or something far more personal an affair? Not at all! For then it would not be part of the all-unity design by God. This impacts upon our life in all its aspects and manifestations, including the social. People ought to learn to live on earth with regard to God? To be subject to the Divine summoning -- this is likewise theocracy, God-power of rule. But how can they do this, if they all live in hostility and disunity? Solov'ev studies the Bible, he studies the ancient Hebrew language (he already knew Greek and Latin). He reads the Old Testament, he translates remarkable bits of it anew. He explains, that the purpose of God's design is this, that people should live upon the earth with regard to God, to rise up moving towards this actual principle, that the Covenant of the Lord was given not simply for the comforting of overburdened hearts, but rather, that within society also and ultimately the lofty Divine outlines should begin to be apparent and realised.

It is impossible to deny, certainly, that with the young thirty year old Solov'ev there was an element of the utopian here. It seemed to him, with the impatience characteristic to youth, that this was something possible tomorrow already. And to the point, he even planned out such a project happening. He thought it over and considered, that the most mighty power in the East -- was the Russian tsar, and the most mighty spiritual centre in the West -- was the Roman pope. And here if they but extend each other the hand, if the Moscow tsardom (or the Peterburg in effect) were to render itself in spiritual unity with the world-wide churchly state, with Rome, then Christianity would be invincible and it would be possible to establish a theocracy upon earth. Solov'ev not only wrote about this -- he even attempted to prepare the practical steps towards it. He journeyed much through the Western lands, he was in contacts with early adherents for the reuniting of the Churches, for example, with bishop Josip Strossmayer, with the [Croatian] canonist Fran'o Racki [Rachki] and others. He did not merely want to establish this idea in an abstract form, a vision of sorts, he actually attempted to realise it.

The Roman pope said concerning this: "A beautiful idea, and all it would take is a miracle, for it to happen". And it must be said, that Solov'ev was absolutely alone in this even in the East. His Orthodox co-religionists began to regard him with extreme suspicion. His articles and books, dealing with theological questions, ceased to be printed, the censor would not approve them, and he had to have them published abroad. And in the West they considered him a visionary dreamer, though they regarded him with love. They said: how is it possible to re-unite two halves of a divided world -- the Eastern Orthodox and the Western Catholic?

But Solov'ev proved to be a prophet, since later on several decades after his death, quite on its own, there began a somewhat uncertain but steady movement towards mutual understanding among Christians in a divided world.

In the social regard, he was always a proponent for democracy and justice. His brilliant articles in defense of freedom of conscience remain fully relevant even today. He felt, that Orthodox Christianity had been undermined for us in our land, undermined in that the state and its censorship were defending it. Solov'ev came out against the harassment of the Old Ritualists, the Old Believers, against the harassment of sectarians. He said: if the truth is actually real, if it is genuinely authentic, if the people who confess it, truly believe in it, then why indeed is it necessary to resort to censorship, to force, to oppression? To censorship, force and oppression resorts only someone, who in the depths of his soul does not truly believe in his own idea. Moreover, Solov'ev spoke also about "the truth of socialism" (his words literally). The "truth of socialism" -- is a partial truth. The word "socialism" Solov'ev understood in very broad a sense, and that yes, it is necessary to strive after the best economic conditions for the life of man. But he was indeed convinced (and argued the point), that economic transformations alone are totally insufficient. That in actual fact man cannot truly be happy, even if he is materially well-off, while being spiritually impoverished and dishonest. All the attempts to decide the question one-sidedly -- whether materially, or spiritually -- evoked protest in him. There is an extreme asceticism, which tended to say: we should get ourself up to heaven and desist in having an hand in matters upon earth, -- a mentality which found in Solov'ev a strident opponent. Freedom. Work. Love. Activity. The constructive, active participation of man. God is not alone in having created the world, man too participates in the worldly creation. And herein arises a colossal responsibility, a colossal answerability. Even the word God-manhood for him was no chance matter, it was indeed taken from a setting of customary churchly useage. Because Jesus of Nazareth is for us the God-Man, and precisely because He is the God-Man, it mean that He sanctifies by the very fact of His dwelling (the dwelling of God) upon earth, He sanctifies earthly labour, earthly life, the earthly human person.

In contemplating the fate of his fatherland, which Solov'ev much loved, and engaging in polemics against the Slavophils (with whom he had much in common, for he admitted many of their presuppositions), he wanted for his country not simply a powerful and mighty state, but something rather other. Solov'ev speaks about this in his poem, entitled "Ex oriente lux" ("Light from the East"). This poem begins with a panoramic clash of two worlds: the enormous army of the aggressive conqueror Xerxes is moving against Greece (about 500 B.C.). The Greek army sparse in number cannot withstand him in open battle, but the Greeks craftily lure the armies of Xerxes into the narrow Thermopylae Pass. The Persians cannot deploy themself in all their might, and they are there forced to engage king Leonides with his soldiers, all of a mere 300 men. (Some years back there was a film about them, "The Three Hundred Spartans", and as a youth I think I saw it). The Greeks would not sally forth against the gigantic army of Xerxes, they would all have to die in this narrow pass, and Xerxes, not knowing, how many of the enemy soldiers still withstood him, was compelled finally to retreat. For Solov'ev this historical event from 2500 years ago was symbolic of the clash of two worlds. And thus he begins his verse with suchlike words:

> From the East light, from the East power!
> And, for all-dominance readied,
> The Iran tsar 'neathe Thermopylae
> Urged on his herd of slaves.
> No but not vainly Prometheus
> The coelestial gift to Hellas hath given,
> Wherefore the servile throngs do flee, in fright
> Afront a mere handful of valiant citizens.

Solov'ev includes in his verse on this struggle of West and East, -- an appeal also to his own fatherland:

> O, Rus! in foresight lofty
> Thou with thought lordly art concerned;
> Which the East thou wouldst be:
> The East of Xerxes or of Christ?

The East of despotism, force, oppression, though amidst outward external might, -- or by spiritual power as first concern? For him this was very important, since the spiritual power always was foremost.

Events tend tragically to unfold in the social-literary life of V. S. Solov'ev. He comes out with a paper on the theme of the Medieval world-view. The paper evokes a stormy reaction, the newspapers take to a regular mud-slinging with it. And theologians consider him almost an apostate from Christianity. There begins all kinds of vicious talk. It would seem, well, what could be so terrible in a mere paper on the Medieval world-view? And what was this fuss all over? Solov'ev came out clearly and said: do not imagine, that the Middle Ages -- was a time of the triumph of Christianity! The Medieval structure and order was something hybrid, which combined within it Christian forms and pagan elements. Moreover, in light of this arrangement, later on, when non-Christian thought began to speak about freedom, about the dignity of the person, about the things that debase man -- as being evil, then this thought in repudiating Christianity was in actual fact preserving the ideals of Christianity. And Solov'ev hurled an indeed audacious thought. He said: who was it that abolished torture, who put an end to the Inquisition -- Christians or someone else? No, it was not the Christians. This is a very pointed and stringent question, upon which if one think honestly, then the conclusion would be problematic. And I well understand, why the press and many others were furious at Solov'ev...

When Solov'ev lived at the Lavra, at Sergiev Posad, he felt more at peace. He wrote, that the monks were very attentive to him, with the intention that he might accept monastic tonsure. "But I got off cheaply", -- he joked. And actually, he was attracted to remain at the monastery for studies, all the moreso, in that his life was so ascetic, and concerned with science. Only science. But this was a temptation that he overcame.

It is impossible fully to take into account, what he did in various areas. He wrote about the ecological crisis, about the poetry of Tiutchev... And whatever he wrote about, it always had deep and interesting thought involved. Let us say, a certain Greek bishop publishes an ancient Christian tract (I-II Cent.). Solov'ev renders it into a translation of his own and provides it with commentaries. And this is not simply a matter of learned commentaries, it is a veritable bomb-shell. Which is because he points out, how things were in the original Church and what changed afterwards. And always was it for the better, -- is the question he poses. A church reformer he was not, but he posed these questions.

Towards the end of his life Solov'ev realised, that his project of the re-union of Churches was futile, that it was not to be. Solov'ev sets about working on theoretical philosophy. He writes an enormous work -- a Christian ethics. A book well worth not overlooking. This large book bears the title, "The Justification of the Good". There is so much of importance and value in it. Solov'ev begins by speaking about the ideals of mankind. What indeed is good, is the good? Merely to be outwardly happy and well-off, hedonism, power, or something yet more? He shows, that all this in the final end proves hollow, breaks down! And furthermore he analyses it -- scientifically, philosophically, theologically, poetically (since he had a poetic view on the world) -- to get at the essence of that, which we term the good.

Some several years before his death he receives Communion from a Catholic priest. By this he wanted to show, that he personally refused to admit of the separation of the Churches. When he told about this to his

Orthodox spiritual father, his priest, the reply was that this was something that should not have been done. They quarreled sharply over it. And when Solov'ev lay dying, he said: "I was in the wrong". He himself had even earlier written, that personal attempts at unia and re-uniting, personal goings back and forth from Church to Church do not aid in the uniting of Christians, but on the contrary, merely introduces redundantly hollow a temptation.

All of you know the park beyond Belyaevo -- this was formerly the Uzkoe/Narrows locale. Here at present it is the rest sanitarium of the Academy of Science. If perchance you happen to be in this area, follow along the path heading far in towards the sanitarium, and you will approach a church. It is under remodeling only on the outside, and inside it has books piled, formerly dispatched for Hitler's chancellor (and laying there since the war). Alongside the church, beyond a garden, is an house, a typical estate house. This was the property of Prince Trubetskoy. Sergei Nikolaevich Trubetskoy, briefly a rector of Moscow University, and dying several years after the death of Solov'ev and still likewise quite young, himself a brilliant philosopher, a sharp polemicist and critic, and very noble a social activist, -- he took in Vladimir Solov'ev at the critical moment, when grievous and numerous illnesses suddenly befell Solov'ev. And actually in his wanderings about Solov'ev was constantly neglecting himself, -- and suddenly this was the result. And in a very brief while he was doing so poorly, that he became unable to travel on, and he died in the hands of Sergei Trubetskoy.

Before his death Solov'ev made confession, and received Communion. He died conscious. He read the Psalms in the Hebrew tongue, since he always loved to enhance his prayers with the language of Christ, to serve in sound as a connection with the ancient Christian tradition. He knew many of the Psalms by heart. Losing consciousness, and then regaining it, he said: "Difficult is the work of the Lord". Simple, like a little child, and at the same time wise. A man, who evoked admiration, envy, hatred, abuse, scorn. A man, about whom they then write hundreds of books and articles, -- a mere ten years after his death his bibliography consisted of several hundred titles. And at present this would comprise an entire book.

And thus, he died and was buried at Moscow. I hope, when you find the time, that you would head out to the Novodevichy monastery. Directly across the entrance, along the first alley, having turned right, you will come to the gravestone of Sergei Mikhailovich Solov'ev -- a white marble gravestone with its bas-relief etching. The cross, certainly, is gone. Alongside -- are the graves of his son and daughter. The gravestones, certainly, are in ruins. At the graves of Vladimir Solov'ev and his sister stand fragments of other gravestones, without a cross. But, glory to God, that things stand even so. At present, for the 90th anniversary of his death, there is the promise on the initiative of our Moscow diocese, of our diocesan administration to restore the gravestone to its original state.

And there, to this grave, have come quite many. Solov'ev had an enormous influence upon Andrei Bely, and upon Blok, who called him a monastic knight-errant. Blok's theme of the Beauteous Woman, certainly, derives from Solov'ev. The whole brilliant pleiade of Russian religious thinkers -- Bulgakov, Florensky, Berdyaev, Frank, Evgenii Trubetskoy and so many others -- would be well nigh impossible, would be difficult to imagine for oneself without Solov'ev. This wanderer was the originator of so much that was original and unique in Russian religio-philosophic thought...

And moreover, when you come nigh this grave, remember, that this was a living man. Not in vain did he write:

> Death and Time upon earth do reign,
> Yet masters call them not;
> All, round spinning, in a trice doth vanish,
> Immobile only tis the sun of love.

This was his deep intuition, this was his profound awareness. This abstract intellectual always lived by faith, always lived by mystical insight, always lived impelled towards eternity. And therefore Vladimir Solov'ev is dear for us not only as a writer, a thinker, a poet, but also as an unrepeatably unique man, indeed very vivid a person, of whom any culture would be proud. And it is comforting, that at present, after so many years of being forgotten, finally again they are writing about him, finally again his works are coming out -- meekly though it be, but the return of Solov'ev is happening today before our very eyes. I would hope, that this small overview might help you, should you want to get better acquainted with the thought of this remarkable man.

Sergei Nikolaevich and Evgenii Nikolaevich Trubetskoy

For us recently there have finally started appearing books of our Christian philosophers. In various journals now appear portions of their religio-philosophic works. Vladimir Solov'ev has appeared, Berdyaev and Merezhkovsky have appeared. Properly speaking, these books are being published directly in consequence of our having meetings with you. And here now are those two remarkable men -- Sergei Nikolaevich Trubetskoy and his brother Evgenii Nikolaevich -- again almost unknown. The sole publication in the last 70 years -- is this article "Maximalism", of E. N. Trubetskoy, which came out in the journal "Iunost'" ["Youth"].

A certain philosopher once justly said, that the brothers Trubetskoy, especially Sergei Nikolaevich, stand their place in line of the trail-blazers of an independent and unique Russian philosophy.

They were both nearly the same age, with Sergei Nikolaevich a year older. Belonging to the ancient lineage of the Trubetskoys, they lived in an unique environment, as princes, aristocrats, but not simply aristocrats -- both belonged to the profoundly intellectual sphere. Sergei Nikolaevich was born near Moscow, in the village of Akhtyrka, along the north road, in 1862, and his brother a year later. They had a splendid upbringing at home, and they studied at the Kaluga gymnasium-school (their father was governor at Kaluga). Their early years were spent in an atmosphere of music, of poetry, love for culture, and love for the traditions of their native land. These were people of balance, tall of stature, immense even, and serious; already in their youth they produced an impression of real solidness. (Andrei Bely wrote, that Sergei Nikolaevich could pass for a camel, and Evgenii -- for a good bear.) I am speaking about them both as it were in parallel, since they had much in common between them not only in birth and upbringing, but also in world-view and developement. Sergei Nikolaevich died early, quite young actually, in 1905, and his brother Evgenii Nikolaevich -- during the revolutionary period, in 1920, having outlived his brother by 15 years.

31

Just like many other people of that era, in youth they experienced the enthusiasms for materialism, for populism, for the denial of all the supreme spiritual values, but very quickly the study of philosophy, and the classics of philosophy, led them initially to the fundamentals of positivism (via Spenser, Comte, Miller), and then, almost without any sort of transition, -- right into a deep understanding of the significance, of what is now expressed as, Western idealistic metaphysics.

Pondering the mysteries of the world started for them with the philosophy of Schopenhauer. Later on, as a student at the law school of Moscow University, Sergei Nikolaevich got into a deep study of the 6 volumes of Kuno Fisher. Kuno Fisher [also Fischer] -- was a German historian of philosophy, having written 6 enormous tomes (which are in Russian translation), under the title "An History of Philosophy". Each of these books, from 600-800 pages, is devoted to various of the outstanding philosophers of Europe: Spinoza, Kant, Schelling, Hegel. This path of study led the Trubetskoys out of the empty, superficial, shallow and tedious world of positivism.

And there is one more important event also -- their acquaintance, then closeness, and finally deep friendship with Vladimir Sergeevich Solov'ev. This friendship continued right on down to the final days of Vladimir Sergeevich, and if you remember, Vladimir Solov'ev actually died in the hands of Sergei Trubetskoy, at Uzkoe, now the Moscow Teplyi Stan micro-district. This was the Trubetskoy estate, at present the Academy of Sciences rest home.

Deeply appreciative of everything abstract, theoretical and subtle, Sergei Trubetskoy gets himself immersed in ancient philosophy. And ancient philosophy, set against the metaphysics of all-unity of Solov'ev, leads him to Christianity and Orthodoxy. And indeed, one of his colleagues from Moscow University writes, that Sergei Nikolaevich was not only Orthodox, but also a man, deeply convinced in his Orthodoxy. I want to offer you several lines from a speech of recollections of Sergei Nikolaevich Trubetskoy, spoken by his colleague Vladimir Ivanovich Vernadsky. This is very important, since later on Vernadsky himself further developed ideas, cast forth like seeds, by Sergei Nikolaevich Trubetskoy. Here is what Vladimir Ivanovich Vernadsky writes: "An idealistic philosopher, in consequence of the mystical basis of his world-perception, and at the same time he appeared immensely learned, having mastered the whole apparatus of the erudite XX Century. I vividly remember, how he profoundly and acutely sensed the age-old connectedness, in pointing out the significance of critiques of the text of the New Testament, and to the establishing of strict and merciless scientific work of the erudite over two centuries, and how he got into this work for an understanding of other areas of the history of thought, such as were more familiar to him". Vernadsky's mention of the New Testament is not by chance. To further his study of antiquity and the history of thought, Sergei Trubetskoy travels on to Germany and meets up there with the noted German historian, thinker and Bible critic Adolf Harnack.

Adolf Harnack (he died 10 years after Evgenii Nikolaevich, in 1930), was a chief spokesman of the so-called Liberal Protestant school. What was relevant is that, very often in churchly circles, both the Orthodox and the Catholic, either they were afraid of a scientific critique, textual criticism, investigating questions as to when arose either this or some other version of the Old or New Testament, or the investigating as to how reliably authentic might be this or that vita [i.e. life] account or ancient report of church historians, -- or else, when this conservative bent proved in the final end intolerant, everything went to the opposite extreme. And thus it was with Evgenii Evstigneevich Golubinsky, who began to write his enormous "History of the Russian Church" (he was likewise their contemporary). Golubinsky's work was set against the backdrop of a pathos of hyper-criticism -- everything, such as is only to be met with in the history of the Russian Church, he subjected to doubt. And essentially his first volume is primarily a matter of question marks and the destruction of traditional notions (beginning with the Baptism of Rus' and everything that follows).

Adolf Harnack found a middle course, a very verifiable and wise path -- he admitted the importance of a keen critical study of the primary historical sources, but he did not allow this to be transformed simply into an archeological pursuit, instead, he always saw in this a searching for the eternal spiritual values -- Christian values. He never surrendered himself to hyper-criticism. He was not a blind follower of traditions (albeit different traditions), but he was also not a blind follower against traditions per se. And if the critical instinct of the scholar (and Harnack was first-class a scholar with world-wide a name and heading an enormous school of thought) suggested, that the investigation was actually affirming the ancient tradition, then he joyfully accepted this as an objective scholar and Christian.

The school of Harnack, and friendship also with this scholar, played an enormous role in the formation of thought in the young Sergei Trubetskoy. He was not yet 30 years of age, and he imbibed all this with an extraordinary quickness. He was a man of colossal capacities, brilliant and with varied talents, sharp-minded, infinitely good, assured, a lover of the old ways, and at the same time, broadly open to the future; a monarchist, but against despotism, having been a committed democrat, -- he always managed a balanced path (as a predecessor, perhaps, to Georgii Petrovich Fedotov).

But with Harnack he also had serious disagreements. Harnack was influenced by the philosophy of Neo-Kantianism, which attempted as it were to separate off the knowing subject from the real object, which in hearkening back to Kant, in actual fact undercut from the authentic Kant the more valuable elements of his philosophy. And Harnack in the final end went the path of adogmatism, of denying all metaphysics.

Somewhat later, the winter of 1899-1900, Harnack read for his students a cycle of lectures at Berlin University, termed -- "The Essence of Christianity" (it afterwards came out separately as a book). And therein the erudite scholar expressed his credo. This book, brilliant in form and content, nevertheless proved incapable of expressing the essence of Christianity. And this was because Harnack was unable to break out of the gnosseological prison, into which he had thrown himself by his Neo-Kantian scepticism. Here -- it was all but a mere word-play, since for Harnack those things, which we know by way of the mysterious and intuitive, vanish as it were; he understood, that science does not know and cannot know answers to the question, of what we live for and why man and the world exist. And irregardless still, he sought for this essence within historical facts, the veracity of which he himself could not be certain. This essence of whatever the appearance is perceived only by an intuitive awareness. History itself provides only a pile of facts.

Trubetskoy understood, that the path to reality for man is not hidden. In this regard he had a serious difference of opinion from Harnack -- he then writes several works, devoted to the particulars of human cognition and the basis for idealism, as he understood it. In refusing to accept the sceptical point of the Neo-Kantians, he at the same indicates, that the concept, developed during the early XVIII Century, according to which man (the knowing subject) is as it were completely alone and in opposition to all the world, -- is a false perspective.

Let me elaborate somewhat. I see here this world, I see your faces, I see the colour of the armchairs, of the ceiling, my organs of sense assimilate this. I rework these perceptions within my thought processes. And this is where the whatever subjective idealist begins. But in the final end he says, that the thing in itself, the thing as it actually is, is unknowable, and I (as subject) am rendered alone in the world. As regards this, Trubetskoy in a whole series of works attempted to show, that man accumulates his presuppositions, theoretical and rational, only by virtue of his having contact with the thought processes of other subjects, that he is not alone, that he is drawn into a certain current of the whole.

And yes, certainly, man -- each man -- is at a centre point of the perceiving of the world. But I must remind you: during the time of Trubetskoy this fact was not regarded as certain. Each of you easily grasps this: all our words, ideas, notions are formed from our childhood years on the basis of contacts. When a little child is raised outside of human society, and with wild beasts let us say (like with Mowgli) [from Rudyard Kipling's "Jungle Book"], -- he did not have properly possible the developing of his subjective "I" and the cognitive process, and all his life, even after having returned into human society, he remained a virtual simpleton. In such manner, even the developement of the person, one's psychic traits and processes of thought are extraordinarily tied in tightly with this, what we would at present term as the spiritual oneness of mankind. Trubetskoy called this principle, -- Sobornost'.

He took this term from the Slavophils, Khomyakov in particular. And absolutely within this was a deep connection for him with those rudiments of the philosophic system, which we have in the early Slavophilism. He was not a political Slavophil, which is to say, he did not feel that for Russia everything Western had to be opposed. On the contrary, in his view, despite the unique path of Russia (and each people has its own unique path), there have to be cultural contacts, a converse cultural connection with other peoples, especially Western Europe, and this -- is something normal. And within the political thinking of Trubetskoy is repeated also his gnosseological conviction: there is no one culture alone, existing apart from all others, but rather it is that a culture develops by virtue of an organic life and in constant mutual-bonds, in dialogue, in borrowings with other cultures. Therefore he reckoned it possible for himself to defend freedom of speech, freedom of conscience, freedom of the press. And at the time this was an acute problem.

There is a sobornost' of thinking process, a sobornost' of mankind, a sobornost' of the people. Let me elucidate further, what Sobornost' in the terminology of the Slavophils signifies. There is individualism and there is its opposite antipode -- collectivism. Individualism tends towards an extreme hypertrophy and shrinking back of the "I", of the individuum, whereas collectivism infringes upon, violates the value and dignity of the person. We know both about the one, and the other. Sobornost' -- is a third path, a central path between the two extremes, which the Slavophils looked upon as the ideal of Christianity, the ideal of the Church, but certainly, not of the empirical church (which the Slavophils very sharply criticised); rather, it is in the true spirit of the Church, in that principle sketched out in the Gospel, where all are united as one, but where no one suffers the loss of his "I".

Starting from this, Sergei Nikolaevich also constructs his own unique gnosseology. He states, that man is involved in thought, because he has received the material for thought from other thinking beings. But all our thinking in toto is possible only because that there exists a certain objectively existing logic, an objectively existent thought, an objectively existent spirit. And here we come nigh to those ideas, which Vernadsky afterwards developed on the basis of nature-knowledge. Sergei Trubetskoy did not pronounce the word "noos-sphere" (sphere of reason), but he clearly pre-envisioned already it in his insights. Mankind -- is singular an organism not only by virtue of genetic code, but also by virtue of spiritual unity and by virtue of connection with the absolute thought process. The absolute thought process by means of facts conveys man to God. Man apperceives knowledge only in correlation with the Absolute.

They accused Trubetskoy of pantheism, but this was unjust an accusation. Regretably, the philosopher having died early was unable to develope many of his thoughts to completion; his brother afterwards attempted to do this. Nonetheless, it is still possible to deduce two views on all-unity from him.

Vladimir Solov'ev taught about the all-unity of mankind and about the Universal within God. With this view Sergei Trubetskoy is fully in accord. We live and strive and exist within Him [God], -- as said the Apostle Paul. But to this Trubetskoy ascribes a certain spiritual essence, which he terms in the ancient fashion of old -- the Soul of the World. The world-edifice is alive. The earth is alive. Mankind is singularly one. the animal and plant world -- is a certain singular organism. And all the

Creation -- is something alive, endowed with a soul. We know therefore, that a soul is present in view of a consciously aware state also with animals, and as regards plants, we have no basis to say no on this, -- wrote Trubetskoy, -- nor that a stone is completely bereft of this. And in the final end he comes nigh to the idea of a certain panpsychism, of a soul-endowedness of the creature, and finds assertions for this in the writings of the mystics, in the experiences of those loving nature, and later on after him we might say, also in the theories of Teilhard de Chardin and Vernadsky. Both Teilhard and Sergei Nikolaevich Trubetskoy were panpsychists.

This perception of the Soul of the World, with which man is connected, in my view appears to be one of the most important grounds for the ecological ethics of today. From which man ought to understand, that he lives in a living world, part of which he is, and in part responsible for, since he has the awareness of this. And that the Earth and the life upon it -- is not simply a chance interweaving of atoms and molecules. And the sufferings of this organic whole (though it be the same thing as with man) ultimately affect man in his fortunes.

Trubetskoy was very interested in the problem, of how this idea of the soul-endowedness of creatures was handled in the ancient world. He thus writes a dissertation, "The Metaphysics of Ancient Greece". This is a beautiful book, in which he is one of the first among Russian thinkers to give an objective, profound and brilliant written account of the developement of spiritual thought in Ancient Greece, of spiritual Hellenism.

He afterwards developed the same idea in a larger work, "An History of Ancient Philosophy". And here he ran afoul of certain of the clergy. Archpriest Butkevich, and archbishop Antonii Khrapovitsky began crudely and in quite uncivil a manner to berate him in the press because of this, that he saw within the thought of antiquity, in the ideas of Herakleitos, of Pythagoras and of Plato, presentiments and precedents of Christianity. And herein he had the same point of view, as had his friend, Vladimir Solov'ev. Solov'ev wrote, that truth cannot be manifest all at once, in a final complete form. Truth is something prepared for, it goes through phases of historical developement. And therefore, if it is that in the Old Testament, in ancient Israel, that we have a readying of the world for the acceptance of the Saviour, then precisely the same, albeit in a different and metaphysical form, in the world of ancient Greek philosophy. And this is not something newly discovered by Solov'ev and Trubetskoy, but rather an accurately faithful following of the tradition of the Holy Fathers. The Fathers of the Church already back in the II-IV Centuries literally thought such and such they wrote.

Sergei Trubetskoy wrote one dissertation and then he moves on to writing a second one, -- "The Teaching Concerning the Logos", his doctoral dissertation. It came out several years before his death. In the history of Scriptural study and in the research on antiquity this is unique a work. The book, which appeared almost 100 years ago (it was published in the journal, "Questions of Philosophy and Psychology", later came out in a separate volume in 1906), has not become outmoded even today, despite a multitude of works in this area. In it Trubetskoy displayed his talent to full effect. He demonstrated, how the human world had presentiment of the Revelation of the mystery of the Divine Word -- the Logos, it had presentiment of the appearing of Christ. Then he turns his attention to the Old Testament world and he did not merely repeat traditional conceptions with a naive sham timidity, all hallowing the Old Testament, but rather employs all the full leverage of the then scientific historical criticism.

We know, that the historical criticism of the Bible back in the XVIII, the XIX and XX Centuries was frequently used for its discrediting and negating. And theologians in a panic therefore were afraid of historical criticism. Moreover, our religious censorship simply and flat out forbade theologians to write in such a key. And even simply the explanation of a Biblical criticism was regarded as something extremely and extraordinarily bold a step. They criticised, certainly, be it Strauss, or Harnack, or Renan and others, but they did not translate them into the Russian language, nor publish them. (This was the picture of things, reminiscent abit of our Soviet style criticism, when they black-listed for us bourgeois philosophers, say the like of Camus, [Erich] Fromm, Freud and others, whom they did not allow to be published nor translated; and the reader, if he remained unable to obtain these books in the original, was compelled to have only an orientation by way of this denunciatory literature.) Thus it was throughout all the extent of the XIX Century in Russia, and not only in Russia -- in the Catholic world this picture of things was much the same [with its "Index of Forbidden Books"].

Sergei Trubetskoy showed, how to combine a naturally and organically bold critical outlook with very profound a pervasiveness into the meaning of the Biblical account and the doctrinal aspect. If they were to ask me, who best has explained the fundamentals of Biblical theology, I would say, that in the Russian language up to the present no one has done it better, than Sergei Nikolaevich Trubetskoy.

In unfolding the panorama of Old Testament history, showing the conflict of ideas, and of the inroads of Revelation several centuries before the Birth of Christ, he boldly approaches the centremost and ultimate idea -- the idea of the incarnation of the Logos within Christ. He speaks concerning Him as a Christian, but also at the same time as a scholar. When Harnack asserts, that Christ proclaimed upon earth only but a lofty moral teaching and faith in God -- that of loving the Father, Sergei Nikolaevich takes exception and disagrees with this. He disagrees, that no, it was not merely a matter of the teachings of Christ -- He was never some mere moralist, simply comforting people with moral sentiments. Christ declared concerning Himself something unprecedented, He possessed as regards history a singular and especial God-consciousness, where the human consciousness within Him became combined and identified with the God-consciousness. He set out not from some high heavenly authority, but upon His Own authority, which He Himself had within Him. And this Self-witnessing, this Self-testifying of Christ, -- says Trubetskoy, -- is a fact of history; Christ is suchlike in the earliest, the most ancient, documents. We can either believe in this or not believe -- but that is a question altogether different, a question not historical, but rather moral, spiritual, mystical; and here the problem of faith comes into consideration.

Further on, Sergei Trubetskoy speaks about how the world has had Christ come upon it, all yet unaware, and that the appearance of God has faced man with a necessary choice; and not only was it the Pharisees or Caiphas that were caught unaware, even today man is caught unaware about all this. And it is because, as Trubetskoy points out in the historical material, people, those in resistance against Christ, -- the ideologues, the scholars, the theologians -- bear within them a typology, are of a type, an inflexible type of piety, self-smugness, authoritarianism, elitism and everything else, which goes with the tide of the times.

The teaching about the Logos/Word amongst the ancient Greeks -- was the teaching about an impersonal force, similar to a law, which directs the world-edifice. In Christ the Word of God, the Dvar Elohim, this becomes a personal force, manifest to man. God speaks. "The Word of God is uttered within the silence of the Absolute".

And then too this man, immersed as he is in ancient texts, in metaphysical quests, emerges also within the societal arena. He cannot remain the scholar hidden away in his chambers, he takes an active part in the social struggle. The struggle for freedom, the struggle for the fatherland was for him vital a programme. In essence, he gave his life in sacrifice for this struggle. And in the then world of his time he stood out by this combination of deep scholarship, a cool and analytical mind, together with a fervent faith. Not a lispingly limp faith! As regards our churchly world, Trubetskoy by no means was one to wimp out with whatever excuse, but often compared us sinners, with the Sadducees. When he was at the Trinity-Sergiev Lavra, catching a glance at how the monks there were goofing off, he said to his brother, that here walk Sadducees (the Sadducees -- were opponents of Christ, the priestly caste in the Judaism of the time).

When Vasily Vasil'evich Rozanov came out against the idea of freedom of conscience, Vladimir Solov'ev burst out with a feulleton, a satire, which he titled: "Porphyry Golovlev on Freedom and Faith". This was very acid a satire written by Solov'ev. He begins it thus: I know the writer Rozanov, he is very talented and intelligent a man, but suddenly there is someone else writing under and using his family-name -- actually, this is the Little Judas Golovlev [character in Mikhail Saltykov-Schedrin (1826-1889) novel] rendering judgements on freedom and faith. Further on, and continuing in the same key, Vladimir Solov'ev leaves not a stone upon stone remaining with Rozanov's murky opinions. And when Vasily Vasil'evich read this, he said: "I am unable to come up with a retort to this. He really murdered me". (Rozanov was a sincere man.)

Trubetskoy also then wrote just as harshly, and in particular, he made a parody of the views of Rozanov in verse, which he titled: "The Prayer of Butonov" (Butonov -- is Rozanov). They tend to say (though it is unverified) that these lines were composed together with Solov'ev. I do not remember it precisely, but it begins thus:

> I set alight my own lampada
> With lofty a soul soaring,
> I do not kill, I do not steal,
> I do not commit adultery.
>
> And, in spirit meek, full of peace,

I do the deed of faith...

(the deed of faith -- is the "autodafe" Spanish-style [torching the bon-fire]).

> ...I set myself up no idols --
> The foreign temples I would shatter...

> Blow up their churches with dynamite,
> And in the air the churches would fly,
> To the far-off Arctic Ocean
> To rain down idols for the reindeer folk.

> And let fall the false faith of cathedral
> Smashed to dusty smithereens,
> And go howling the ancient jackals
> Over those desolate places.

> And so, I make my way, humble in spirit...

And it finishes:

> And so I pray, humble in spirit,
> For our Orthodox people,
> For the wafting of healthy salubrious breezes,
> And for the Mostholy Governing Synod.

Trubetskoy's frame of mind is quite clearly apparent from this parody poem.

Particularly important for him was the issue of the autonomy of the university. Sergei Nikolaevich was a professor at the Moscow University. He felt, that this is a place, where the intellectual elite from the whole country should be able to collaborate, and it should be a place of freedom. This is because the problem of the autonomy of the university, its independence from the government, from the police and other institutions -- is verymost important a principle for culture. And for it Trubetskoy struggled desperately, boldly; he recoursed to the tsar, he turned to the Senate, the struggle was very severe. In the final end, though, it took its toll upon him. They elected him rector of the University. But his health was seriously undermined, despite his young age. Sergei Nikolaevich spent all of 27 days in the position of rector. He had journeyed to Peterburg, in order to again get involved in these matters, and there suddenly he died from a stroke, outliving, as I said, his friend Solov'ev by all of five years.

From him there remain five enormous volumes of his collected works. The first tome comprises published articles, among which is the brilliant sketch concerning the French thinker Renan. The second tome -- is theological and historico-religious articles, among which is the brilliant work, "Dogmatics and Ethics" -- brief but precise, wherein Trubetskoy indicates, that ethics (as we now often tend to think) cannot be merely something suspended of itself up in mid-air, but that it is obliged to set forth with roots within a religious basis; that man cannot find a truly viable justification for ethics within nature, within logic, within law, within advantage, ultimately since that in one instance what is advantageous, in another instance is not, in one instance it might correspond to nature, whereas otherwise -- it might not. Therefore ethical principles derive from higher a spirituality. The third tome -- involves the metaphysics of Ancient Greece, and the fourth tome -- the teaching about the Logos. The final tome -- is "The History of Ancient Philosophy". And as the majority of our philosophers and historians of Russian thought tend to assert, Trubetskoy did not get to completely work out his views, he did not accomplish it before his end. But all his fundamental principles are lodged therein. Those of you, who love clear and fine thought, who love a free and open approach to actuality, will find tremendous joy, when you get to read the works of Sergei Trubetskoy. He writes without obtuseness, precisely, lucidly, just like his friend, Vladimir Solov'ev. And I indeed hope, that in the closely impending future we will again have Sergei Trubetskoy published (since all our time spent with you is with the intent, that after my talks about the philosophers their books should also come out).

And yet here he dies. At the University was formed a society in his name. At the gatherings of this society various people tended to stand out, and some, to my recollection, had gotten published, among whom was Vernadsky. And there is the pithy comment by Sergei Nikolaevich Bulgakov, then a mere assistant professor (in political economics). Stepping forth, Sergei Nikolaevich proclaimed: "Though I but little knew the reposed S. N. Trubetskoy, his star gleamed bright upon my spiritual horizon, pointing the way... at a point in time, when I was experiencing an implosion of world-view, traversing that lengthy path from Marxism to

Christianity, Prince Trubetskoy, amongst other religious thinkers, proved to be a strong and courageous source of support, so needful for a man, forcing his way through the thicket of modern non-belief, or oftener still even of all the religious indifferentism". And Bulgakov goes on further to say, that the precious thing in Prince Trubetskoy was his Christocentric world-view. Which is to say, that for him in Christ was revealed something quite centrally foremost, which is only contained within Christianity. And on this note Bulgakov quotes then the words of Sergei Nikolaevich Trubetskoy concerning Revelation and its critique: "I am firmly convinced, -- writes Prince Trubetskoy, -- that Revelation can never cease to be Revelation, I am not afraid of history nor do I look to turn it all around back... In vain do we think to fence in and guard Christianity, isolating it from history, for in such manner we would be leading astray those, who would face up to the facts and see, that it is at a mere mid-point of history. Christianity lives and acts upon the earth, it sprouted upon the earth like the tiny grain of mustard seed, it has grown and will grow further, until it attains fully its stature in Christ". Thus, in the words of Bulgakov, Prince Trubetskoy has become a Russian successor to the Greek, the Egyptian, the Syrian Fathers of the Church, who taught about the significance of the reasoning ability, of knowledge, of science, of philosophy, for a proper contemplating of the Christian world-view.

Evgenii Nikolaevich Trubetskoy -- was a man of somewhat different an outlook, he was not so attracted to metaphysical problems, but still the influence of Solov'ev upon him was quite strong, and he had to assert his own freedom from this influence. As the result of this inner struggle to assert his own independence as a thinker, the erudite scholar Evgenii Trubetskoy (a professor likewise of the Moscow and Kiev Universities) writes a two-volumed profound work, replete with an enormous amount of factual material, concerning the societal-religious ideal of Western Christianity. I remind you: Solov'ev felt, that Christianity ought to realise upon earth a theocracy -- a God-power rule of authority, a certain ideal arrangement, in which the Divine laws would be the foundational basis of society. For there to be any justification for this order of things, Evgenii Trubetskoy attempted to perceive it in context of history and in this vein he examined two points: the teachings of Blessed Augustine concerning the state and the teachings of Pope Gregory VII, the creator of the theocratic papal power in the XI Century. With Trubetskoy there were no earlier pre-conceived notions on the matter, and he came to the conclusion, that herein lurked a multitude of dangers.

During this time at Moscow there lived a fine lady, a very wealthy woman, Margarita Kirillovna Morozova. She had several houses in the Arbat quarter, and in particular, one house with a beautiful salon along the Mertvyi lane. She deeply loved Prince Evgenii. But this love also thus remained Platonic, nothing happened between the two of them, except for a sincere spiritual questing. But I make mention of this purely personal aspect, since for Russian philosophy it played an enormous role. Margarita Kirillovna was a wealthy woman, and she provided Prince Evgenii the financial backing for religio-philosophic publishing, as well as hosting religio-philosophic gatherings at her home.

There, on Mertvyi lane, began gatherings of the finest, and the then still young, representatives of Russian religious thought and with sizeable also an audience. The house was beautiful and old-fashioned, the halls had entertainment for guests, with a special chamber for lectures and discussions; the walls were adorned with icons, then still but beginning to be uncovered in the restoration process. In these years (the beginning of the XX Century) the restorers first uncovered for themself and for the world the vivid palette range of colour in the ancient Russian icon. Indeed prior to this it was considered, that the icon -- is something basically blackish, with dark faces (as you know, the darkness occurred simply from chemical processes, from the dulling of the oil, with which the icon was preserved). And so here we had these restored icons hanging, and right there we had talks being given, papers and reports being read. And in this setting was forged that unique Russian religio-philosophic movement, which afterwards was eradicated by the Revolution, physically eradicated, though part of it succeeded in making its way West creating there its own school, the literary and spiritual inheritance of which now is returning home for us.

At the gatherings of the Society were deliberated quite varied a scope of questions, and it was decided to form a publishing effort under the logo "Put'" ("The Way"). Under this publishing firm there first appeared the two-volume work of Evgenii Trubetskoy concerning Solov'ev (this was both a biography, an history of his life, and an history of his thought). Trubetskoy points out in the book, the points in which he is in agreement, and also those in which he is not. Also under the publisher "Put'" there first appeared Florensky's book, "The Pillar and Affirmation of Truth", then the collected works of Kireevsky, and for the first time, more than seventy years after being written, the collected works of Chaadaev were published. It seems impossible to enumerate the endless number of books, which came out through the funding of Margarita Kirillovna, this is an entire bibliotek of a library, which is precious even today.

Under Trubetskoy's editing quite seriously important books came out, and when the Revolution had already started, he summed up his world-view in the book, "The Meaning of Life". On the title page he set the imprint of the publisher "Put'", though this publishing firm had already been liquidated in the raging tempest of the revolutionary years. Then also under publisher "Put'" there came out his small book, "Two Beasts".

Who are these two beasts? These two monsters -- are the monsters of reaction and the monster of the unrestrained tyranny of the "left" (the so to speak "left"). He said, that these two beasts are alike dangerous for the love of one's country, and for our Russia especially. But his most brilliant works of this period were brochures, setting a basis for all the thought involving the ancient Russian iconography right up to the present day. From three of these brochures in particular there begins quite new an understanding of icons. These works are entitled "An Intellectual Intuition into Colours", "The Two Worlds of Ancient Russian Iconography", and "Russia in its Icon".

Very interesting is a basic insight of Evgenii Trubetskoy. He says, that this world -- is a world of devouring, and he recollects, how he once had seen pictures about a water beetle, which devoured everything it found in the aquarium. "This reminded me of our life, -- he wrote during the time of the First World War. The iron war machine devours everything -- is life possible amidst such? Is man doomed to exist thus? The human spirit reveals a different realm, a different vision of things, and this vision of things was what with genius the old Russian iconographers reflected the imprint of. And for us it was revealed freshly anew, when they removed the adornment covering, the over-frames, when they cleaned the icons. He writes about how the over-frame -- was the result of piety, but primitively and in vulgar a manner: the icon had become dark, and it was felt necessary to adorn it, in order to brighten it up. He poses the question: how would the Madonna of Raphael or Botticelli thus appear, if it was buried within an adorning over-frame? Is it even possible to imagine? Certainly not. And yet the way we have adorned the Vladimir Mother of God, and the Trinity, within an over-frame! Actually, for Trubetskoy, just as for many people, this was all on the order of a revelation. Icons, which initially had seemed but gloomy dark markings in the background of the gilded covers, actually instead had brought into play all sorts of heavenly colours, and it became apparent, that each colour possesses its own especial characteristic; that the solar light is signified by gold, and intensity of spirit -- by bright red scarlet a colour; that all these lines, which seemed simply to be drawn in ignorance by wandering artists, are rather indeed melodious lines -- symbols, as it were the notes of a mysterious vision, which came to the saints and was transmitted through symbol and music, the artistic music innate within the icon.

"The Two Worlds of Ancient Russian Iconography" -- what are these two worlds? The first -- is the world of fierce struggles, a world of hostility, a world of discord, and this world is the world of death. But the icon opens before us a different world, a coelestial world -- the world of light, the world of beauty, a world the opposite of our black world, our black world of death and hostility. And in this -- is the seeing of light and harmony.

That which Sergei Nikolaevich had called the all-unity, sobornost', became for his brother a spiritual mystical reality, reflected within iconography. And he emphasised, that in the old churches, which have preserved their original schematics, there exists a certain unity throughout all the composition, and all the movements, all the faces, all the hands of the saints are oriented towards one central aspect -- and this is the harmony of the world. Actually given to people. But it was lost, the walls were repainted, the golden cupolas rising heavenward vanished, replaced by bulbs on narrow stems, steeple-spires -- this reflected a loss of the vision. And the fact that Trubetskoy was aware of this and speaking about it to people, was a sign of the transition to another perception of the icon, and to another perception of the world as a whole. And if one tends to speak about the asceticism of the old Russian icon, then the asceticism here is not something gloomy, not as Vasily Vasil'evich Rozanov tended to speak about it, but is rather the surmounting of the maliciousness of this world.

Evgenii Trubetskoy was writing a multitude of pamphlets and articles, all the time by this asserting meaning in the face of meaninglessness. The world War, Revolution, the Civil War -- these are all bereft of meaning, but meaning -- signifies love and unity. Such was a chief point of his outlook, his feelings. If we tear a picture into pieces -- it becomes at a loss for meaning. Only the integral wholeness of the organism possesses meaning. If we cut off from the organism a part, then the part dies, it loses its meaning. And suchlike here is the organic unity of the world.

Evgenii Trubetskoy believed, that the country would have to pass through intense a cleansing by suffering. His friends already during this time had forsaken their native land, but he dreamed only, that he might die upon his native soil. And thus it happened. He had journeyed south, joining in with the White Movement and he died at Novorossiisk in 1920. And from that time his works were no longer republished, his name was stricken from the history of Russian culture, and only today do he and his brother begin to return to us again.

This is a very short and abridged an outline of that, which might be said about these two remarkable people.

The Religio-Philosophic Views of Lev Tolstoy

Lev Nikolaevich Tolstoy was not a philosopher, nor a theologian in the full sense of the word. And at first I did not intend to devote an entire meeting of ours to his religio-philosophic views. But I see nonetheless, that this is necessary. And today we shall focus upon him in our interesting and nowise simple journeying into areas, for a long time hidden away from people, such as are interested in Russian religious thought.

When we speak about Tolstoy, we first of all then have in view the writer, the author of novels and tales, but we tend also to forget, that he was a man of thought. Can he be called immense as a thinker? He was immense a man, he was a great man. And even if we cannot accept his philosophy, each of us is still thankful to him for some happy moments in our tribulations, when we read his tales, his artistic works. One finds but few people, who in general have no love for his creativity. At various periods in one's own life Tolstoy suddenly opens for us some new and unexpected aspects.

If this be so, then have we the right to think, as certain people tend to think, that Tolstoy was a genius in literature, but that in philosophy and religion he was tedious and boring a writer, -- material better left untouched, and a good thing also that this material is not included in collections of his works, except on the academic level? (The academic indeed -- there is a little accessible 90 volume collection, with which literary specialists and historians deal). It is amazing therefore, that over the whole extent of time elapsing since the death of Lev Nikolaevich, especially in the Soviet period, that so few have turned serious attention to this side of his creative activity.

But, my friends, this is extreme an ingratitude! I tell you this in all sincerity. Being an Orthodox priest, a member of that selfsame Church, which published a decree, excommunicating Tolstoy from the Church, I nevertheless stress, that this nowise means, that we ought to be unjust to this man and be disdainful of what agitated this departed giant of life, moreso perhaps than with his artistic works. This reflected his inner life, matters which tormented and delighted him across the expanse of his long life.

Those few of you, who possibly have read his diaries, easily can concur, how early Tolstoy began to analyse his courses of action, how early he began to ponder the meaning of life, how he thought upon death, about the ethical aspects of human existence and human society. And thus it would seem, that he was not simply a writer, but actually some synthetically mighty a person.

About 90 years back Dmitrii Sergeevich Merezhkovsky wrote a book, "Lev Tolstoy and Dostoevsky". He wanted to present Tolstoy (and justly so) as a full-blooded giant, as a rocky crag of a man, as some great pagan-like figure; whereas Dostoevsky -- was for him only as a Christian, as a fanatic, an inspired and spiritual preacher of spirit. The seer of spirit and the seer of flesh -- is an antithesis of which Dmitrii Sergeevich Merezhkovsky was fond. And there is a grain of truth in this. And usually we tend to say: the pained eyes of Dostoevsky, the tortured muse of Dostoevsky, the tormented genius of Dostoevsky, life as suffering. But Tolstoy -- courses deep and full-blooded.

This is a mistake, my friends, our mistake where like children we are indifferent to the sufferings of our fathers. Because Lev Nikolaevich Tolstoy was a man no less tragic, than was Dostoevsky. And I tell you straight out -- more tragic, far more tragic. Both his contemporaries, and many later on also have seen this. I shall not go into details. But if you think on it, that here was a man who, in having created one of the greatest Russian national epic works -- "War and Peace", -- came out against patriotism. This was a man, who wrote passionate and immortal lines on love (which even in old age he wrote: remember the novel "Resurrection", the moment when Nekliudov and Katya meet, when they are still young; it is an old man writing this and how indeed he writes!), this is a man, having described love in its various nuances and aspects (uplifting love, passionate love), who in general considered marriage as some sort of misunderstanding and in "The Kreutzer Sonata" he stressed this.

Here was a man, who for a large part of his life was a preacher of Gospel ethics, and the final 30 years of his life he devoted to preaching of the Christian teaching (as he understood it), which brought him into conflict with the Christian Church with the final result of his being excommunicated from it. A man, who preached non-resistance [from the "non resistere malo" Gospel teaching -- "resist not evil"], but who was a mighty militant struggler, like in identity to Stepan Razin or Pugachev in hurling down the gauntlet to the whole of culture, consigning it to the likes of mere feather-down and dust. A man, who stands forth in culture as a phenomenon (comparable only with Goethe, if one consider Western Europe), an universal genius, with nothing that he did not tackle -- be it plays, publicist articles, novels or tales -- everywhere capable! And this man then came to scorn art, wrote it off and in the final end came out against his brother in art Shakespeare, in considering that Shakespeare wrote his works at random without purpose. Lev Tolstoy -- was one of the greatest phenomena of culture -- and was also one of the greatest enemies of culture.

And finally, let us give some thought to his personal fate. Call to mind Dostoevsky: a figure tragic, in youth sentenced to be executed, a bitter lot. But with him there was love and harmony with Anna Grigor'evna. And though his life was arduous, even so, it corresponded to his spirit, his thought, the style of his life. But Tolstoy over the years was tormented by this, that the style of his life was contrary to what he was preaching, the years brought out a revolt against this -- and he was compelled to suffer it to the end of his days, one might say, right down to his flight and hour of death. A man, who fled his home, -- a figure, without question, deeply tragic. And this goes only a little way towards how we might describe it. And it is precisely because of this, that we along with you ought both with respect and caution also to approach that which tortured and tormented Tolstoy. That which transformed his life into a tragedy, into a drama.

Now let us turn to the question about his religio-philosophic views. Tolstoy wrote, very often repeating this in various places: "Only in childhood did I have a traditional faith, and from age 14 I fully left off from it and lived devoid of it, as did all my contemporaries". Certainly, it is not necessary to accept these words literally. He did have a faith. But it was a faith hazy and indistinct, a type of Deism. You know, surely, that alongside the cross young Tolstoy hung a portrait of Jean Jacques Rousseau. And this was not by chance.

Jean Jacques Rousseau -- was a great, an enormous figure of the European and world stage. He set before people the question, which up to the present is not fully dealt with (though Rousseau, actually, was not ultimately correct), -- the question, of whether civilisation is our enemy? And whether or not the path backwards, towards the simplicity of life, is the sole salvation of mankind? Jean Jacques Rousseau spoke about this in the XVIII Century, when there were no atomic power-plants, no poisoned rivers, nor densely congested cities, which at present transform the capitols of the world into a sort of mindless man-killing anthill. But back then already Rousseau, as we are accustomed to write in school books, foresaw with genius all this abracadabra of the XX Century, and Tolstoy sensed this, he sensed it with all the fibres of his being, of his soul, and it was not only from the French tradition that he imbibed this (though the French was innate for him, since he was European by upbringing), but also from the Russian tradition.

Remember for a moment what Pushkin's drama, "The Gypsies", is all about. Here also it is the selfsame question of Rousseauism. But Pushkin wisely decided it otherwise, since the colossal instinct of this superhuman of a man allowed him to open the truth before us: nowhere can man flee from himself, neither in whatever the gypsy-camps, nor in whatever the forests. Pushkin in his character of Aleko performed also this experiment -- a flight from civilisation. But from sin one cannot flee! Thy sin will haunt thee even in the wilds.

But Tolstoy (however, just like many other writers) is unable nonetheless to part with this fanciful dream. It was and will be a fanciful dream of mankind, though it be fifty percent illusion. When did it appear? Three thousand years ago, actually. Way back still in antiquity Chinese philosophers said, that time flings aside everything artificial and passes over to the natural. And already the ancient [Greek] cynics, (these were not cynics in the sense in which we now use the term), the cynic philosophers lived under the slogan: "Back, to nature" -- and they walked their way about and appearing however they might, thinking, that in so doing they were returning nigh to the natural life. And those laughing at them gave them the name "cynics" from the Greek word "kunos" -- meaning a dog, since they lived life literally like a dog. And all of us even at present, when we escape the city, tend to breathe a sigh of relief along with a nostalgia for nature. But as regards Rousseauism, this is not the solution. For Tolstoy, however, this was a solution.

Tolstoy's work, "The Cossacks": I shall not run through the whole plot, since surely you will have read it and remember it. But who actually was the character Olenin? Actually Lev Nikolaevich Tolstoy, as a young officer. Whence were his yearnings? To return to nature, to merge himself with it. And the character Maryana -- this was the image of Mother Nature, the Earth. To return to this sky, to these vineyards, to these hills, to the wild critters, for which Uncle Eroshka hunts, just as wild, and even the wild-boars, rustling about in the underbrush, and those mountaineers, shooting them with arrows... whither and whence all the moral norms have vanished, and where the law of nature becomes the morality. But then suddenly it becomes clear for Olenin, that all this has been an illusion, and that he cannot go back, he cannot. And for him this is a realisation bitter, shameful, sad. Olenin grieves, as actually Lev Tolstoy himself grieves, that there is no way back, that the movement here is all one-sided.

And hence here, long before his spiritual crisis, Lev Tolstoy begins to seek for a way out of this dilemma. He seeks for it in work, in family, in that which we tend to call happiness. But remember his likewise early piece -- "Family Happiness". A sweet notion, but a dreary thing. He sings its praises, like a genuine artist, very dear, sacred, and then it all somewhere goes to pieces, and he buries it.

In "War and Peace" also, that absorbingly immortal great vignette of the onward rush of history, Tolstoy emerges not as some sort of a man without faith. He believes -- in fate. He believes in some mysterious power, which inexorably leads people thence, whence they want not. The ancient Stoics said: "Destiny leads the consenting, but the resistant, destiny drags". And this destiny or fate is here active within his works. How can we not love "War and Peace" (I am very fond of this work, having essentially read it ten times), but what always amazed me, was how Tolstoy, such a great writer, had no feeling for the significance of the person within history. For him Napoleon was only a mere pawn of sorts. And the mass of people act, basically, like ants, which move along by certain and mysterious a sort of laws. And when Tolstoy attempts to explain these laws, I think you will all agree, that his digressions, the historical interludes, seem far weaker, than the actual full-blooded, mighty, many-faceted picture of the events happening -- on the field of battle, or in the maids of honour salon, or in the room where sits one of the heroes.

What kind of a faith is still therein, except for mysterious fate. A faith, which again can meld together with nature, this is again the Olenin dream. Remember Prince Andrei, how he inwardly converses with the oak. This oak, is it simply a notable old tree? No, it is likewise a symbol, a symbol of eternal nature, for which the soul of the hero strives. The searchings of Pierre Bezukov. Likewise all bereft of meaning... It would seem, that none of Tolstoy's heroes manages to find in mind a genuine

Christian path. Why is this? Well, because the finest of the people of the XIX Century, after the catastrophes of the XVIII Century, happened somehow or other to get cut off from the great Christian tradition. And in this both the Church, and society, suffered tragically. The consequences of this split bore their bitter fruit in the XX Century -- as a terrible event, almost nearly destroying the whole of civilisation in our land.

And where indeed does Pierre Bezukhov seek his exit, his way out? He goes to the Masons. Their rituals (you remember -- the blind-folded eyes and all manner of words) -- what was this? An attempt to imitate the Church. The general overall crisis of the Christian Church of the XVII-XVIII Centuries led to chaos enough, true, but also to attempts everywhere to create an imitation of the Church on the basis of the most simplistic dogmas: God, the soul, immortality. These are the dogmas of Deism, which denies Revelation, and the Incarnation, and the Person of Jesus Christ as the Revealed Word of God upon earth, viewing Him as a seer-like teacher and prophet.

Deism spread with an extraordinary strength, and we know, that outstanding people of the XVIII and early XIX Centuries got caught up in these ideas: among the Masons were Mozart, and Lessing, in Russia Novikov, Bazhenov and many others. And Tolstoy's hero also. He goes not to the Church, but rather to the pseudo-church which, in place of the sacred symbols of nearly two thousand years of Christianity, -- instead has people going through a system of these artificially contrived and intellectual home-made symbols and rituals. And certainly, all this very quickly for him grew stale, just as it did with Pushkin, who likewise started with Masonism and likewise went through the ritual, and then cast it all aside, just as did Karamzin.

And then -- "Anna Karenina". Another tragedy. I think, that those of you who have read Tolstoy at depth, tend to know, that he wanted to depict the moral downfall of Anna and show, how this fate, this destiny, this mysterious God, which rules over all, tends to deal with a transgressor. And therefore Lev Tolstoy began his novel with the words from Scripture, with the Words of God: "Vengeance is Mine, and I will repay, saith the Lord" [Rom. 12:19]. These words signify the appeal of God to man not to seek revenge. Prior to Christianity, indeed, revenge was regarded as a sacred duty. And sometimes this "sacred obligation" devastated whole tribes of people, since if someone was murdered, then his relatives were obligated to kill someone from the murderer's family, and thus this blood-feud vendetta went on uninterruptedly, until whole villages were laid waste, particularly in the hills. And thus here, God speaks through His prophet, saying: "Revenge is Mine, and it is for Me to exact it". But Tolstoy interpreted these words differently: fate, or God, takes revenge on man for sin, and punishes.

Tolstoy traces out the history of the woman. And the paradox! Who of us can be unsympathetic towards Anna?! The author succinctly comes out on her side, and not on the side, let us say, of her husband, when he attempted to describe objectively, though at certain moments we might feel abit for Karenin, and particularly when he attempts to forgive Anna -- as he touchingly and suddenly reproaches himself: "I am so at a loss for words", -- he says. And here this stammering -- of an august senator, accustomed to weigh each word, suddenly shows, that beyond his cold exterior there beats a living heart. But the sympathies of the reader remain nonetheless with the unfortunate Anna! Tolstoy had nothing more to suggest. Logic, the inner logic of life and of the heroine, the threading of life entered into the matter and clashed with his intent.

And then there ensues a crisis. I wanted to read you what he writes about this crisis, but -- I shall not. You are all literate people, read it for yourself. It was nauseating for him. When he was at the town of Arzamas (and this was a time of his flourishing), he had a feeling that he might die. This was terrifying! Some psychiatrists would say, that he had an onset of acute depression. But why however was he thus? For what reason?

Some people tend to say: it is in the difficult moments that a man finds in himself both God and faith. But there is also the well-known saying, that "faith -- is for the weak", that only in misfortunes do people find their way to the Church, a saying discredited by merely this one example here. I know of such examples by the hundreds, but this example is sufficiently clear and convincing. When did Tolstoy begin to seek, finally, for God and faith? It was when he became a noted writer, when he was already the author of great novels, which thundered their way throughout all the world. When he already had a beloved wife, a loving family, and a regular choir of grateful readers. And moreover, he was a rich man. He had everything of what today for whatever modern man would seem the epitome of happiness. And suddenly at this moment he comes to a standstill.

Tolstoy writes about this with an extraordinary sincerity in his first religio-philosophic book, given the title "Confession". This book afterwards was to serve as a prologue to his tetrology, a four volume collection, a name for which Lev Nikolaevich failed to come up with; but in the tetrology was included the "Confession" (as a prelude), "An Investigation of dogmatic Theology", a translation and interpretation of the four Gospels, "In What is My Faith?", and afterwards a fifth and supplemental book, entitled "The Kingdom of God is within You". This is the chief religio-philosophic book of Tolstoy. It summarises his world-view, provides the dynamics for it, and indicates by what manner Tolstoy arrived at these views.

The "Confession" -- is the most intense of these books. I have to inform you plain out, that to read the religio-philosophical works of Tolstoy is difficult. And this is not, my friends, because it is some sort of a lofty, convoluted and subtle metaphysics. And not because, as it is with Florensky, a text rigged with various sorts of peculiar wordings, copious foreign notes and quotes, an enormous apparatus. But rather it is because that, however odd it may seem, this is a literature endowed with immensely less power, than the artistic works of Tolstoy. Already back then many people, who had objectively an appreciation of Tolstoy, feeling that here was a winged and mighty talent, a veritable eagle soaring high over souls and fates, events and persons, -- they however suddenly quit Tolstoy, when he attempted to expound his teaching. And do not think, that I am saying this merely out of a sense of bias, that somehow I would want to trivialise the philosophic views of Tolstoy. A great man ought not to be trivialised. But objectively we have to tell it, like it is. And the truth of my words you can easily prove for yourself, in reading these books.

At present a small volume of Tolstoy is being readied for printing, to include particularly these works. Do not ignore it, read it, even if only some of it. I tell you this, unafraid of seeming to sow seeds of temptation, since I believe, that you are sufficiently mature of mind and of critical an ability, to think it through, separating the genuine grain of wheat from its chaff.

Some of my Christian friends and colleagues say: why even bother to have this republished? We have read his novels, so just leave this for the literary specialists and historians. But only someone afraid of truth could tend to say this, and one mustneeds not fear truth. The truth can stand on its own. And then too, are we not sick of the censoring attitude towards literature, thought, art, culture, religion? For myself, I think we are fed up with this, we have had enough of everything snipped at and trimmed, enough of having them distort the picture. Why indeed continue with this vile practice! Here he is before us -- a great man. This can please one, or not please one, but still he created this, and if towards him we have a tiny bit of respect, we have to engage it all for what it is, to evaluate it, to think it through. One might topple it, capsize it -- and Tolstoy would never take offence at this. But to go at it with the scissors of the censor -- this is a degradation of the genius, a degradation of human dignity in general and a debasing of culture.

And well, thus, his most successful thing -- was the "Confession". Why? Because Tolstoy did not therein resort to deliberations of things remote and abstract, things quite tedious, but rather speaks about his own life. He tells, how it came to a stop, that one day he simply died as it were. Look here, I shall possess so many horses, I shall own so much land. And why? And what for? Well, I shall be a very famous writer, I shall be celebrated, like Moliere, like Shakespeare. And then what? And here is that terrible, that soul-chilling question -- it shakes him to the very depths, since it was quite justly a proper question.

In what is the meaning of our existence? This is a question that has to be faced. We tend to try to suppress and drown it out. These eternal questions have been suppressed and smothered for two to three generations by all kinds of shrill fanfare. But the moment just when this fanfare ceases blaring so loudly, this question arises anew and facing each person. Why and for what? One's offspring? They are likewise in the grip of death. The future? Completely unknown, for whom it will be. And then too, is there anything better for the present? Why is all this? And thus, at the crest of success, at a period of life and a condition, which the ancient Greeks called the "acme", the point of highest flourishing, the prime of a man's life, comparatively young, nowise infirm, rather healthy a man, who would hop onto an horse, and who loved physical work, who each day walked and journeyed about, a man, immersed in the whole of culture (he indeed spoke German so well, that even Germans would not guess, that he was a foreigner); it would seem, that here was a man who had it all! And suddenly it proves to be -- nothing. It all burst like a pretty bubble. And life stops as it were, and he says: "And I am like dead". And it is among the greatest service, the greatest merit, of this thinker and philosopher Tolstoy, that he puts before us this tragic question in all its harsh alacrity: what is it all for?

As an erudite and learned man, he began to seek within literature, within the history of human thought: perhaps, there is something there? He turns to science -- and discovers, that science is unable to provide the solution. Science does not know, why we live, science is involved only with the processes, and processes -- are insensitive a thing, they are fluid-like towards whatever their course and unable to provide any sort of actual meaning in themself, since such categories as meaning-bearing thought is beyond the proper scope of science.

Tolstoy turns towards philosophy, he reads the ancient seers. But certainly, he reads them very selectively -- do not forget, this is Lev Tolstoy we are speaking about. He seeks for what he needs, and finds it. He opens the Bible, and opens it, certainly, to Ecclesiastes, to where it is said, that it profits not the man, which toileth his day beneathe the sun, a generation cometh and a generation goeth, but the earth abideth forever, and the wind doth wind its way about and returneth whereof it began, all the rivers flow hence to the sea, and the sea doth remain unfilled; and all is vanity of vanities and a chasing of the wind. He opens the scriptures of India and hears the words of Buddha, that everything will fall apart: everything that is, what comprises it, will disintegrate. The world is a projection like unto a mirage. He turns to modern philosophy, which is the philosophy of his century, the XIX Century, and certainly he comes upon Arthur Schopenhauer -- a very talented, I would say, a genius of a writer, but an absolute pessimist, who in his brilliantly written books asserts, that the world -- is all like rubbish and that the sooner it all ends, the better. And Tolstoy surrounds himself with this pessimistic philosophy. And on each page he gets to repeating: "I, Buddha, Solomon and Schopenhauer have perceived, that this is all useless". "I, Buddha, Solomon and Schopenhauer"... (Solomon -- was the legendary author of Ecclesiastes.)

Science does not help. Philosophy says, that everything is useless. Faith, perhaps? And, perhaps, in spite of it all there is meaning? Perhaps, there is the God, about which always all the generations speak? And suddenly, at the very moment when Tolstoy caught sight of this thought in his heart, he suddenly felt for real, that he was alive again! Life again had returned into his soul, into his awareness... And then he said to himself: but indeed religion teaches about such absurd things, and it is all expressed so crudely, so strangely. And just as this thought arose, he again felt like dead. All had become empty and cold. And Tolstoy then makes a primary and verymost important deduction: faith is life, and without faith a man is not alive.

I have made several citations from his collected works. It stands to reason that I should not want to inundate you with this, but some of the words are very important. I shall read a passage from his youth's diary, in order that you understand, how far back these thoughts perplexed him. A quarter century already prior to his exodus, before his spiritual crisis during which time his "Confession" and the other books of the tetrology were written, back on 5 March 1855 he writes in his diary: "Conversing on the Divine and faith have brought me to a great and vast thought, the realisation of which I sense myself capable of devoting my life to. (You see this, and yet later on he tells us, that he had no faith!) Here is the thought -- the founding of a new religion, correlative to the growth of mankind: a religion of Christ, but cleansed of faith and sacramentality, a religion of the practical, not promising a future bliss, but giving bliss upon earth".

And therefore, "faith -- is a matter of this life" -- is completely accurate an axiom. And secondly -- this striving of Tolstoy to create a new religion, such as would correspond to the contemporary (XIX Century) thought, the popular rationalism, for which reason -- is the supreme highest judge in all things. This is that aspect of reason, about which Pasternak spoke of, that it has no need for the perceiving of truth, but merely that we do not get cheated at the bakery, -- for Tolstoy this sense of reason becomes the supreme arbiter.

But all the same, -- what to do with this faith in reason? How to put it all together? And so he makes an experiment, fully in his own spirit. This experiment is not new. Think back on Platon Karataev. Indeed when I think back on the heroes of Tolstoy, I am ashamed for my generation, since they made a mess of all these "images" for us in school, so that now, when one turns to the novel "War and Peace", one tends to remember a tedious series of parts and grumbling teachers, who drudged over them, to give us a proper horror for Russian artistic literature and moreover for all culture entirely.

And so here, Platon Karataev for Tolstoy -- is a true seer, a true wise man; he has in himself something higher, than does Pierre and Prince Andrei. Howso? The people -- do believe! (The people, as Count Lev Nikolaevich conceived of them for himself -- he had his own concept of the people; he loved the aristocracy, as his brother-in-law Bers recollected, and he loved the people. It was the in-between ones that he did not acknowledge: he had no love for the merchants, nor the clergy -- these were all people not of his circle. Either the aristocrats, or the people. Such big childishness.)

Tolstoy honestly begins to make the following effort. He gets himself involved externally with the churchly faith (just like some of our neo-Orthodox now tend to do), he begins to go to church, although he does not understand what is happening there; he begins to observe the fasts, and the pre-Communion fasting; he journeys about to the monasteries, to churches, he converses with archimandrites, with bishops; he visited at the Optina Pustyn monastery, where he conversed with the Starets/elder Amvrosii (now since enumerated to the rank of the Saints), and was quite annoyed at him, but all the same he could not admit, that this sickly old man could be giving greater comfort to the thousands of people, coming to him, than others who were healthy. But very soon this farce (I use this word, since in the recollections of contemporaries, it was indirectly felt, that this was all a farce, and that Tolstoy wanted to show, that this was all superfluous and unnecessary) ended up nowhere: Tolstoy casts aside the churchly faith in the name of reason. Well, he was a rationalist-philosopher in the spirit of the XVIII Century, was he not? Yes, indeed! Not the XIX and not the XX, but the XVIII Century namely, with his so extreme naive faith in the all-encompassing power of healthy reasoning -- that healthy reasoning could grasp all the Universe.

And could the theology and religious philosophy of these times quench the thirst of Lev Nikolaevich? Perhaps. Already there had occurred the age of Khomyakov, of Chaadaev, already there had appeared Russian religious thinkers -- like the first swallows of Spring. Tolstoy was a contemporary of Sergei Trubetskoy, one of the most significant Russian thinkers. But chiefly, he was well acquainted with Vladimir Solov'ev. Here indeed was a knightly palladin of reason! But reason did not hinder Solov'ev from being a Christian! Solov'ev was universally erudite, a poet, a metaphysician, a political writer, an historian, an exegete. And all this nowise proved an hindrance for him.

And here now they happen to meet. And again I have to share with you a remarkable anecdote. There was a certain eyewitness present at this conversation of Lev Nikolaevich with the young Vladimir Solov'ev. This young man with his iron-like logic literally forced the gigantic Lev Tolstoy back into a corner. "At first, -- writes the eyewitness, -- Lev Nikolaevich was at a loss for words. Solov'ev had him all caged in". And only the modesty of Vladimir Solov'ev relieved the awkwardness of the whole situation, wherein the great and seemingly unquestionable figure of authority had been forced to yield. True, he did not yield in words, he continued to hold onto his own very same arguments, since it was not at all a matter of reason, but of will. And as to why, it was because he did not want to see it otherwise. He wanted to have the simplistic faith of Deism to proclaim as the sole truth.

And then Tolstoy turns to the Bible. Initially he extols the Old Testament as an artistic work, and then he casts it aside. Then he take up the New Testament -- and casts it aside. Only the Gospel! And here it comes to him like a revelation, that the Gospel is the true teaching. But do not think, that he is speaking about it as the teaching of Jesus Christ. Tolstoy is insistent, that there is a singular worldwide true teaching, which likewise was well expressed by Marcus Aurelius, by Seneca, by Confucius, by Buddha, by Dante Alighieri, by Kant -- by whomever. Such a vapid and general faith.

How to explain it? Man conceives himself part of something, part of the whole. We call this whole, this wholeness, -- God. God is our master, our owner. He sent us into this world. Immortality does not exist, since the person -- is something insignificant and small. When a man dies, he dissolves back into this wholeness. In whatever strange manner whether this be God, or some sort of higher being, or fate as precisely it tended to be with the Stoics, it bids man to conduct himself morally. And these recommendations of an higher being -- are elementary, they have always been given through all sorts of teachers, through all, but especially -- through Christ.

When Tolstoy attempts to explain the Gospel, he does not merely translate it, he literally redoes it. God preserve you when seeking the Gospel in the book, which goes under the title, "A Translation of the Gospel by Tolstoy". Here is a literal quote, that I copied out especially: "The teaching of Christ, -- he writes, -- possesses an overall human significance (in a certain sense accurate). The teaching of Christ was very simple, clear and practical in significance for the life of each individual man. This significance can be expressed thus: Christ teaches people not to do stupid things. In this consists also the very simple meaning of the teachings of Christ, accessible to all. Christ says: "Be not angry, regard no one beneathe thee -- for this is stupid". And further on thus: "If thou be angry, thou wilt offend people -- and thou wilt be the worse off for it".

I shall not quote further. But this is how he tends to view all the remaining points dealt with.

My friends, if you were to reduce the Gospel to such an elementary, and moreover still I would say, utilitarian based sort of morals ("thou wilt be the worse off for it"), then it would be nowise distinct from other ancient aphorisms. And moreover, if Lev Nikolaevich had said, that here too is a teaching of Confucius, and a teaching of the Stoics, and it is a teaching too of Lev Tolstoy, -- well then, it would serve as added material to a system of moral teachings. And would thus cause no sort of tragedy. This teaching actually is close to aspects in Buddhism, and (to a large degree) -- to Chinese type views (and not fortuitously did Tolstoy happen to write a preface to a translation of Lao-Tze, while under his editing efforts appeared the dictums of Men-Tze and other Chinese thinkers).

Chinese pantheism, the Indian -- likewise pantheism (I simplify somewhat), and finally, the Stoic pantheism -- all this was close to the teaching of Lev Tolstoy. Certainly, it would be difficult to say, what sort of a logic there is in all this: how a single impersonal principle could order man to do something, let us say, could give the command to be good. But Tolstoy thought so. And he termed God with the cold and detached word, -- "Khozyain", the "Master", the "Boss".

Therefore and in actual fact, Christ brought nothing new -- although Tolstoy in his book "The Kingdom of God is Within You" says, that this was a new teaching, since it spoke about non-resistance to evil by force. The elements of this teaching were however already there in India, and so there was actually nothing new in this. Tolstoy was not only remote from Christianity, but, as Nikolai Akeksandrovich Berdyaev tends to note, rarely has there been anyone so far removed from the Person of Christ, as was Tolstoy. He had a sort of pre-Christian consciousness, external and outside the Christian. Even Maksim Gorky after a conversation with Tolstoy reminisced: "He spoke much about Christ and Buddha. About Christ quite negatively, sentimentally, deceitfully. He advised reading a Buddhist catechism. About Christ he spoke condescendingly, and clearly had no love for him".

Irregardless of how we feel about Gorky, he nonetheless was an observant man, and with this he was accurately on target. Even the droll Renan, in describing the life of Jesus Christ, lowering it to the level of the vulgar taste of the French everyday average of the past century, still always had a love for Christ. Even Renan! We find nothing similar in the books of

Tolstoy, for he always writes about Christ coldly and with detachment. The chief thing for him -- was the teachings of Christ, only the teachings, -- and he repeats this word a million times over the sweep of a few pages.

And what comprised the teachings? A younger contemporary of Lev Nikolaevich, Prince Sergei Nikolaevich Trubetskoy, a rector of the Moscow University, a Russian great thinker, who is too overlooked up to the present, as if in reply to the thesis of Tolstoy, wrote that the Sermon on the Mount -- is central to Christianity. He hence wrote: "The Sermon on the Mount -- is not at all a moral preaching. The moral teaching of Christ derived from the awareness of Christ, unique in history, and His Self-Awareness was something singular within the world -- a consciousness of identity of the Divine and the human. Thus, when Christ is quoting words from Scripture, He gives them straight and forthright, as One possessing authority, and He says: "formerly it was said (said in the Bible) -- this, that, or another thing. But I tell ye..." And furthermore He gives a new commandment, as One, Who has this right to do so, an inner, mysterious, mystical right, a metaphysical and moral right to do so".

All this seems to have eluded Tolstoy. And here is why, when we read the first words of the Gospel of John: "In the Beginning was the Word" -- the Logos, the Divine Word addressed to the world, and "through Which all was created", -- we find Tolstoy translating it as: "In the beginning there was a reasoning intellect" -- and it all just dissipates. "We beheld His Glory", -- writes Matthew. Glory -- this is a shining radiance, a mysterious radiance. But Tolstoy puts it down as "teaching". Fine it may be, that alongside his own translation he puts the traditional translation and the Greek text. Any of you can check for themself, how far he tends to stray from the meaning of the text.

Moreover, it was not only the Gospel that suffered this fate. For surely, some of you have chanced upon a book by Tolstoy, "A Round of Readings". It contains the expressions of tens of teachers from all ages, lands and peoples. And I remember, when I first read it, still in school, I thought: why is it that they all say something almost alike? There was almost no difference, in what Kant said, or Dante, or Pascal. All terribly similar. And then, later on, many years afterwards, When I happened to check up on but a few of the quotes (Tolstoy gave them all without source references), it seemed, that this man had calmly gone about distorting them. He was indeed a creative fellow! He would hack away at it to the very core, and from this would construct his own material. Here it is not

Socrates, nor Pascal, nor the Gospel, nor the Talmud, which he is citing, but rather Lev Nikolaevich building his own edifice from the chopped-out stones of all the teachings, which chanced to fall under his hand. Is it necessary therefore to read the "Round of Readings"? It is necessary. This is an interesting book. But do not expect to find there the thoughts of great people or the genuine dictums of the sacred books. There it all begins with Tolstoy and also ends with him.

What happened between Tolstoy and the Church? I repeat: if he had simply said, that he had come up with a new teaching, no one would have condemned him. In Russia there were millions of non-Christians -- Moslems, Jews, Buddhists -- none of them excommunicated by the Church. But they did not go around saying, that they were preaching the Christian teaching, as Tolstoy tended to say. It was not enough that this man, teaching about the good, tolerance, truth, justice, respect for man, a man who taught, that in each religion there is its own truth, on which he made only one exception and for only one religion -- for Christianity as it was revealed by the Church. Here he was pitiless, and his wrath knew no bounds! Vile blasphemies, which offended the sense of a countless number of people, flowed from the lips and the pen of this "non-resister". And besides, all this occurred under the refrain: this here is the true Christianity, and the Church is distorting it.

Moreover, having made assault upon the Church, he attacked also the whole of contemporary civilisation. He consigned it all to the devil: not only art, but also jurisprudence and the laws. Apparently he had deduced this from the Gospel. Christ says: "Judge not", which is to say, do not make moral judgements about the blunders and courses of action of other people. Since "whoever of you is without sin, -- demands Christ, -- let him cast the first stone". And this is understandable, this is natural, this is profoundly just inwardly; but how does this attitude relate to jurisprudence, to the laws, which have to uphold society? Tolstoy consigns to the devil the army, and the courts, and the Church. (True it is, that he cast aside the taking of oaths, and I completely agree. Christ actually outright forbade the making of oaths in the Name of God. He said: "For your word let it be: yes, for yes, and no, for no" [Mt. 5:37].)

And lastly, a final thing: the non-resistance to evil by force. What was the intent of Our Lord in saying this? His intent was to say, that human evil, to which we stand opposed, by in like turn ourself resorting to evil, in the final end will not prove victorious. Ultimately in the end only good can vanquish evil. And when Christ with a whip chased the money-changers out of the Temple, He indeed was not of a mind of reasoning and arguing with the money-changers, -- no; He simply chased them out. The Apostle Paul, in precisely expressing the thought of Jesus Christ, said: "Not with evil can we win, but rather conquer evil with good".

This however does not relate to jurisprudence. Christ speaks about the ability to forgive, and if they have inflicted upon you a grievous loss, if (I offer an extreme example) they have murdered someone close to you, and you, having manifest some supra-human nobility, and perceived things as they were and yet forgave, -- you would be very lofty of soul. But the law cannot merely forgive. The law is only then moral and empowered, when it follows its own letter of the law. Between personal ethics, between personal morality and societal morality there still cannot exist a precise identicalness. Even in the third millennium, and perhaps even in the fourth -- it will not exist. It is because that we, as people, -- are spiritual beings, and we have a private life. But society still half lives in accord with the natural laws of the struggle for existence. And society is obligated to isolate the murderer and contend against this with mechanical means. And to imagine, that this all can just harmoniously happen -- means living in illusions.

If one attentively read the Gospel, then one can note, that Christ never said, that the social and legal means of suppressing evil are unnecessary. Concerning it He simply said, that evil cannot be totally eradicated. And in actual fact, prisons have existed for thousands of years (I cannot tell you, when the first prison was built, for indeed in ancient Egypt, in the third millennium before our era, they already existed). And moreover, has the morality of mankind improved over the last thousand years? No. But this nowise signifies, that the law ought not to act. Certainly, and unconditionally, the law ought to come nigh close to human principles, but all the same this represents two polarities, which still are quite remote from any sort of conjunction.

Yet indeed, the anarchistic viewpoints of Tolstoy on society, on the Church, upon all the structures of mankind -- ought we to toss this all away, to regard it the profound error of a genius, an unsightly black spot upon his beautiful soul and life? But here I tell you -- no, and yet again, no. The Church was obligated to testify, that Tolstoy was preaching not the Christian teaching, but rather his own. And hence the declaration of the Synod, about which you all know.

Some of you, surely, have read the tale by Kuprin, "Anathema": where some poor wretch of a deacon had to cry out an "Anathema!" at Lev Tolstoy, but instead of this the lout shouts to him: "Many Years!" Even the film had it such many years back. But this was all fictitious. There was no sort of an anathema pronounced. There was a decretal of the Synod -- a small text on two printed pages, where it was said, that Count Lev Nikolaevich in his arrogance is slandering the Church, the Christian faith, and in betraying this as a true teaching, the Church can no more regard him as its member. In reply to the Synod, Tolstoy asserts to the correctness of the Synod. He says: yes, actually, I cut myself off from the Church, which calls itself Orthodox; for actually, I am not its member.

Bishop Sergei Stragorodsky (who forty years later became Patriarch of Moscow and All Rus') said concerning this, that it was unnecessary to excommunicate him: he himself by his teachings stood already outside the Church. This whole scandal actually was provoked by Pobedonostsev, a man complex and of great contradictions. He, so to speak, whispered to Alexander III, that he should take action against Tolstoy, but Alexander III, having good personal relations with Sophia Andreevna, did not want a scandal. But Nicholas II, being a student of Pobedonostsev (Pobedonostsev read him his lectures), did however get him involved in all this.

I am not convinced that by way of form, that all this was very successful. But the Church was obligated publicly, openly and honestly to testify, that this teaching of Tolstoy's -- was not authentic to the Gospel, nor was it Christian, in any sense as understood not only by the Orthodox, but also neither by the Catholics, nor the Lutherans and other Protestants. Ask any Baptist, for if he opens the Tolstoy Gospel, he will readily see, that this is not at all the real Gospel. Even those Protestants, who considered Christ simply a man of genius, a prophet discerning of God, they still likewise all the same relate otherwise to the Person of Christ: as uniquely manifest. For Tolstoy, however, Christ was not unique.

I repeat my final question: is not all this just something unnecessary for us? No, it is necessary. And it was necessary back then, precisely because in his struggle Tolstoy set before the conscience of a society, which regarded itself as Christian, some very acute questions: hunger, prostitution, poverty, oppression... The man, who wrote "After the Dance", -- was he not a Christian? The man, who wrote the many pages of "War and Peace" with a profound spiritual penetration into the religious life of people; the man, who wrote "I cannot be Silent!" -- was a true Christian. He was a conscience of the land and a conscience of the world. And therefore Russia, independent of the literary achievements of Tolstoy, ought still to be proud of such a man, just as at present it ought to be proud of Sakharov. Because it is that Tolstoy fecklessly made bold to come out against the established iniquities, against the abasement of human dignity, against that, which prevailed within society.

Certainly you will say: things were not then, as they are now. Yes, certainly, back then it was a matter of far lesser iniquities, than in our day. But then too, Tolstoy managed to survive. Ah, but if he had tried to open his mouth in thirty-seven! I think, generally he would not have survived prior to 1937. If he had been a young man at mid-century, he would not have survived, they would have thrown him out of the country or would have eliminated him even back in the first quarter of our century. I think, you would all agree, that it would have been so.

The man, who challenged the views of the social evil of society, the man, who spoke the truth about the situation of things (granted that he erred in certain questions), was a bold man. And always, when I think about Tolstoy, I tend to remember the pervasive words of Anatolii Kon, a reknown publicist, advocate, having known many of the remarkable people of his time. He wrote thus: the wilderness at evening seemed dead, but suddenly there sounded forth the roar of a lion, he was come out on the hunt, and the wilderness came alive; certain of the night birds cry out, some of the beasts answered him back; the wilderness came alive. Here thus in the wilderness of a stale and one-sided and oppressive life there resounded the voice of this Lev, this Lion, and he woke people up.

And therefore I add in conclusion: Sergei Nikolaevich Bulgakov (the economist, philosopher, afterwards archpriest and noted theologian, dying in the emigration) wrote, that although Tolstoy was excommunicated from the Church, there is still a certain churchly connection with him. And it is precisely because there was so much in him of searching for the right, so much in him that dealt with the most critical problems of mankind. And we believe, that not only on earth, but also in eternity he is not totally sundered off from us.

The Encounter and Meeting

On 29 November 1901 at the location of the Geographical Society on Fontanka in Peterburg occurred an extraordinary gathering.

The narrow, corridor-like hall is crammed full. In the corner -- is an enormous, squat calico statue of Buddha. At the presiding table are people in clergy riasas and klobuks. Alongside on the loft -- are the secular, primarily the young. And amazing is the absence, such as is customary for public gatherings, of having someone appointed, with the right to cut off the orators. There is an atmosphere of excitement. And everyone has the feeling that this is an important event.

Thus began the Peterburg Religio-Philosophic Gatherings.

Heading it, Bishop Sergei Stragorodsky, right off defines his position: "It is my most sincere wish to be here not merely in clergy riasa only, but in actual fact as a servant of the Church, to truly express its confession". At the time of speaking he attentively glances through the assorted participants. It was all truly extraordinary. All sorts were here -- students, and professors, and women.

Here too is a significant fellow in snipped-beard goatee, Dmitrii Merezhkovsky. At thirty years of age he is already a noted writer, poet, translator, critic. Alongside is a red-haired woman with lorgnette eye-glasses -- the poetess Zinaida Gippius, his wife. Here is the brilliant theatre director, Prince Sergei Volkonsky. And figures from the "World of Art" journal: Sergei Dyagilev, Lev Bakst, Aleksandr Benua.

Almost all of them were fated to die in the emigration, and only many years afterwards would their creativity return home to their compatriots.

Here is the churlish and loud archimandrite, Antonin Granovsky. He would become a bishop, twenty years later at Moscow heading the Reformist Movement Church Schism and departing life in 1927 an unrepentant rebel. But presently he is working on the censorship committee: he has the task of controlling the publication of the reports of the Gathering.[1]

Here is the unassuming in appearance Vasily Rozanov, the author of essays of genius, an inimitable stylist, a thinker, tormentively shifting between a passionate love for Christianity and just as passionate antipathy towards it. He later expires from starvation at Sergiev Posad in 1919, at peace with the Church. Here is Anton Kartashev -- son of an Ural miner, now a rector of the Spiritual Academy. He is twenty-six years old. In 1917 he occupies the position of Minister of Confessions in the Provisional Government and opens the Local Sobor/Council of the Russian Church. In the emigration up until his death (1960) he will be a professor of the Paris Theological Institute, the author of fundamental works on Church history. And amongst the public, having come from Moscow, is a nineteen year old mathematics student with long bushy hair. This is Pavel Florensky, in future to be a noted theologian and a man erudite. He will perish in the Gulag.

And finally, presiding, is the forty year old Archbishop Sergei, author of theological research bold for these times; he already has had success working as a missionary in Japan, and had just shortly before been appointed rector of the Peterburg Theological Academy. But hardly anyone would expect, that in some twenty odd years he would stand at the head of the hierarchy of the Russian Church and afterwards become patriarch.

But all this was in the future. At the time, at the outset of the XX Century, these were just a variety of people gathered at Fontanka for the first open encounter between representatives of the Church, on the one hand, and literary figures, artists, publicists -- on the other. Many outstanding figures of Russian culture were convinced Christians, but the form of life, of lifestyle, the interests of the basic masses of the Intelligentsia were all involved on the outside of anything churchly. A characteristic example was offered at one of the gatherings by Prince Volkonsky, describing the general awkwardness with a visiting priest at the home of a marshall of the nobility. "We had nothing in common with him,

---

[1] The stenographic reports were published in the journal of D. S. Merezhkovsky, "Novyi Put'", and later on appeared in a separate edition: "Notes of the Religio-Philosophic Gatherings (1902-1903)". Spb [i.e. Sankt Peterburg]. 1906. In the text are a series of addenda of the censor. a portion of the stenography is omitted.

nor was he able simply to converse with us: he was, as one might say, "ignorant" of our general life, for which are needful special themes, a particular manner of conversing; in the presence of the batiushka [priest] our life as it were ground to an halt, and only on his leaving could we return to it with a sigh of relief".

The chief thing, unintentionally inherited from Christianity by the Intelligentsia, was a devotion to lofty moral ideals, a readiness for sacrifices in the name of the good of the people. The Church itself however, as an institution, subordinate to the state, evoked protest and distrust. Positivism, the expectations in progress, and populism became symbols of the faith of the Intelligentsia. The clergy, and the theologians, on their part, could not find a common language with the Intelligentsia, and not without basis were the Intelligentsia viewed as free-thinkers. Literally, the sense of confrontation was reciprocated. Quite indicative of this, is that when in the mid-XIX Century Archimandrite Feodor Bukharev attempted to throw a bridge across between the Church and culture, it first of all met resistance within the churchly setting itself. And amidst this, any secular writers, coming out in defense of religion, wound up as lone voices amongst "their own".

One of the few "windows", through which the Intelligentsia glimpsed into the Church, was Optina Pustyn. But, as the rare exception, its connection with the figures of culture were mere episodes and inconsistent. Even Dostoevsky and Solov'ev journeyed there on an occasion all of three days. Both of them -- the great writer, and the great philosopher, had devoted themself to a revealing of the Christian ideal, -- having oriented themself to the Intelligentsia, to which they themself belonged. The secluded churchly medium, the world of the religious schools, the churchly thought and life was in much distantly remote even for them. They however prepared the groundwork for that sort of dialogue, which became possible at the Peterburg Gatherings.

The Gatherings started up somewhat a year after the death of Vladimir Solov'ev. Their format became lectures on philosophy, oriented towards a secular audience. It was Dmitrii Merezhkovsky and Zinaida Gippius who conceived of having the Gatherings.

In September 1901 Merezhkovsky with his wife, as always, spent the time out of town. And as always, they talked much, and made plans. During this while Merezhkovsky was working his way from positivism and Nietzsche towards that of the Gospel, though in his novels "The Death of the Gods" and "The Resurrection of the Gods" he asserted, that Christianity renounces "flesh", "earth", culture and that there is needed its synthesis with paganism which, in his opinion, contained within it the "revelation of flesh". Without dwelling in detail on this idea, we might mention in passing only this, that the paganism of antiquity was however pervaded in much by world-denial and spiritualism. But for our account it is important to note, that Merezhkovsky wanted in all its alacrity to put forth the question about the problems of the "world" for the Church and its official representatives to address.

Zinaida Nikolaevna thereupon expressed the hope, that the matter might get somewhere, if it were "various people gathered, who never had gathered nor would tend to gather". This thought took an extraordinary hold upon Merezhkovsky. Actually, it would be the very best thing for discussing the themes of the Church -- and to hear thus the living voice of "historical Christianity".

Having returned to Peterburg, the spouses energetically set about the realisation of their plan. They thought, that for them it would be impossible to get it past the "master of the situation", the mighty K. P. Pobedonostsev, the Over-Procurator of the Holy Synod. Everyone knew him as a man of conservative views, with no love for change. Aleksandr Blok wrote about his "owl wings".

Not without trepidation in setting about it was a group of five delegates of the future gatherings. These were: D. Merezhkovsky, V. Rozanov, the publicist D. Philosophov, the journalist V. Miroliubov. And herein important especially was the presence of "curly Valentin", as they called their friend V. Ternavtsev. He was a vivid, easily enflamed man, on the one hand being close with the Intelligentsia, and on the other -- with churchly circles, since he served on the Synod.

Detailed accounts about the meeting with Pobedonostsev have not been preserved. But in any case, he consented to hear out the delegates. The very same day they set off to the Aleksandr-Nevsky Lavra monastery to Metropolitan Antonii Vadkovsky. Joining in with them was the poet Nikolai Minsky, and the artist Aleksandr Benua and Lev Bakst. The metropolitan, a pre-eminent member of the Synod, was reputed to be a liberal and was noted for his mild character. He responded heartily to the idea of the gatherings. And actually by virtue of this, Pobedonostsev, albeit grudgingly, gave permission. He however set the condition, that at the gatherings should participate only "active members". "...This rule was circumvented, however, -- recollected the art-critic Sergei Makovsky. -- for I, first of all, never comprised a member of the Society, and was present at the gatherings".

And thus were gathered for a first time in many years, in open discussion -- clergy, academic teachers and representatives of the creative Intelligentsia reflecting very different views.

Various also were the intentions of those gathered. Some were ready to stand in defense, others -- to go on the offensive. The editor of the "Missionary Review" journal and a Pobedonostsev fellow, Vasilii Skvortsov, rejoiced over the possibility of "bringing the errant to their senses". Merezhkovsky strove to draw the audience into a cycle of disquiet with his ideas and mental schemes. He stood forth as a Christian, "questioning" the Church. Rozanov from time to time dispatched notes with insightful thoughts. He did not like to aggressively step forward.

Zinaida Gippius later on tended to remember, how surprising the meeting with churchly people was for her and her friends. "These truly were two different worlds. Making closer acquaintance with the "new" people, we passed from surprise to surprise. It is not even the inward difference I am speaking of, but simply rather the mannerisms, the traits, the language itself: everything was quite other, an altogether precisely different culture. Neither lineage, nor direct belonging to the religious calling -- the "riasa" -- played here a role. A man of the then "churchly" world -- whosoever he might be: an official, a professor, writer, teacher, a theologian simply, alike either smart or stupid, talented or ungifted, courteous or unfriendly, -- all the same however bore upon himself the imprint of this "other" world, dissimilar to our own intelligentsia -- customary, "mundane" (a churchly expression) world". It united the awareness of belonging to a common history, to the same land, the same people, the same society and in the final reckoning -- to a same culture, irregardless of how distinct might be its separate parts. Essentially, it made apparent the absence of experience in such a sort of discussions. At times the talk wandered far afield from its basic theme. And not seldom someone would tend to speak about "his own thing", with little concern in it for others. And thus, the archpriest Ioann Yanyshev constantly came back to spurring the growth of philanthropic institutions, for him the panacea for everything.

Characterising the role of theologians at the gatherings, Sergei Makovsky recollected: "Not everyone participated in the discussions, but there were also those, especially from among the monks, who were evidently pleased to speak and shine with erudition, and they were sincerely interested by the points brought out by the questions, being favourably disposed towards "mundane" theosophia (the least receptive in the disputes were the non-riasa erudite lay theologians)". The artists, the theatrical people and poets remained mostly a passive audience. The Church was of interest to them, chiefly, in connection with the new trends in art, with the re-evaluation of avant-garde realism, and the rebirth of an archaic and mystical symbolism in creativity.

And for the churchly people, there was the unaccustomedly heated talk of the writers and publicists, who then in their turn, complained of the "narrowness", and the "obtuseness" manifest in the theologians. Bishop Sergei, in presiding, exerted great efforts to reconcile the disputants.

And yet overall the atmosphere was one of inspiration. Everyone valued the possibility to openly talk about vexing matters, to put forth acute questions, to discuss and to listen, not glancing over one's shoulder at the "administration".

After the opening speech of Bishop Sergei the gatherings were started with a report by Ternavtsev entitled, "The Great Task Facing the Russian Church", which in much defined the character and style of dialogue.

Ternavtsev noted the growth of a deep spiritual crisis within the land. He connected it with this, that the idea of secular progress from the 1860's had hit an impasse: "Their creative energy (the idea of progressivism) exhausted, their resulting fruits did not provide answer to the eternal questions of conscience, nor to the decisive demands issuing from life". And further on Ternavtsev said, that the rebirth of the land should occur "upon religious a grounding". Enormous responsibility lay with the activists of the Church. But were they prepared and ready for such a task? For the giver of the report, this was to the highest degree doubtful, since, in his words, "the preachers of the Russian Church were instructed in the faith at most one-sidedly, often falsely enthused, they know little and even less understand the whole significance of the mystical and prophetic side of Christianity. And chiefly -- within Christianity they see and understand only a next-worldly ideal, ignoring the earthly side of life, with the whole cycle of societal relations standing empty and devoid of an embodied truth. This one-sidedness, moreover, hinders them also from becoming "fishers of men" in our own day".

In the opinion of the giver of the report, the potentialities lodged within the Church would be revealed more fully, if it were to act in concert with the Intelligentsia of Russia. The Intelligentsia were active, sacrificial, striving to serve the people. And all the while clearly in contrast to the Church. These people, who boldly criticise the power of property owners, who always struggle against injustice, who strive towards a surmounting of life on mere personal principles, cannot accept the Church, if it remains primarily caught up within itself, whilst remaining indifferent to problems cultural, civil, and socio-moral. The task of the Church -- is to make a turnabout in terms of facing the world, and revealing its spiritual treasures. "If it (the Church) should become aware of and accept this task and show forth its resolve to the degree of its religious duty, it -- now stifled and impotent -- would instead then be manifest as the centre of irresistible moral allure at the head of all the intellectual forces of the land. Then only would it prove itself by faith as regards its own inner essence".

Ternavtsev did not call for Russian Christianity "to adapt itself" to the novelties of the age, but he insisted on this, that the creative influence of the Church upon the world serves as a realisation of its genuine universal nature. "...for the whole of Christianity, -- he said in conclusion, -- there ensues a time not only verbally in teaching, but also with deeds to show, that within the Church is contained not merely an other-worldly ideal".

After the report discussions began, which in much were directed towards particular questions: what precisely is the Intelligentsia? What is the role of the clergy in the life of the people? Has Ternavtsev accurately reflected the position of the Russian theological discipline? Most significant, in my view, was the short response by Bishop Sergei. He noted, that in proclaiming the heavenly aspect, the Church already by this itself tends to transform earthly life, and that it ought not to set the cornerstone of its service into dealing with social questions. The bishop offered an historical example: "The Church did not immediately rise up against slavery, but rather preached the truth of the heavenly ideal and of the utmost dignity of man. By this, and not by other means did it gradually attain the abolition of slavery".

At the second session there was a report by D. Philosophov. He insisted, that at the foundational core of the Church -- are the two chief commandments, indicated by Christ: love for God and love for neighbour. The Intelligentsia, in the opinion of Philosophov, had assimilated only the second commandment. "In our doctors, our students and women-students, going out in a famine year in service to neighbour, there was an unconscious "religiousness", insofar as they were faithful with a true love towards the "earth". But "religiousness" -- is not religion. For them the faith in God was replaced by a faith in progress, in civilisation, in the categorical imperative. And here before our eyes has grown an awareness of society, while the old ideals have ceased to satisfy it. Their futility has been graphically shown by Dostoevsky and Nietzsche, in ignoring spiritual writers. In the name of love for neighbour without love for God there cannot be a true doing of activity upon the earth. Without God there cannot be an authentic culture, encompassing all the fullness of the being of mankind... The Church, in contrast to the Intelligentsia society, has consciously been mindful of and admitted only the first half of the commandment: "Love the Lord Thy God with all thine heart and all thine soul". And by not embracing the second, it began to deny it, to reduce it to its love for God, its service to Him -- to the point of hatred for the world, and a contempt for culture. Historical Christianity, right up to the XX Century, has concentrated all its attention to the ascetical side of the teachings of Christ, on service to God, disdaining in its one-sidedness the themes of God's world, a part of which -- is that of neighbours toiling in the sweat of their brow".

This thought, having arisen way back with Chaadaev and Solov'ev, later on became one of the pivotal aspects in the Russian religio-philosophic literature of the XX Century. But at this time back then at the gatherings, everyone seemed quite far from understanding Philosophov. Even Ternavtsev spoke out against him, in advancing analogous thoughts about the common oneness of "truths of heaven" and "truths of the earth".

And most acute was the reaction of Vasily Rozanov. He agreed, that making a dichotomy between the sides was meaningless and dangerous, that rather it was necessary to strive towards unity; moreover, Rozanov emphasised in particular, that the split between the Church and culture -- is a phenomenon not only Russian, but general also throughout Europe. "The whole of Europe, -- said his note, -- decries the dissociation of "the cultural classes" from the Church. But these selfsame "cultural classes" also grew forth, regretably, into their own antipathetic and frivolous features, since they grew streetwise and theatrically, and they grew thus because, that they were split away from the Church".

But Rozanov went even further, and he presented the question about the loss of the spirit of community within the Church itself. Preachers call people into its fold, but those, who enter, find not the expected. How extremely different modern churchly life is in contrast to the freedom and simplicity of the Gospel life! "God, -- exclaims Rozanov, -- back then was nowise similar to what we have now! And it makes one want to weep at the comparison. We scurry about amongst chancery-clerks and say: Hey, deign to give us a look, we're -- Christians too". Rozanov was speaking on behalf of the believing Intelligentsia, those people who, in the words of Ternavtsev, having come into the Church, were unable to become "typical-sort parishioners". This bitter reproach was accurate in much. However, it is unknown what was said in response to this. The answers indeed were purged by the censor, and hence the answer was silence.

The third and fourth sessions were devoted to consideration of the problem regarding Lev Tolstoy.

The theme of "Lev Tolstoy and the Church" was particularly pertinent, insofar as quite recently, a few months prior to the start of the gatherings, there had appeared a "Deliberation" of the Synod, in which it was stated, that "the Church does not regard him (Tolstoy) as its member and cannot regard him as such, as long as he remains unrepentant and does not renew his association with it". Passions flared around the "Deliberation", and there were related and touching accounts written about the "anathema", to which the venerable old writer had been cruelly subjected. Amidst all this Tolstoy himself had unambiguously admitted in his "Reply to the Synod": "that I am cut off from suchlike the church, terming itself pravoslavnoe/orthodox, and this is quite justly correct".

It would seem, that everything was clear. The author of "War and Peace" had created his own teaching, quite distinct on principle from the teachings of the Church. The teachings of Tolstoy were closer to Confucianism or Stoicism, but the writer nonetheless asserted, that this was the true Christianity. The Synod established the fact, sufficiently evident, that the teaching of Tolstoy was not identical to the churchly teaching, and publicly witnessed to the fact, that Tolstoy had set himself outside the Church by his blasphemous scoffings and anti-churchly writings. But within society there still resounded a chorus of voices, reproaching the Church with intolerance and abuse against a great writer.

The debates at the gatherings began with a paper read by Merezhkovsky, who was working on his book, "Lev Tolstoy and Dostoevsky". Merezhkovsky pointed out, that the assault by the writer against the Church -- was only one link of a chain in his total denial of culture. "With Tolstoy the nihilism of the entire post-Petrine culture of Russia, in the expression of Dostoevsky, -- "stands at a sort of ultimate precipice, swaying over an abyss". Thinking, that to struggle against the Church, to struggle against history, against the people, for its salvation, -- is in actual fact to struggle unto one's own ruination: a terrible struggle, like to the struggle of a would-be suicide against someone trying to hinder the person's hand".

Merezhkovsky did not dispute the correctness of the Synod's "Deliberation" and he agreed, that the Church ultimately had to state: Tolstoy as a thinker had fallen away from Christianity. And he himself termed Tolstoy -- a great pagan, a "seer of the flesh". But this was in regard to his own dialectical schema: paganism (flesh), Christianity (spirit) and their synthesis in a certain "Third Testament" -- whereby he expressed the suggestion, that Tolstoy as an artist could be accepted by the Church, similar to how ancient paganism had enriched it.

Yet it is characteristic, that the basic debates revolved not around the teaching of Tolstoy, but rather were connected with the question: how much the Synod had the right to express the spirit and teaching of the Church? It was stressed, that the Synod per se is not something churchly, but essentially rather an official department of the state, instituted by tsar Peter I.

During these years there had begun a movement for the restoration of the patriarchate as an authoritative power, more canonical for the Church, than the Synod. Concerning this Ternavtsev however noted, that the tsars also approved the patriarchs, and on the other hand, even without the patriarchate the Russian Church lived a full life and had great ascetics.

But all this was a swerving off the theme. And Bishop Sergei essentially rephrased it. He pointed out, that the Church had not "excommunicated" Tolstoy, since excommunication is a sort of banishing of a man for this or that reason from the churchly community. This was not applied towards Tolstoy. He himself left the Church, similar to the emperor Julian the Apostate, whom no sort of Church Sobor had excommunicated, but rather he abandoned Christianity of his own free will. "The serious aspect of this question, -- said Bishop Sergei, -- can be seen, for example, from the observation of Vl. Solov'ev: -- L. Tolstoy offers us a Christianity without Christ. Each of us, consequently, has to decide, do we remain with Christ or do we want a Christianity without Christ? This is the pertinent question, whereas those regarding the person of L. N. totally recede into the background".

However, as might be imagined, disputes on the role of the Synod and about the relationship of the Church to the autocracy overshadowed everything else. The censor did not approve the stenographer notes for the fifth and sixth sessions.

The discussions on freedom of conscience had also a stormy character. The basic report was read by prince S. Volkonsky, who later on in having emigrated, became rector of the Russian conservatory in Paris (he died in 1937). A man of broad an outlook, erudite, a moderately-conservative representative of the Orthodox Intelligentsia, the prince posited with all its alacrity the problem of freedom for the Orthodox Church. He asserted, that there is not and will not be this freedom, as long as the Orthodox are not free from the police "protection" on the part of the ruling authorities. He offered a series of facts, regarding when sectarians were deprived of their native rights, and non-official groups were persecuted for their studying of the Bible. He reminded those gathered of the words of Peter I: "The human conscience is subject to God only, and no sort of state is granted by its power to compel a different faith". If the churchly administrators and clergy, -- said Volkonsky, -- do not understand the necessity of freedom, then this "only but shows the inner weakness of the Church, compelled to grapple for constant help and to recourse to alien measures, in order to bolster the impotence of its own fading authority".

The meaning of the report was not at once accurately understood by its opponents. Antonin Granovsky declared, that Christianity, being the absolute religion, does not tolerate a "co-existence" with other religious teachings. Volkonsky meanwhile had not in view a conjoining of religious teachings, but rather a renouncing of the juridical idea of "governance" as a state religion. The missionary Skvortsov offered an example of another sort, relating, that the laws of the empire were sufficiently tolerant towards the heterodox and other faiths. Merezhkovsky in reply pointed to legal rules, permitting the persecution of sectarians.

The atmosphere became charged. "The principle of freedom, -- thundered Antonin, -- masking the caprice of will lies within a demonic power. And there hence arises a question of compromising Christ with the demons". And only afterwards, when Bishop Sergei stressed, that the freedom of conscience is organically present for Christianity, and with also other theologians supporting him, that Antonin finally understood about what he was saying, and he agreed, that coercion in matters of conscience is impermissible. His position he defined thus: "When Christ said: "Whoso takes up the sword, by the sword also perishes", then by this He said, that the Church alike suffers ruin, in defending its life by the sword... When priests appeal for police protection, or when they send summons to the house, saying: come and do your Communion duty, then the Church alike loses its inner power".

The tone at the tenth and eleventh sessions was set by Merezhkovsky, who had been working on an investigation into Gogol. There was quite a bit of a dispute over how negative upon the writer was the influence of his confessor, Fr. Matfei Konstantinovsky. Opinions differed, and the dispute soon passed over into broader a theme: the relationship of Christian asceticism and culture. The theologians -- priest Ioann Egorov, and Sergei Sollertinsky, professor at the Vladimir Uspensky Academy -- pointed out, that in assuming an healthy asceticism, the Church does not disdain art, or literature -- "the flesh", or culture in general.

At the final meeting was read a message by the participants of the gatherings, to Bishop Sergei, in which they stated their deep appreciation for his felicitous role. The Intelligentsia, -- it said in the message, -- at first expected from their contact with the hierarchs merely "perplexity, pettiness, and lack of understanding". But the people of the Church, and particularly the presiding bishop, had dispelled these worries: "The good spirit of the pastor has made it all happen, and already after the second gathering the whole literary segment of the gatherings had decided, that the matter was settled, that it was something solid and that neither the clergy nor the representatives of society would run away, nor were they driven away. How had this occurred? The bishop by his spirit had shown, how one mustneeds conduct oneself, and yet too to heed the other... It was not a presiding hierarch at the head that the members of the gatherings saw, but rather a Christian, who in overseeing matters, said: "and in everything be ye Christians, -- and while being Christians may ye accomplish everything, may ye eternally go forward, and in everything be successful".

However, not everyone concurred in the same opinion.

Zinaida Gippius twenty years later reminisced with not small a bit of sarcasm: "The "fathers" already long before had become alarmed. No sort of "aligning" of the Intelligentsia with the Church had occurred, but rather only that the "worldly" had often pushed them to the wall -- defeated. In writing for help (from Kazan?) there was archimandrite Mikhail, famed for his glibness and acquaintance with "worldly" philosophy. But Mikhail -- oh alas! -- after two of the gatherings he evidently went over to the side of the "Intelligentsia", and instead of helper the archpriests found in him a new questioner, and sometimes even, accuser".

Gippius, regretably, was looking at events through the misty prism of the past, and provided a picture not altogether accurate. Over the course of the gatherings there had been perfected the "art of the debate", and people began to hear one another. And as regards archimandrite Mikhail Semenov, he was not from Kazan (though he studied there), but rather from Voronezh, where he taught theology in the Theological Seminary, and the aim of his journey was in a defense of his dissertation.

In her reminiscence Gippius did not spell out the character of the upheaval, occasioned by the testy archimandrite. At the very first he actually mistook the Intelligentsia for an enemy of the Church and he began an attack against it, and evidently, with success. In the words of Andrei Bely, Merezhkovsky in his "own circle" was constantly exclaiming: "Oh, how I hate him -- that Mikhail!" But soon the twenty-five year old monk saw, that in front of him were not enemies, but rather sincere, searching, at times distraught people, with whom it was possible to have serious dialogue.

And actually, Fr Mikhail sensed his affinity with "the prodigal children of culture". He himself was a radical, ready to take matters to their end. A gifted and prolific publicist, in the revolutionary year of 1905 he emerges as a proponent of a Christian socialism. He winds up being expelled from the Academy, sent to a monastery, and in 1907 he goes over to the Old Ritualists [Old Believers] as a sign of protest against the state church. A year later Mikhail becomes a bishop and later tragically perishes in Autumn 1916.

At the gatherings he actively participated in the deliberations on the theme of marriage, which found disagreements even among the theologians. This fact was stated by Uspensky in his closing statement. "All the chief questions, -- he said, -- set forth at the gatherings, have thus also remained questions. But their "questionability" possessed a nuance other than had been earlier, it became more filled with content, and its scope -- broader". The people, regarding the Church "from within", had been convinced that its teaching would remain all simple for any discussion of problematics.

But why over the course of seven sessions, being left for the last, was the issue of "dogmatic developement"? It tended to involve whether the dogmas of the Church are something ultimately complete or whether there is possible the appearance of new teachings, which the Church would come to accept as its own.

To the chagrin of the "worldly side", the theologians were inconspicuous in wanting to engage the issue of suchlike a possibility. And first of all, Bishop Sergei pointed to the essential natural aspect of considerations of faith, its interpretations over the span of centuries. In his words, religious speculations -- are "various bridgelets, across which human reason attains to truth. The movement of theologising thoughts is always possible, nor are there ever limits to this. And since we are alive, there ought thus also to be theological thinking".

The priest Ioann Slobodsky attempted to express more concretely the thought of the bishop. He pointed out, that the dogmas are like trees, growing up from out of seeds. At their core basis is an enduring constant truth, but the verbal formulae, in which it is clothed, cannot be considered something frozen solid. And indeed all these formulae did not come about spontaneously, but gradually tended to crystalise within the experience of the Church. "The developing of dogmatic formulae there had definitely to be, -- said Fr Ioann, -- otherwise human history would have remained completely in the dark".

This position was basically distinct from the wish of the secular writers to introduce certain things of their own hypotheses, albeit eccentric and debatable in the extreme, -- within the guise of a churchly dogmatics. Gippius was ready to accuse the other side of a positivism in outlook.

It would have been extremely interesting to get into the stenographer notes for the final two sessions (and in general also for all the preserved texts to have been published). But they were not published.

Over the gatherings, clouds had already thickened. All of Peterburg was speaking about the disputes in the hall of the Geographic society. If the first meetings had presented but a series of restrained monologues, they then gradually came to be a field of genuine intellectual battling, although people attentively heard each other out and adopted a corrective tone. But the themes could not but alarm the "guardians".

The Over-Prokurator was following events with a growing mistrust.

And finally, as Gippius notes in writing, "Pobedonostsev was watching and watching, and he then forbade the gatherings". Merezhkovsky dashed over to the Lavra monastery to Metropolitan Antonii, reminding him, how willingly he had supported the idea of discussion. But pleading proved fruitless. The metropolitan answered in the negative, mentioning himself as "being subject to the secular authorities", specifically, to the Over-Prokurator.

On 5 April 1903 it all ended. And now, at present in the modern historical perspective, the time has come to give an objective appraisal of the gatherings. On the one hand, within the gatherings there appeared much lacking in maturity, beclouded and vexing, but on the other hand -- it would be inaccurate to regard the gatherings merely as a momentary episode within the cultural history of Russia. The twenty-two meetings, occurring over the span of a year and somewhat, was of no small consequence and bore definite fruit.

Nikolai Berdyaev, who then had only just emerged upon the literary scene, remembered the gatherings as "an as yet unprecedented phenomenon within Russian life". After the wintry censorship "suddenly freedom of conscience and freedom of the word were for a time asserted within a small corner of Peterburg", -- he wrote. And on Berdyaev's own admission, he got quite much out of the sessions. It can even be said, that to a remarkable degree it defined the problematics of his early works. And quite a few other noted figures of Russian culture "emerged" from the gatherings, which likewise helped them find their own particular paths. Among them were poets and theologians, philosophers and artists, writers and critics.

N. Berdyaev and Fr. S. Bulgakov, Fr. P. Florensky and S. Frank, L. Karsavin and Vyach. Ivanov, V. Rozanov and G. Fedotov, D. Merezhkovsky and A. Kartashev -- were people, whom for us now we have had "opened" anew, -- and in one way or another lead back to the Peterburg Religio-Philosophic Gatherings.

At the gatherings also, for the first time after many long years, various currents of culture intersected. And to a remarkable degree there were dispelled prejudices, mistrust and biases, which each imputed to the other "side". The Intelligentsia were persuaded, that the theologians and clergy -- were not a bunch of idiots. The representatives of the Church came to see that within the secular society were people, vitally interested in spiritual problems, and capable of dialogue. And quite literally, the possibility of a mutual enrichment was at hand. And especially so, through the vital interaction of opinions, whereof to build a full-blooded spiritual and cultural life.

Indeed, Zinaida Gippius may not already have been so mistaken, when towards the end of the 1920's she wrote: "If the questions, so acutely presented at the gatherings, had at the same time actually been heeded, if thereafter not only the Russian Church, but also the enormous mass of the Russian Intelligentsia, had not forgotten about them overall, -- perhaps, the Church would not have found itself in such a "miserable position", and the Intelligentsia would not have tasted at present of the "woe of banishment". But, it would seem, that Gippius rather underestimated the role of the gatherings. The tradition that they established was continued thereafter by the "Religio-Philosophic Society in Memory of Vl. Solov'ev". It arose after 1905 and existed up to the Revolution. And its successor of sorts was the Free Academy of Spiritual Culture, founded by Berdyaev. The spirit and the ideas of the gatherings was reflected also in Merezhkovsky's journal, "Novyi Put'", wherein stenographer notes of the sessions came to be printed, and also in books of the Moscow publishing house "Put'", and in suchlike journals, as "Voprosy zhizni" ["Questions of Life"], "Voprosy philosophii i psikhologii" ["Questions of Philosophy and Psychology"], and in the Berdyaev-edited journal "Put'", which came out in Paris (the final issue, No. 61 was dated Spring, 1940). The gatherings in Peterburg served as an important impulse for the developing of thought in Russia, for the movement initiated by Vl. Solov'ev, and which came to be termed "the Russian Religious Renaissance of the XX Century".

And the gatherings showed, that under conditions of freedom, though even not fully so, the spirit is capable of revealing its inexhaustible wealth and creative possibilities. And one could indeed hope, that these historical lessons will prove of benefit to our own critical times, so fraught with disputes and hopes.

Dmitrii Sergeevich Merezhkovsky and Zinaida Nikolaeva Gippius

Dmitrii Sergeevich Merezhkovsky occupies an unique place within our country's history, philosophy and literature. He was totally forgotten about in our land, or more accurately, they forgot him totally (or as I might say, -- they did the forgetting aggressively, "with a vengeance"). And here now he again returns to us.

And why ought we to speak with you about him? If Vladimir Solov'ev was factually the first professional philosopher in Russia, if let us say, Berdyaev within the history of Russian religio-philosophic thought was an outstanding figure, a giant -- mighty in his character, scope and talent, then Dmitrii Sergeevich Merezhkovsky -- was a figure of lesser magnitude, I would say, in the order of things. But we ought to know him, we ought to know this remarkable man. And, as the selfsame Berdyaev tended to recall of him, Merezhkovsky was one of the most culturally educated people in the Peterburg of the first quarter of the XX Century.

And what has he left us? This was a man, as it were still from the past century (at the beginning of the XX Century he was already 35 years of age), having his formative years from the era of Populism, he was personally acquainted with Lev Tolstoy and with many of the noted names of these times. And he died early on during WWII, in exile. This long life, on the one hand, rough, since Merezhkovsky was a lonely figure; but on the other hand, he also was not alone, since he was inseparable from his wife. The history of literature and of thought, perchance, knows no second suchlike instance, when two persons comprised such a degree of oneness. Both he, and his wife, Zinaida Nikolaevna Gippius, admitted, that they did not know, where his thoughts ended, where her thoughts began. They lived together, as she writes about in her memoirs, for 52 years, not being separated for a single day. And therefore both his works and hers -- perchance, are basically the same thing. And to speak about Dmitrii Sergeevich Merezhkovsky without speaking about Zinaida Nikolaevna, for me is totally impossible. I think, that their souls now almost are as one, and it is impossible to separate them apart whether in culture, or in thought, or in history, or in their biographies.

Merezhkovsky has left us 24 volumes (true, not very thick) of his works, published prior to the Revolution. These include: verses, poems, translations from all the European languages, translations of ancient tracts; novellas in the spirit of the Italian Renaissance; the trilogy "Christ and Anti-Christ" -- his first major literary effort, comprising the novels: "Death of the Gods" ("Julian the Apostate"), "The Gods Resurrected" (Leonardo da Vinci) and "The Anti-Christ" (Peter and Aleksei); another trilogy -- "Kingdom of the Beast" ("Beast from the Abyss"), comprised of the drama "Paul I" and two novels: "Alexander I" and published already during the time of the Revolution in 1918, "14 December". The "Kingdom of the Beast" -- is about the crisis of the Russian monarchy, about culture, about the people, about the future of Russia, about tragic fates. Merezhkovsky further on has a novel about the Egyptian pharaoh Akenaten [Amenhotep IV], written already in the West. There is a very interesting, brilliantly written book, "Napoleon". Later on, a curious, but very controversial trilogy about the religious fates of Europe, beginning with ancient times: "Tutankhamun at Crete" -- half-novel, half-essay, half-history, "Mystery of the Three" -- about Babylon, Egypt and Crete, and "The Messiah"; there is a book, evoking rather broad a notice in the West, entitled "Jesus the Unknown" -- a large two-volume book about the life of Christ and about His personality; there is still another book -- a series of biographies of saints, Western and Eastern: the Apostle Paul, Augustine, Spanish mystics, Theresa of Avila, John of the Cross, Joan of Arc. Rather later were published books (abroad, certainly) about Western Saints: about Luther, about Little Theresa -- a French saint, Carmelite nun, dying at a young age at the end of the last century; this book was already twice published abroad. The most impressive book, perchance -- was "Lev Tolstoy and Dostoevsky".

Merezhkovsky received his greatest celebrity as a thinker and critic, but as a thinker he was very unique. And this was quite altogether a different matter, than with Berdyaev, Florensky, Frank -- classical philosopher types. His thought rather was a matter of caprice, subject to schemes, original thought. I cannot come up with the right words for characterising the books of Merezhkovsky, nor suggest for them the proper gendre: it involves biographies of writers, and religio-philosophic, even theological thoughts, as well as brilliant literary criticism -- all in one. This indeed was a sort of synthetic gendre of enormous essays. He was an essayist and a brilliant master with quoted citations. In the history of Russian criticism no one was as superbly a master of quotation: sometimes it indeed seems, that he is doing a juggling act with quotations, like an experienced acrobat, always getting his hand to the right place. Certain critics have accused Merezhkovsky of too often coming back to his same themes, but this was a style of the beginning of the century, this was an aspiration there also with Andrei Bely, -- just as one might repeat a musical arrangement, a musical phrase, beginning with a particular thing and ending with the same, returning constantly back to the same themes.

Dmitrii Sergeevich Merezhkovsky was born into the family of a decently well-read and educated official, a man, not adverse to literature, in youthful years remote from the clergy, but nonetheless interested in various religious problems. And in the early years, when the young Merezhkovsky had already begun to write verses, the father, a very direct man, decided to put it to the test: is there a gift of talent or not, is it of any merit, or merely the usual type scribblings. He takes the young Dmitrii and sets off to none other than Feodor Mikhailovich Dostoevsky. This was not long before the death of Feodor Mikhailovich. Merezhkovsky himself then, I think, was not yet even fifteen years old. They come to the quarters of Dostoevsky, the corridors cluttered with copies of "The Brothers Karamazov". Feodor Mikhailovich emerges, pallid with sickly eyes, and in front of him the trembling boy nervously reads his verses. "Poor! Poorly, -- says Dostoevsky, -- nowise satisfactory. Nowise suitable. In order to write, it is necessary to suffer! To suffer!" "Well, Feodor Mikhailovich, -- says the father, -- it is then better not to write, merely to suffer not. Is this to be thus for him?" But Dmitrii Sergeevich did happen both to write much, and to suffer.

Merezhkovsky actually was a man of much writing. He worked at it amazingly. Andrei Bely, who was a friend of his in their youth, venomously described his manner of working: a reserved Peterburg person, he worked only "from the height of the day" (though, generally, this was not so), and when they shot the cannon (to mark the precise time -- back then in Peterburg they shot a cannon), and Dmitrii Sergeevich would throw aside his pen in mid-phrase, get up and go out to stroll along the Neva.

This was a diminutive man, shorter in height than his wife, strongly slurring over the letter "r", -- he did not produce the impression of some sort of mighty creative thinker and as such was not, though nonetheless he aspired to this. In this frail body, within the diminutive man beat tremendous passions. But these were not passions of the vitalistic sort. Moreover, we can reckon as a paradox of sorts this fact, that his remarkable and happy marriage was, evidently, to a certain degree even Platonic. He wrote much about love, about sexuality, about passion. But he himself was a man, evidently, quite dispassionate. In order to better show the peculiar aspect of his lengthy life together with his wife, I want to share with you a small extract from her memoirs, written not long prior to death, in Paris.

The war, the chill in the heart. In an awful way she survived his death, madly bereft. I would tend to say, that this as yet living woman was as one dead... She said: "I have died, and only the body remains yet to die", and when this happened, it was during the German occupation in France in 1941, with the chambermaid rushing in and saying: "Madam, it looks bad for the gentleman". This was such a shock, that in reading her diary, one senses, how strongly powerful was her love. But this was not simply love as passion, in this love there was not passion. This was a perchance unique occurrence betwixt great people (and moreover very notable people within our culture). You will have occasion to read their verses, their novels, their essays, but today I want you to have a sense of them, the feel for them, as people.

And thus, several lines of remembrance, in which Zinaida Nikolaevna -- when the delicate, pretty, red-haired, venomous, clever-minded woman (she forever went about with her lorgnette eye-glasses) -- when after the death of her husband in occupied Paris she relives again that Spring, when they met. This is a slightly amusing bit of history, but it is also very important for understanding the character of both Zinaida Nikolaevna and Dmitrii Sergeevich. He is older than she, he has finished with the philological school, he is already writing verses, and he is friends with Nadson (I think, that few of you know about this man, but towards the end of the last century this young officer, sick with tuberculosis, dying at twenty-four years of age, writing sad verses, was quite popular; Merezhkovsky had become friends with him, being nearly the same age). And Zinaida Nikolaevna, a young person, was from a Russified old German family. They meet, and they begin their novel (however, I would not exactly term this a novel).

"Basically, the whole period of the initial acquaintance with Merezhkovsky was brief -- the final few days of June, when we journeyed to Berzhom [Caucassus Borjomi], and the first ten days of July, whereas 11 July started the beginning of the change in our relationship...

11 July, St. Olga's day, at the rotunda there was an evening of dance, not our usual thing, rather childish. The whole Summer it was done only one time, and we all likewise certainly had gone to look it over. D. S. Merezhkovsky, though not dancing, however, had been at the Sunday evenings; we met him also at this. The ball with dancing was very nice, but while for our mothers watching their children was certainly happy an affair, I however quickly grew bored. And D. S., certainly likewise. Indeed, in the hall -- it was stuffy and crowded, but out in the night it was remarkable, bright, a cool freshness, the trees in the park stood silver under the moonlight. And with D. S., we imperceptibly happened together, along the park pathway, that runs along the bank of the noisily rushing rivulet Borzhom [Borjomi], remote along the narrow ravine. And imperceptibly we went along all the further, til the music was but barely audible. I cannot remember, how exactly our strange conversation began. And strangest of all, that it then did not seem so strange to me. More than once already I had received, as the saying is, a "proposal", and even more often had heard a "declaration of love". But this was neither a "proposal", nor a "declaration": we, both of us indeed -- suddenly began talking, as though it long ago already had been decided, that we marry and all well on with it. He began and set this tone, very simply, and finally, I likewise for myself imperceptibly and quite naturally assumed the same tone, as though nothing unexpectedly had transpired. Afterwards, remembering this evening, particularly during the time of our tiffs (and no little of these occurred later), I even asked myself, whether of not it was out of flirtation that I had not repulsed him, and whether I actually wanted to be married to him?

<...> From this point we constantly met mornings in the park, the two of us; daytime, if we were not going off somewhere with an entire group, D. S. was with us. There was no sort of "explanation" about our future wedding, nor how it should be, evidently. <...>

During this period we tended to quarrel, though not such, as in the days of our early acquaintance and in the first year after the wedding, but often all the same. We both had a character childishly stubborn, me particularly. But on this, that the whole this of a big "wedding" and "reception" -- we were against, and that out of a need so as to simplify matters, we would dispense with the white gown and veils -- on this we were in agreement. The wedding ceremony was set to occur on 8 January (1889), but to head out on that day, or even on the next, we could not: we got the tickets for the coach only on the tenth. I did not even want the wedding attendants, but it seemed, that they were necessary: the wedding-crowns were not to be worn directly upon the head, they needed to be held over the head. <...> There was hardly anyone else, yet on the other hand bright and lengthy plays of sunlight shone from the upper windows -- upon all the church. Upon a rosy red carpeting we entered together and -- circumspectly: certainly not in white slippers, -- from the street, and overall just following after the priest. How dissimilar this wedding was in contrast to that of Tolstoy, which he described in "Anna Karenina" -- in the wedding of Kitty! When they gave us to drink from the common cup, alternately by turns, I the second time around looked to finish it, but the priest excitedly whispered: "Not all! Not all of it!" -- finishing it was for the bridegroom. After this the ceremony rapidly continued, and then here -- we were already at the portico, talking with the attendants.

<...> Afterwards the guests (auntie and the attendants) went home, and our day went on, like the day before. D. S. and I continued to read a book from the day before in my room, and then we ate. In the evening, towards tea-time, my former French governess chanced to come by. One can imagine, how she almost fell off her chair in surprise, when Mama, pouring the tea, happened to mention: "And today Zina went out and got married". Dmitrii Sergeevich had himself gone off to the hotel quite early, and I fell asleep and forgot, that we were married. Indeed so very forgot it, that the next morning, I barely remembered anything, when Mama, through the door, shouted to me: "You're still asleep, and your husband is already here! Get up! Husband? How amazing!"

An hundred years have passed since this little amusing incident.

And here you see, how strange it all was: a wedding, inconspicuously made, on the go, such that Zinaida Nikolaevna in the morning did not even remember, that she had gotten married, and yet this marriage proved to be something not only durable, but rather exceedingly durable. Over the span of 52 years not once, not for a single day were they apart. And they were to think in unison. In constant a spiritual communion. Whether it be within history, within literature, within philosophy they were inseparable, and therefore always, when we speak about Merezhkovsky, we involuntarily tend also to speak about Zinaida Nikolaevna Gippius.

During this period Merezhkovsky traveled quite abit, and he not only happened to vividly tell about his travels with his companion, and later wife, -- he likewise described it in writing. And though perhaps not the best, but fine still a thing in his creativity -- are the essays, which he then combined under the common title, "Eternal Companions". He describes his visit to Greece, to the Parthenon. The beauty of ancient Greece always charmed him: the azure blue sky, the white columns, a beautiful, perfect sort of world. And certainly, this was a myth -- a myth, deriving from the XVIII Century. But he lived this myth. All the same while that within him there was unquenchable the flame of a Christian faith.

How to unite all this? In those years, beginning his life together with Zinaida Nikolaevna, he conceives of a philosophic, historiosophic novel, in which there was a need, in his thinking, to contrast two truths. What indeed is Christianity? This is the great Revelation of God. But this is indeed also asceticism, this is a renunciation of the flesh, this is an extreme spirituality, which in the final end loathes everything of beauty, such as is in the world. With paganism however -- is a song of the flesh, a song of love, a song of the earth. Christianity is completely disinterested in human life, in the social order, in the problem of art or of family. But in paganism art is deathless, immortal, and paganism has acclaimed love way back still from the time of the ancient poets and philosophers: Sophocles, Anacreon, Plato.

And here then appears his first novel, he gives it the title, "Death of the Gods" -- about the decline of paganism. There are two chasms of the deep, as Merezhkovsky loved to term this: the abyss of Heaven and the abyss of the Earth, the realm of God and the realm of the Beast. Paganism was worn down with exhaustion. And the emperor Julian (IV Century), in facing an emerging and already triumphant Christianity, attempts to turn back history, attempts to affirm in the empire subject to him a renewed and transformed paganism -- under the banner of the cult of the Sun, which combined within it all sorts of Eastern and ancient religious traditions.

Merezhkovsky traces out the Christian youth of Julian. The fierce cruelty at the Christian imperial court, witnessed by the young Julian, -- all this is traced with rough strokes. True, if one were to speak from a literary perspective, the living images of Merezhkovsky almost never succeed. He was a master with words, but never a master of creative image, -- these are different things.

I remember, when I myself was quite young, when I was age fifteen, when I chanced upon this book. L knew nothing, just like all my peers, about Merezhkovsky: he was nowhere in the dictionaries, in the history of literature he was absent -- he had evaporated from our culture. I set about reading this strange novel, "Death of the Gods". And I have to admit, that despite the inexperience of youth, I at once perceived its chief defect. In showing the clash of two worlds, Merezhkovsky had not accurately shown Christianity. Christians for him -- were gloomy, nasty, rudely vicious people. And the pagans, here was Julian -- this person, with whom he is most of all sympathetic.

I understand, that there was herein deep an historic and literary meaning. Julian was a man of a genuine religious awareness. And the fact, that he arrived at paganism, -- is not by chance (but this is a different history). I perceived that Merezhkovsky, who had lived there (he journeyed through Italy, he journeyed through those lands), was seeing everything through the prism of quite subtle subjective suggestions. Yes, Julian and his circle had grounds for accusing the Christians of much. There is shown in the novel, for example, the Church Sobor/Council, where theologians and clergy dispute each other with an intensely hostile and repulsive viciousness. And he provides the emperor Julian the possibility to enter into a session of the Sobor and gloomily, with a smirk of satisfaction to gaze at the throng of hierarchs and theologians, who had all anathematised one another, and then with a silence ensuing -- when they all catch sight of the emperor -- he spiels forth the bitterly ironic words: "Here is your Christianity!..." Christ is not there.

The contemporaries of Julian were great, and truly verymost noble figures in the history of our Church: together with Julian at the Athens University had studied Gregory the Theologian, the greatest poet of Christian antiquity, very refined a soul, wise and holy, and also his close personal friend Basil of Caesarea, called Basil the Great, a man, whom not in vain does the Church continue to read over the expanse of fifteen hundred years. Yes, Merezhkovsky makes mention of them, but it is as it were only through clenched teeth, only slightly. He devotes merely two-three lines to the images of these people, who were connected with Julian, who had studied at the university at the same time as him.

The trilogy was to be called, "Christ and Anti-Christ". Yet nothing of this emerged. Because Julian was not the Anti-Christ. In the novel (yes indeed, regretably, also in life), Julian was a passionate soul, a tragic personage, unfortunate, who tried to go against history, but he was nowise the Anti-Christ. And of Christ in this novel there is even less. This is a biased, an unobjective book. But the question, which it raises, -- is an important question: does Christianity actually spurn the flesh? Nikolai Aleksandrovich Berdyaev, who for a certain while was close with Merezhkovsky, answers it thus: "In actual fact in our churchliness there is too much flesh, too much earthiness, too much typical lifestyle, and not too little". And antiquity is not necessarily to be portrayed as an hymn of the flesh. Indeed, all the one-sidedness of the extreme negativity in relation to the body, to matter, to life, -- came also into Christianity from paganism.

I have to remind you of a remarkable high-flown Greek expression concerning this, -- that the body is a "tomb", the live body as such. Why a tomb? Well, indeed because, that according to Plato and the Neo-Platonists, the spirit is locked up and trapped in the body, just like in a tomb. The body -- is a tomb, something negative. A follower of Plato, living several centuries after him, Plotinus (III Century) was even hesitant to disrobe, he was so ashamed of his body! All in the selfsame era as when the Apostle Paul termed the body a temple of the Holy Spirit. And the Bible never had contempt for the body -- since the body was created by God, and just like the whole creation, it could be beautiful. Certainly, in paganism there was also the opposite: in art, actually, there was an acclaiming of the body. But those pessimistic, gloomy, life-denying elements, which Merezhkovsky attempted to link to Christianity -- they existed already parasite-like upon it and were present to a sufficient degree within the prior paganism. Hence, this attempted antithesis is a false one.

Afterwards, in the preface to his trilogy, Merezhkovsky wrote: "When I finished this book, I already perceived, that heaven and earth are co-united, that they are not in opposition each to the other, but that in the person of Jesus Christ they have found their fullness". This was soon after his marriage. He had become a consciously convinced Christian and remained such to the end of his days, to his last breath.

The second novel, "Resurrection of the Gods", -- is about Leonardo da Vinci. Merezhkovsky had traveled much throughout Italy, and had an excellent knowledge of art and of the history of the Renaissance. But he committed an act of violence against history, since he depicted the representative of the authentic Christian Renaissance, the preacher Savonarola, under the mannerism of a sort of hysterical madness: here, said he, -- is the ascetical Christianity. And Savonarola there is depicted as some sort of idiot, beguiling the wits of other idiots, like himself. But Savonarola actually was one of the greatest sons of Italy, a poet, an activist of culture. He was a monk, but also an absolute defender of democracy. And when the tyrant, ruling his city, lay dying and summoned him, so that fra Girolamo Savonarola should absolve him of his sins, that one said: "I shall absolve thee thy sins, only if thou give thine native city its freedom, if thou cease with the tyranny (and there was an hereditary tyranny there). Savonarola perished on the scaffold, defending the idea of Christian freedom, and he was one of the great cultural geniuses of his land. But Merezhkovsky depicted him in a way, that even to read, is shameful.

His chief hero, Leonardo da Vinci, he sketches out in the form of a certain abstract model, which Dmitrii Sergeevich derived from reading Nietzsche: Leonardo da Vinci -- is a man, living on the other side of good and evil, beyond good and evil. With suchlike an interest he sketches the pretty faces and gaping mouths of the crowd, gathered round the bon-fires, where at the instigation of Savonarola they were burning great works of art. Yes, certainly there was burning. But Savonarola called for the burning of so-called "vile things" -- of all the trash, pornography, he never burns genuine works of art. Yet Merezhkovsky in the novel directly asserts, that the "Leda", a remarkable picture by Leonardo da Vinci, stands atop the pyramid, which they set afire, and the dispassionate Leonardo with pencil in hard sketches the facial expressions of the madmen raging about. Yes, this reflected the influence of Nietzsche, but Merezhkovsky gradually got beyond it. He wanted to better comprehend the dignity of man, and this was a great impulse and aspiration. He desired, that Christianity should bespeak the truth about the earth, about life, about love.

And so it was (the Autumn of 1901) that Merezhkovsky and Zinaida Nikolaevna were living in the suburbs; they were taking a stroll, and she asked: "Well, what shall we do this Winter? It is time to stop talking, and to start doing something". They were both frail Intelligentsia figures, little capable of action, but always wanting to assume action. "Let us, -- said Zinaida Nikolaevna, -- pull together people of quite opposite ideologies, and who never chance to encounter one another. We all live apart. Let's get them together". "Excellent!", -- said Dmitrii Sergeevich. Joining in with them was the poet Minsky, the creator of a strange philosophy, somewhat reminiscent of existentialism. And joining them also was Ternavtsev, a burly, red-haired man, dreaming about the Kingdom of God on earth as a sort of utopian communism. And with them also was

Vasily Vasil'evich Rozanov, a genius and man of contradictions, eternally suffering under his miserable outward circumstances, constantly writing about sexuality, sex, love and the domestic home life, and that within this can be resolved all the problems of the world. He wrote brilliantly and always contradicted himself. He was quite particular a figure, and deserves to be spoken of separately. He was an essayist and thinker of genius, who never thus however connected all the end pieces together.

And thus it was that Vasily Rozanov, Minsky, Ternavtsev and Dmitrii Sergeevich also set off to the dread Pobedonostsev, a man, whom Berdyaev said, was a man who did not really believe in anything good. Pobedonostsev was for all practical purposes the head of the Russian Orthodox Church. He was a refined, intelligent, profound, and in his own way inspired a man, who somewhere in the depths of his soul was endowed with complex an inner life. Not by chance did he carry about a book by Thomas a Kempis, a Catholic (and Pobedonostsev was intolerant towards Catholics), entitled "The Imitation of Christ" -- one of the great books of the Christian world, and up to the present it appears in Russian translation namely, by Konstantin Petrovich Pobedonostsev. Pobedonostsev -- was a bald-headed, droll, dispassionate official, wearing his spectacles. There is a picture by Repin, "Session of the State Council", and Pobedonostsev is there amidst all the regulators, in stiff shirt collar, as worn by senators. He was behind the excommunication of Lev Tolstoy which, certainly, had a definite purpose, but I would tend to say, was handled rather badly (but this is already getting off the subject).

And here comes in our group to Pobedonostsev -- for permission to organise the Gatherings. Pobedonostsev is decidedly against it. They start all kinds of approaches, and making a fuss, and suddenly and unexpectedly Pobedonostsev consents. And in Autumn 1901 is initiated the unusual legislative measure, the honour for the creation of which belongs, namely, to Dmitrii Sergeevich Merezhkovsky.

On Fontanka there is the hall of the Geographic Society -- a narrow edifice, wherein during their time appeared Semenov-Tyan-Shansky and other noted travelers. It was a narrow and lengthy hall, and therein stood an enormous statue of Buddha, a gift from some one of the Eastern peoples. And here they set up a long table, all veiled in green cloth (as was done in official places). At the head of this sat an archbishop, not overly long having been a bishop, 40 years of age, in his spectacles and long beard. This was Sergei Stragorodsky, our future patriarch, who was chosen as such during wartime, in 1943. Alongside him was a rector of the [Theological] Academy, the young academy professor Anton Kartashev, the future Minister of Faith Confessions in the Provisional Government, and afterwards abroad -- an immense historian of the Russian Church (he died in 1960). The hall was crowded. Officially at these disputations only members of the Society could come (but certainly, everyone came, whosoever wanted to). A big thing was that there was no police inspector, and in the old days, in those times (don't forget, that this was at the beginning of our century) there was supposed to be a police inspector present at any such social gathering, and if a speaker were to say something not allowed, then the police inspector had the right to interrupt him and demand that he be silent. But there was no police inspector here. There was only Buddha, whom, so that he not distract the Orthodox Christians, was covered round about with calico cloth, and he stood there wrapped up, like some sort of a stuffed critter.

The discussions were opened by Bishop Sergei, who said, that he had come hither for the purpose of finding a common language with the Intelligentsia. Then Ternavtsev gave a brilliant speech. The tone for it all was set by Dmitrii Sergeevich Merezhkovsky -- he was putting questions to the Church -- and now not simply an abstract Church, but the rather to concrete theologians, concrete bishops and archimandrites. And this manner of tone set well with those in attendance: the dialogue was congenial, and it was indeed great an encounter, a great event within history.

Berdyaev later reminisced: suddenly, in a corner of Peterburg -- there was freedom of speech, freedom of conscience -- though for short a time! These gatherings continued for hardly little more than a year. And then Pobedonostsev came to imagine, that things being said there were so capricious, that it was necessary to put an end to it. There were twenty-two of these gatherings. And I have to remind you, that although afterwards this was forgotten, but the whole movement of Russian religious thought in one way or another emerged from these gatherings, initiated by Merezhkovsky -- or more accurately, by Merezhkovsky and Zinaida Nikolaevna; over and over I want to stress, that this was her idea, and she all the while pushed for it into life, although she herself did not step forth at the gatherings, since it was basically the men that stepped forth. Men who were on the order of professors at the Spiritual [Theological] Academy, and clergy, literary figures, critics -- including an entire cohort from the "World of Art": Sergei

Diaghilev, Lev Bakst, Aleksandr Benua [Benois]. And it was with an extraordinary interest that they had come -- a new religious world had opened up for them!

Sergei Makovsky, a later literary critic and art-expert (he wrote a book, "On the Parnassus of the Silver Age", published in Munich in the early 1960's), likewise came out to these gatherings. Makovsky in his memory mentions, that at the first session was sitting a young student of the first course mathematics, named Florensky. He had not yet chosen his path in life, and I tend to think, that being present at these gatherings (at which he only kept silent and listened), it positively influenced him in his further directions in life and spiritual developement. These gatherings even up til now have not been sufficiently evaluated nor studied, though after 1905, when a stop was put to our censorship, whole new societies were created and named for Vladimir Solov'ev -- at Moscow, at Peterburg, and at Kiev. But the start of it all was done by Merezhkovsky.

His third novel, already written after the close of the Gatherings, was entitled "Anti-Christ". This is a novel about [tsar] Peter I, a novel both theological and philosophic. A ponderous and tormentive book. Everything black and gloomy that can be said about Peter, was therein gathered and expressed with great knowing effect. Here finally he succeeds in pointing to the Anti-Christ. But there was no Christ there. In spite of all his desire to show Christ in the person of those, who opposed the Reform of Peter, it did not succeed. The Old Ritualist Old Believers? He did not succeed at depicting them, though they much interested him. Tsarevich Aleksei? Yes, with Merezhkovsky he figures in as a bearer of faith. He has a conversation there with Leibnitz, the noted German philosopher, who says: "Why are you in Russia all so unfortunate?" And Aleksei answers: "well, yes, we are hungry, drunken, impoverished, but in us -- is Christ". In the novel, however, this is not evident, though there is a frightful scene, when the tsarevich, perishing in prison in the presence of his father, Peter I, curses him, predicting, that all his line, all his dynasty, will perish in blood. And remember, this was written at the very beginning of the century.

Merezhkovsky searches for truth. He makes a study of Gogol. Because Gogol represents for him -- a sacrifice to a Christian narrow one-sidedness. Fr Matfei Konstantinovsky, who was the spiritual father for Gogol in his final years, is depicted by Merezhkovsky in near demonic a guise; he is made to represent the historical Christianity, with which the writer [Gogol] could not find a common language and which obstructed his creativity. This was likewise inaccurate, and unjust. Fr Matfei, upon whom they have heaped so much abuse in history and literature, nowise had it in mind to obstruct the creativity of Gogol. The crisis for Gogol was something inward, and spontaneous. And what Fr Matfei said in actual fact did not play a decisive role. He did not look negatively upon the writings, on the contrary, he praised what Gogol had written earlier. Fr Matfei was not pleased with the form of the second volume of "Dead Souls". He was not a literary critic, he was a simple priest, an archpriest from the city of Rzhev. Gogol had taken to him the second volume of "Dead Souls", and that he did not like it -- that was his privilege. And indeed Gogol himself was unhappy with it -- do you think, he burns it, because he had gone out of his mind? No, he burns it, because he is not pleased with it. And at present, in reading what remains of this book, we sense, that actually there was something out of kilter there, that he could not set right.

A book, which I have mentioned, "Lev Tolstoy and Dostoevsky", tends quite much to posit a problem concerning Christianity and paganism. Who here is the pagan? -- Lev Tolstoy. A seer of the flesh -- is how Merezhkovsky presents him. And Dostoevsky -- is a seer of the spirit. Again there is that simplistic schema, and over it here "hovers" Hegel in a very simplistic form. The thesis: is flesh, paganism -- in the given instance this is Lev Tolstoy. The antithesis: is spirit, jolting the flesh -- in the given instance this is Dostoevsky. The synthesis? The synthesis lies ahead. There was the Old Testament. The Old Testament spoke to us concerning the flesh (together with paganism). Then came the Son of Man, and He gave us the New Testament, but He spoke only concerning the Spirit. A Third Testament is necessary, however, in which in its fullness will be revealed the sacred plenitude of the Divinity.

Merezhkovsky has entered here upon the path of a strange theology. It seems, that quite independently of Rozanov he has arrived at the thought, that the love of man and woman reflects the archetype of a sort of Divine mystery. In the broad theological sense of the word this is undoubtedly so. Because the designs of God, as we know, is a co-uniting of the separated within the world: not by absorption, nor by leveling down, but rather a co-uniting. All that which dissipates and separates -- reflects a Satanic death. And harmony, unity -- this is something of the Divine. And therefore love is a verymost great power. It can be compared with the inner-core forces, such as obtain within matter. They have to be enormous, and not without reason at their setting loose do they give such a colossal destructive effect.

If such a colossal power is necessary to unite matter together, then in order to unite the human spirit, human persons, indeed no less a power is needed. When there appeared the film, "Hiroshima, My Love", where it spoke about the tragedy of Hiroshima and about the love of two people, -- this was no less an explosion, only on a different plane. But Merezhkovsky in his "theology" (I term it theology within quotation marks) transferred this mystery into the inseparable Trinity. He seized upon the fact, that in the ancient Hebrew and Aramaic languages the word Ruah (Spirit) has feminine a gender. And for him this became a triadic mystery: the Spirit, co-united with the Divine Father, begets the Son. In the triangle of father-mother-child (son) is reflected the eternal triadic mystery. Throughout the threading of all his works he returns to this thought. In it is very little of a theological or philosophic basis -- this is a matter of allusions, of emotional overtones.

First of all, the birth of a man is not necessarily the fruition of love; the fruition of love indeed is an unity of souls, such as there was, let us say, with Merezhkovsky and Zinaida Nikolaevna. The birth of a man can happen, just as the conception and birth of any living creature, without love. Besides which, it is not obligatory that there should be the three -- of children there can be many. In brief, this analogy does not work out completely, but it was a matter tormentingly pursued all his life.

The thought later arises for him, that the old world has to be destroyed, and for the Third Testament to draw nigh, there is necessary a revolutionary transformation of the world. It conveys with it the idea of a religious and theological basis for revolution. And he is all the time saying, that there is coming the kingdom of Ham. He has a very interesting book -- "The Approaching Ham" -- the title alone of itself deserves attention. "Not Peace, But the Sword..." -- is thus his assault within it upon historical Christianity.

And yes, we have to be sufficiently honest: we have to admit, that Christianity over the span of centuries has constantly been pervaded by elements of world-denial, which do not correlate to the Gospel. And this has yielded bitter fruits. But to rise up and revolt against historical Christianity -- means to rise up and revolt against Christianity in general, since that it lives and is manifest within history, and not somewhere in a world of abstract ideas.

Merezhkovsky continued to live abroad, and there he wrote his final novels, particularly, "The Kingdom of the Beast" -- about the destruction of the empire. The unbalanced Paul I -- is a figure very contradictory. In my opinion, Merezhkovsky did not succeed in connecting the two sides of the person of Paul. The second part, notably, -- is about the Decembrists, and is entitled "Alexander II"; this book was written under the strong influence of Dostoevsky. And the strongest part -- is "14 December" (likewise under the influence of Dostoevsky). This runs through a course of events, reminiscent of much in our times. The people were not ready for it, those who came from earlier times, -- just like gazing into a mirror in our own era.

The Merezhkovskys, husband and wife, often journeyed abroad and sometimes returned to Russia only briefly. This kept them somewhat cut off from the societal scene, as well as from philosophic life and the Church. They had their own small sacramental-type mystery (almost no one knows about it, and in literature there is almost no mention of it). Zinaida Nikolaevna thought this up. She said: the once historical Church is incomplete, let us create a new church. Such a thought could only be born in the head of a dame. And they set about creating it -- a small circle at first, with some of the finest people of the era coming: Berdyaev, Kartashev, Rachinsky among many others. Then she created an altogether intimate inner circle: Dmitrii Sergeevich, Dmitrii Philosophov -- their closest friend, and herself. And they began to make at home something on the order of small-time divine services. Wine was provided, with flowers, grapes, some improvised prayers were read -- this was as though a make-shift eucharist. When Berdyaev learned about this, he became furious, and this served as the impetus to give him the final push of involvement into Orthodoxy. He said, that he was Orthodox and had no patience with some sort of an at-home do-it-yourself church. These peculiar events, and his reaction, pushed him to the Church.

The critics reacted to Merezhkovsky quite coolly, and people often did not understand his problematics.

In the book, "The Onset of the Century", Andrei Bely provides a grotesque image of Merezhkovsky's appearance in the halls of the Moscow University. His revelations seem absurd to the philosophers and professors, and he himself in the satirical depiction by Andrei Bely is simply ludicrous.

This grotesque vision of how Merezhkovsky appeared in Moscow indicates, how foreign he was from the academic scene. They actually did not understand him, and even he did not understand, whither he was going. Here it was a matter of two worlds: the world of the XIX Century -- classical in its way -- and his own, oriented towards some sort of future horizons, as they then loved to say.

Merezhkovsky reacted quite unambiguously to the onset of the Revolution. Of all the Russian writers and thinkers, he was the most resolutely anti-Soviet. Just like Evtuskenko said as regards to Gumilev, "from songs leave thou not out the words...". Gumilev was a monarchist, yet he however served and considered it his duty to serve in the state, the principles of which did not especially suit him. But Merezhkovsky was, I think, under the definite influence of Gippius, who was totally irreconcilable, and died such. Irreconcilable to a paradoxical extent. For a certain while they were close with Boris Savinkov, and in 1919 they fled from Russia, and were close with SR [Social Revolutionary] circles, then left them and remained extraordinarily alone in the emigration. The Rightists regarded them as revolutionaries, the Leftists did not know for what they stood, -- they tended to fit in with no one. They were constantly searching for a certain political point of refuge. They were for Pilsudski, and then they became disillusioned with him. Even Mussolini, when they were living in Italy, evoked the hopes of the Merezhkovskys. I have read their correspondence; Dmitrii Sergeevich writes: "Caesar" promises to be acceptable to me ("Caesar" -- was a conventional title of Mussolini). But even "Caesar" disillusioned them.

When WWII, the Fatherland War, broke out, many of the emigres, among them Berdyaev, and Bulgakov, assumed a patriotic-front position. Gippius however did not share their views. She wrote a book, "Realm of the Anti-Christ", wherein she depicted revolutionary life, the events in Petrograd and in general in Russia, in Moscow, with very negative a point of view. It was unnecessary to embellish or claim it otherwise -- and thus it was.

What was the point that Merezhkovsky was trying to make in his subsequent philosophic-literary-historical essays? To further develope the quite particular thought: Christian ideas have not been realised in the world. Within the Gospel is lodged the idea of the brotherhood of mankind -- a great idea! Yet who is it that attempts to realise it? Napoleon, a man with demonic a destiny! He has a very interesting, and vividly written a book about Napoleon. A man, not having within him a Christian spirit, attempts to form an unified mankind. It is uncertain, how historically true this may be, but this is how Merezhkovsky depicts it.

And thus for him it becomes time already to surmount the Old and New Testaments and head towards a new one, a third one. And into this drama he portrays both the Apostle Paul, and John of the Cross, a noted Spanish saint.

A central sort of book by Merezhkovsky, written in exile, was published in 1932-1933 in Belgrade, -- "Jesus the Unknown". It is one of the strangest and most original works on the Gospel theme. The writer attempts to shed new light on the mystery of Christ, employing an enormous arsenal of apocryphal sources, to which prior to this no one had attached suchlike a significance. And note also, the particular title: "Jesus the Unknown". The world has not known Christ, the world has not understood Him. This actually is a Gospel expression, but then too in the Gospel it is said, that He was in the world and the world knew Him not, but whoso hath accepted Him is whoso that hath perceived Him. For Merezhkovsky, Jesus was understood neither by the Church, nor by the world. One of the Paris critics titled his review of this book, "The Forgetful Church" ("Jesus the Unknown, and a Church Forgetful"). If the spirit of Christ has not been realised in the Church, neither would it be, in anything that Christianity has given to the world. Merezhkovsky, excellently and on immensely erudite a level, knew all the New Testament historical literature. The book was vividly written, and from very subjective a perspective. This is an enormous three-volume essay, which begins with a description of the appearance of the shape of his personal gospel, which he had carried with him even while still back in Russia, heavily used, but which he is hesitant to have rebound, since he does not want to be in lack of it for even a single day.

Merezhkovsky focuses in on the mystery of sex. He found in one of the apocryphal sources the words of Christ: "When will be the Kingdom? It will be then the selfsame one: the feminine wilt be masculine, the masculine wilt be feminine".

Back in those times, at the beginning of the century, times which defined the philosophic thinking of Merezhkovsky, there was popular a certain, and in my opinion not altogether psychically healthy, Austrian writer, who indeed later committed suicide -- Otto Weininger, having written a book, "Sex and Character" (it also had been translated back in those years, and enjoyed great popularity). He discussed at length the polarity of the two sexes, and further, that in each person is lodged a certain bit of the other sex (if a man -- then in him is an element of the feminine, if a woman -- then in her is also an element of the masculine). There had been a great deal of debate on such things even back from the times, when Vladimir Solov'ev had come out with his book, "The Meaning of Love".

But in actual fact Merezhkovsky tended to stray in some of the very simple things. Sex is not eternal a phenomenon. A man is capable of being seen as such fully and completely. And if this individuum, which belongs, let us say, to the masculine sex, it nowise necessarily follows, that he has to bear within himself also a feminine element. Man spiritually stands higher than sex, since as the Apostle Paul says, in Christ there is neither man, nor woman. But for our oneness, for our love for each other, there certainly have to be differences: in character, in the type of thinking, in the type of emotional life. But in actual fact this is not so essential a matter, that it should have to be written about and consume the whole of life.

The truth about the earth -- this is actually worthy an issue in the legacy of Merezhkovsky. We (whether as Christians, or theologians) ought honestly to admit, that he was particularly correct in this, that over the span of the past twenty centuries often it has obtained, that Christians and the directions of churches have not devoted sufficient attention to the problems of life, to the problems of this world. A possible explanation in trying to understand this is that people wanted to preserve and develope within themself the inner power of spirit, in order then to go out into the world. But in the process of developing the growth of the power of spirit they forgot, they forgot the reason they were doing it for, and so neglected to go out into the world. Indeed, many of you know about St Seraphim of Sarov. For many years he lived in seclusion, but when the spiritual power had matured in him, the power of the grace of the Spirit of God, -- he opened the doors of his dwelling to people. He opened his heart, filled with the Holy Spirit, to people. Herein also is that dialectics of a Christianity, which does not deny the world, -- nor embrace it wholesale, does not become worldly, merely a thing of this world. This is a synthesis, which is accomplished within the history of the Church and will continue to be accomplished, just as it was once and forever accomplished in the Person of Jesus Christ. But in the philosophy of Merezhkovsky the synthesis is conceived of and presented as something separative, sectarian-like, rather than unifying, as something, that will become unitive only in a certain coming of a third testament. We today however say to him: no, for the New Testament, the New Covenant, is the eternal Testament and Covenant. Neither the Church, nor the world, needs a third testament, for Christianity of itself today, just like yesterday, bears within it this potentiality of sanctification, and of comprehension, and of penetration into all the spheres of the world.

No, my friends, there is ultimately nothing mundane, worldly per se, there is nothing found outside of God. Outside of God -- is only non-being. Everything has its connection with Him, and all comes before His Face. A number of centuries ago B.C., the Lord gave Abraham, our father Abraham, the father to all the believers upon earth, the first commandment: "Walk thou before Me and be blameless" [Gen. 17:1]. "Walk thou before Me", -- here is the basis for Christian activity, for Christian love within the family, for a Christian upbringing, for Christian art -- for all that, which is. "Walk thou before Me", that whatever one is doing -- be it splitting firewood, sitting sick in bed or telling friends tidbits of history, in order to lift their spirits, to keep them from becoming despondent -- all sorts of nonchalant matters. Everything, which is not a sin, is wrought perfect before the Face of God. But we still have to be grateful to these sincere people, who with torment have suffered and approached these questions.

In conclusion I want to recite for you several lines from one of the finest, in my opinion, of the verses of Merezhkovsky. This verse bears the title, just like the ode of Derzhavin, -- "God". And it is regretable, that in Russian literature scarcely can there be found similarly simple a verse, without any decadentist elements, a verse about most important, most ultimate, most beautiful, most essential an aspect of our life, and about God, before the Face of Whom we ought all to walk.

> O my God, I give thanks
> For this, that Thou gave my eyes
> To see the world, Thine eternal temple,
> And the night, and the waves, and the dawn...
>
> Let the torments threaten me, --

I give thanks for this moment,
For all, that with heart I attain,
About what the stars do tell me...

Everywhere I do sense, everywhere is
Thee, O Lord, -- in the stillness of night,
And in the remotest star,
And in the depths of my soul.

I thirsted for God -- and did not know;
Still did not believe, but, loving,
Whilst of mind denying, --
I of heart had sense of Thee.

But Thou revealed to me: Thou -- art the world.
Thou -- art everything. Thou -- art the heavens and waters,
Thou -- art the voice of the storm, Thou the aether,
Thou -- art the thought of the poet, Thou art the star...

Whilst I live -- I pray Thee,
Thee I love, Thee I breathe,
When I die -- with Thee flowed back,
Like the stars with the morning dawn.

I want, that my life should be
Non-silent praise of thee.
To Thee -- for the midnight and the dawn,
For life and death -- I give thanks!...

Nikolai Aleksandrovich Berdyaev

In Peterburg at the beginning of the XX Century there occurred an important event -- the Peterburg Religio-Philosophic Gatherings began their work. These meetings of the most brilliant representatives of the Intelligentsia together with the representatives of the Church happened on the initiative of the outstanding activists of Russian culture -- Dimitrii Sergeevich Merezhkovsky and his wife Zinaida Nikolaevna Gippius.

Nikolai Aleksandrovich Berdyaev journeyed there, and afterwards over the expanse of several decades, the themes, which had been debated at the Gatherings, remained constantly present in his works.

The first collection of his articles was entitled, "From the Point of View of Eternity", or "Sub Specie Aeternitatis". He puts forth the question about the importance of spiritual culture, about the importance of human worth. This for him was not a conditional perhaps and maybe, these human aspects of worth flow forth from the utmost upreaches of the spiritual nature of the human "I", of the person. Berdyaev afterwards called himself a personalist. He felt, that within the person spirit expresses one of the chief properties. Not in the mob, not in the sum total, but -- in the person. It is person that accomplishes the greatness of man, which is manifest of his nature. In the mob, when people lose control of themselves, they fling themselves backwards. He ponders in this book over the destinies of Russia, over the fate of the Intelligentsia, -- questions, which agitated him always.

Berdyaev journeys on to Moscow. For a certain while there he roams about, but in the end he finally settles in the Arbat quarter, on Bol'shoe Vlas'evsk, and he gets together with the young, with original and energetic people, who seek a return into the bosom of the Orthodox tradition. Here both is Rachinsky, a very original translator, and homegrown thinker; and here also is the known writer Vasilii Vasil'evich Rozanov, who tosses about between a passionate love for Orthodoxy, for Christianity, and just as passionate an hatred for it. Here is Sergei Nikolaevich Bulgakov -- a Marxist (not simply in the peripheral circles, like Berdyaev, but fundamentally so), the author of an enormous investigative work "Capitalism and Agriculture", a man, who at the beginning of the century traversed the path from Marxism to Idealism, and then from Idealism to Orthodoxy, to Christianity. They got together so much, that people often began to call them the brothers Dioscuri, the Gemini twins Castor and Pollux, but here these were people quite different.

Bulgakov, raised in Orlov province, the son of a provincial priest, having made his way upwards, having broken away from the backwaters, and keen for knowledge, tremendously erudite, haughty, fiery, a bit naive, despite his political learning, -- and Berdyaev, the aristocrat, who never was able to join anything as a follower, and even the word "we" was awkward for him! This was, certainly, the tragedy of his life. He departed the revolutionary circles. After the Revolution of 1905 he was already quite definitely a Christian, for him truth manifests itself in the Person of Christ, in the Person in Whom is incarnated the personal Divine principle, and in front of the Divine Person there stands reflected within It this Divineness of the person of man. Therefore, having become a Christian, Berdyaev could not become a man churchly in the typically usual sense of this word. He journeyed to monasteries, he prayed in the churches, he communed the Holy Mysteries, but when the repentant Intelligentsia went to various startsi-elders and lovingly accepted their words as on the order of the utterings of an oracle, -- Berdyaev could not bear to do this, he considered that this was not his pathway. And he always remained not so much a theologian, as rather a free philosopher. He spoke thus: "I think independently, I proceed from my own "I" and its own intellectual experience and intuition".

In 1911 he gets together with the group "Put'" ("The Way"). In Moscow, not far from the church of Christ the Saviour, was the stand-alone house of the millionairess Margarita Kirillovna Morozova, who provided capital to the benefit of both Russian and translated books of religio-philosophic content. Under the publishing activity of Put' there first came out the remarkable work of Florensky, "The Pillar and Bulwark of Truth", under this publisher there first came out the almost complete for those times Chaadayev, in it there appears also Solov'ev, dead but a short while, and also Bulgakov, and Berdyaev...

In his house many people constantly gather, and he himself is a ready and willing participant in various circles. In 1911 he writes his book, "The Philosophy of Freedom". This is the book of a young man, still not yet age forty. But it seems to me, if we go not into details, this book contains within itself everything, that throughout the distant future would be themes of Berdyaev. And he wrote much indeed. He died in the year 1948. And over these years he penned tons of books, and hundreds, if not a thousand articles. His Bibliography (only an enumeration of his works) itself comprises an expansive book (it came out in Paris)[1]. Nikolai Aleksandrovich has been translated into twenty languages, and in many lands they gather together symposia and congresses, devoted to the study of his creativity. He himself before death spoke somewhat woefully: they consider me for the Nobel Prize, I have now the title of Doctor, I have become known throughout all the world, except for my "Rodina" native-land. And here now after the space of forty years his vision returns to his Rodina to be realised.

"The Philosophy of Freedom" has only recently come out in our country. And for each of you, who want to become acquainted with the fundamentals of Christian philosophy, I would heartily recommend reading this book with all due attention. Berdyaev -- is a brilliant stylist, he is a journalist, he writes vividly, aphoristically, but there too is his fiery temperament, his spirit, which all the time bubbles up like a volcano, he provides it words, and he can repeat one and the same word fifty times on one and the same page. He literally, as some of his friends say, "shouts out" with some of his books. And therefore because of the absence of a certain systemisation, of deduction, of connection of the parts, because of this it is not easy for everyone to read him, but this is indeed great philosophical poetics, deep wisdom!

The book "Philosophy of Freedom" developes the chief thesis of Berdyaev: at its basis lies spirit, spirit is that which is impossible of definition; spirit -- this is that genuine real power, which is hidden within us, and never can rational abstract cognition be in any condition to contain it fully in any sort of mere points of definition. Spirit realises itself within life. But always, when it realises itself, or as Berdyaev expressed it, "becomes objectified", it loses something. I would add also a similar comparison (I do not remember, if it was from Berdyaev, but it is fully in line with him): spirit -- is the inexhaustible flowing waters of a river, whereas objectification -- is the same waters, but frozen in place.

---

[1] trans. note: the YMCA Press 1978 Tamara Klepinine Berdiaev Bibliographie lists 483 separate Berdyaev entries, plus those "sans signature", and articles missed here by Klepinina have also surfaced.

Berdyaev had a certain sense... of repulsion from life, from reality. It quite pained him to see the degradation of man, the ugliness of life, everything dirty and stifling, even that which is stiflingly oppressive in our flesh. This was a spirit, who could be termed "a chained-down spirit" (and thus Marina Tsvetaeva termed Andrei Bely, an acquaintance of Berdyaev). So here also, this was a "chained-down spirit", which languished in its prison. And therefore he had a very unique understanding of love. Read his letter to his spouse Lydia, it is printed in a small collection of the works of Berdyaev, published by "Prometheus" Press, under the title "Eros i lichnost'" ("Eros and Person").

Love for Berdyaev was also a spiritual act. In general he was as it were on the outside of everyday life, on the outside of matter. He always was weighed down by actuality, but amidst this he loved the world madly. He was neither an anchorite, nor a man of renunciation, he took delight in nature, he loved it. As one of his acquaintances remembers, he could not pass by a single dog on the street, without talking to it. Another of his acquaintances related to me, that when they lived in Paris, Berdyaev was always out on the street with a dog or two, and the dogs he had were huge. And there was the cat (in Paris still), Muri (i.e. Purry), which he loved powerfully much. This cat died in his arms. Berdyaev experienced the agony of this living creature such that he wrote about this and tells about his cat with complete seriousness in a profound philosophical book of his, how through the death of this beloved living creature he comprehended the terror of non-being, the terror of dying.

People tended to see Berdyaev differently. The majority loved him during these years. There was in him, certainly, something haughty, but on the other side, as Marina Tsvetaeva reminisces, there was no man more gracious and open. He could mix in beautifully with peasants, with craftsmen, he went to "Yama" ("The Pit") and there he conversed with various sectarians ("Yama" -- was an inn where various God-seekers from among the people gathered). And as an aristocrat he was keener to the language of the simple people, than were the Intelligentsia.

One time (I speak here about the period before the First World War) Berdyaev was close with Dmitrii Sergeevich Merezhkovsky. But gradually the circle of Merezhkovsky became stifling for him. And Merezhkovsky, having become disenchanted with historical Christianity, with the historical Church, conceived a plan with his wife Zinaida Nikolaevna Gippius (to say it more accurately, the wife thought this up) to create their own "Church". And they gathered together at home and made a sort of do-it-yourself divine-service: they set out flowers, they offered up wine -- a sort of pseudo-Eucharist... remember, this was an epoch of decadence! An epoch, when the Symbolists were all the rage, and after them came the Acmeists, all the rage! Merezhkovsky actually brought Berdyaev to Orthodoxy. How so, you ask? Merezhkovsky began to invite him to these vigils of his, these gatherings. And suddenly Nikolai Aleksandrovich sensed, that this was false, that this was something abnormal, a do-it-yourself sort of thing, and that he needed the genuine, the authentic Church. And so he did as it were just the opposite, he became an Orthodox man (to the very end of his life). Such was his paradoxical pathway.

At this point you will hear several lines about him from the mouth of one of his contemporaries, Evgenia Kazimirovna Gertsyk (Herzig), an authoress, who was very fond of him, and esteemed and understood him. As she herself said in her writings, of everything she lost in those times (the beginnings of the 1920's), her loss "most of all" was him. Several lines, so that you can see this person, this man. This is from her memoirs.

"Evening. The well-known Arbar alley-ways -- to Berdyaev. The square room with the red wood furniture. The mirror in the antique oval frame, over the couch. All that are there are but the two beautiful and gracious ladies -- Berdyaev's wife and her sister. He is not at home, but with a casual step I go into his study. I go over to sit at his large writing table: of a creative disorder there is none. Everything is set out tidy on the table: only to the left and right are piles of books. How many there are! Closer -- are the ones being read, bookmarked, and farther -- the supply for the future. Quite various: the Kabbala, Husserl and Cohen, Simeon the New Theologian, works on physics, a little pile of French Catholics, and further off likely a novel for the night, something found second-hand... I walk about the room. Over the wide couch, where at night it serves him as a bed, there is a crucifix of blackwood and ivory -- we bought it together with him in Rome. Farther on the wall -- is a water-colour: a depiction of a starets-elder's cell, drawn by the reverent hand of Berdyaev's grandmother, a Kiev native. Quite recently a Christian, in Moscow Berdyaev sought association with those, not inclined towards the literary salons, but with the genuine people's life of the Church... And how different Berdyaev is from the other newly-illumined, the newly-converted, who are so ready to renounce both reason as well as human pride! He stands firm in this, that forswearing reason would not be true to the Glory of God. He stands for the might and the way of life of thought, he fights for it. A sharp dialectician -- he gives blows right and left. There is nothing stuffy or ultra-holy about him. And his sense of humour never left him. On occasion we smile with him past the head of his then like-minded fellows, the ever so devout Novoselov and Bulgakov. The philosophical thought of Berdyaev one might characterise as that of the knight chivalrous. The decision of the problem of love for him is never dictated by smouldering insult, by fear, by hatred, as there was, we might say, in Nietzsche, or Dostoevsky... And in life he bore his own dignity as a thinker, as did once his ancestor, the ernstwhile Count Choiseul: brandishing the fancy laces, reckoning, that a sharp word of deep thought -- is nothing reproachful; without effort, without strain, preserving for himself a certain throe of contradiction, sometimes -- of philosophical desperation. In this is his strength, and his weakness".

When this period was coming to a close, Berdyaev wrote one of his books in summation of his pre-war period, which he titled "The Meaning of Creativity". Creativity was for him not a simple function of human thought and life, but from life itself. He wrote: "Spirit is creative activity. Every act of spirit is a creative act. But the creative act of the subjective spirit is an egress from oneself into the world. In every creative act there is an element of freedom introduced, an element, not definable by the world. The creative act of man, always issuing forth from spirit and not from nature, presupposes the material of the world, presupposes the manifold human world. He descends into the world and bears into the world the new, the formerly non-extant. The creative act of spirit has two sides: an ascent and a descent, spirit in the creative impulse and taking flight soars upwards over the world and conquers the world, but it likewise also descends into the world, it is pulled downwards by the world, and in its products it conforms itself with the condition of the world. Spirit objectifies itself within the production of creativity and in this objectification it associates itself with the given condition of the manifold world. Spirit is fire! The creativity of spirit is fiery! Objectification however is a chilling down of the creative fire of spirit. Objectification within culture always signifies accordance with others, of a leveling of the world, with the social middle ground. The objectification of spirit within culture is its socialisation".

Further on Berdyaev speaks about, how that our customary concepts about God, about the duty of man, is very often sociomorphic, that it is built upon the example of social life, reflecting affliction or self-affirmation, or still other yet moments of the human manner of life. It is necessary to snatch off the sociomorphic trappings, so as to penetrate into the depths of being, both of man, and of the Divine.

For Berdyaev the mystery of God was always a mystery unfathomable. In this he was in full agreement with Christian theology. But the mystery of man also remained just as unfathomable. The mystery of man for him takes on extraordinarily close a connection with the mystery of the Divine. Here is one of the vulnerable sides of Berdyaev's metaphysics. He writes: "According to the Bible, God breathed into man the spirit. Therefore the spirit is not a creation, but is rather that begotten of God". This is very imprecise. This is extremely disputable. This is practically an identification of our spirit with the Divine Spirit. But Berdyaev speaks about this in the heat of polemics, trying to exalt spirit, which is constantly being degraded by both materialism and by religious thought. And he in his paradoxical polemics reaches to suchlike an expression: "For us the path is not only Golgotha, but also Olympus". Certainly, at the first glance by a reader it would seem strange what this has in common. But he wanted to point out, that the beauty of the world, the beauty of the flesh has value for God (even if it be embodied in pagan Olympus), since that it likewise is a form of creativity.

Is salvation the manifest goal of the life of man? -- he asked. If by this there be understood something purely utilitarian and namely, whether man wind up in the "better" place after death or in the "worse", whether he wind up in paradise or in hell, -- Berdyaev radically comes out against such an understanding of salvation. He said, that the task of man -- is altogether not in suchlike a salvation, not ego-centric, nor egoistic, not the search for some sort of bliss, but rather creativity. God has lodged within man a tremendous potential, and man ought to create, and then from this would flow forth both an utmost moral understanding, and a nobleness of spirit. It was difficult, certainly, to hear out these keen, paradoxical, not always successful expressions of Berdyaev within the circle of his colleagues.

He then writes his book, "The New Religious Consciousness and Society", and he tackles there questions of sex, social questions, and he ponders the Revolution. He says about it, that revolution can be reactionary. He, having already a certain record of revolutionary struggle, he brings out here and quotes the remarkable words of Mikhailovsky, the populist, with whom he had much engaged in polemics. And in these suchlike words, Mikhailovsky says: I am impoverished, of my house there is nothing, besides the shelves with books and the bust of Belinsky. If even this the people, in whose service I devoted all my life, were to rush in here, in order to burn my books, and to smash this bust, I would defend this to my last breath. And here these words of Mikhailovsky were to prove extraordinarily true for Berdyaev. He spoke about the violence, which happens above on the side of those having power, and also of that below, on the side of those, who are not given to think over the rights of the person of man -- the trampling of freedom is possible from both sides.

And here ensues the Revolution. Berdyaev awaited it. And he awaited many a stormy event. Still back in 1909 he had participated in the anthology "Vekhi" ("Signposts"). He was not a poor prophet. In the year 1917 he participates in the anthology "Iz glubiny" ("From the Depths"), which undertakes a sketch of all the elapsing epoch. He actively participates in social life. They elect him into the university. I have people close to me, who heard Berdyaev lecture, they saw, how he stood out. He produced a tremendous impression upon his audience. (The sole thing, which interfered, was the nervous tic on his face, which spoilt it somewhat). He participated in the Vol'phila (Free Association of Culture), the Free Spiritual Academy. He thought intensely.

During these years the German philosopher Oswald Spengler wrote a book, "The Decline of the West" (or as we tend to translate it, "The Decline of Europe") -- a book, which shook Europe and the world. It spoke about the inevitability for civilisation of a period of decline: just like an organism passes through periods of childhood-youth-decline, and just like in nature there are the seasons Spring-Summer-Autumn-Winter, so also it is inevitable that civilisation will pass into decline, which nothing and no one can stop. The West today, wrote Spengler, is in decline. But Berdyaev together with his like-minded compatriots answered this book brilliantly! He pointed out that fate, historical destiny, -- which actually can lead a civilisation to ruin, that it is not something singular, which stands before mankind. Spirit can conquer fate. Christianity, Berdyaev writes, hurls challenges to fate and never can it be reconciled with the mechanistic, the morbid, the fatalistic.

It can be said, that in Berdyaev immortality lived as an actualisation of that, which is always present. Within him there was constantly a tempest of thoughts. He was able to bring interesting ideas to the masses, ideas that came to mind for him. We might speak, for example, of his viewpoint on the division within the Church. There existed various viewpoints: Khomyakov's -- that the sinful Latins fell away; the Old Catholics -- that it was the unworthy schismatics, the raskolniki, who fell away; and there were those, who wanted to re-unite these fragmented parts and grieved on account of the division of the Church. Berdyaev was the first to genuinely to take a profound look at this problem. He pointed out, that the Christian West and the Christian East each had their own particular consciousness and realisation of spiritual life. In the West there was always a strong striving towards God, as up and above, as though, in Berdyaev's expression, a falling in love with Christ, an imitation of Christ externally on the outside. From this, he says, is the striving and stretching upwards of the Gothic churches, and the arrow-shaped windows. In contrast to this, the East senses Christ as being here, and intimately close. Therefore the Eastern churches as it were embrace a going-inward, the light burns within, the Spirit of God is present within. These two types of spirituality had to develope themselves independently, and the evil of the separation of Christians was not a matter of Divine Providence wherein Christianity should be all jumbled together in an impersonal one-sided massive-lump throughout all the earth, but rather that the concreteness of the multiple-blossomings of Christianity should flower forth ultimately, in spite of the sorrow of division.

Eventually, in the year 1922 they threw Berdyaev out of Russia and banished him. By this time he was already the author of numerous articles, the author of the books "The Meaning of Creativity" and "The Philosophy of Freedom" and a series of others. For a certain while he settles then in Berlin, and then he winds up in Paris. At Clamart, near Paris, he stays a long time. And there he writes his most important works, their number being too long to list here. I shall mention only the chief ones.

The "Philosophy of the Free Spirit", a work in two volumes,[1] written with an extraordinary acumen, -- this is a developement of the idea of his philosophy of freedom. He turns especial attention in this book to his metaphysical treatment of freedom. He says about it, that freedom is situated within the depths of God, that this is an unique mystery. In this he had investigated the sources of the XVII Century German mystic Jacob Boehme about a sort of Abyss, which lies at the basis of everything. For

---

[1] trans. note: published in English in one volume under title "Freedom and the Spirit".

Berdyaev this concept was not altogether precise, and sometimes he identified it with God. God is situated on the other side of the understanding of good and evil (as with Boehme). But Berdyaev then separated God from the Abyss and identified the Abyss with that fitful, monstrous, irrational, incomprehensible, but mighty and impulsive freedom, which cannot be defined, save only as nothing. This dualistic representation is scarcely perhaps distinct from Christianity, since Berdyaev said, that God created the world from nothing, but the "nothing" -- this is not "nothing", but rather that dark chaotic world of uncreated freedom, like God uncreated.

We stand from Biblical times from the point of reference, that nothing uncreated exists, except the Creator. At one of the congresses, studying the legacy of Berdyaev, at Paris, it was said that the striving of Berdyaev to give such an interpretation was rooted in his desire to create a new theodicy, a conception, which would reconcile the mystery of God and the mystery of suffering. The mystery of evil was for Berdyaev exceptionally acute, and all his life was tormented by it. And he spoke thus: God is not culpable in worldly evil, God is not all-powerful in this. He does not rule within the world, but He conquers the dark chaotic principle, which is co-eternal to Him, having been always.

You say, and how then does it manifest itself? Berdyaev answered: as nothing, for this is impossible to name, this is that which is situated beyond the bounds of thought. Actually the mindless, irrational striving towards evil is sufficiently difficult to bring into any sort of logical order. And Dostoevsky, whom Berdyaev so loved, often pointed out the irrational and mindless character of evil. It is mindless... And thus here, if God be not somehow almighty, but only conquers the darkness, Berdyaev advances another concept, disputable from the Christian point of view, that God has need of the world, that He seeks us out, seeks out mankind, to sustain Him. Berdyaev one time heard words of the French writer Leon Bloy in regard to this, that God -- is as a Great Loneliness, and he experienced this as some sort of inner experience. In this he had the sense not in the plenitude of God, but in a certain Divine metaphysics of suffering. And the suffering of the world he experienced as... a break with the Divine Unity. For us the Creator is necessary, but we are also infinitely needful for Him. There is much that is striking, profound, enigmatic and subtle in these discernments of Berdyaev, although from the theological point of view there are, certainly, debatable aspects.

Berdyaev was of a deeply eschatological outlook, and for him the essential condition of the world is as something deadened, objectified! History -- is a matter of statues and corpses... Everything then and only then will realise itself, when the world casts off from itself this here ossification resulting from objectification. Therefore the meaning of history -- is in its annulment, its taking away; it is in that, what we aspire to, like an arrow, towards the future, where the mortality of objectivised being will be conquered, where the creative spirit will triumph fully, where it will come into play, where it will blossom! Eschatology therefore, which is a teaching about the end of the world, for Berdyaev is not something ominous, dark, terrifying. He said about it, that man mustneeds come nigh the end of the world, that man ought to strive towards this moment of the transfiguration of being. And everything dark would be annihilated.

People have an incorrect understanding of the idea of Providence, Berdyaev says, they understand the words of Christ the Saviour literally, that He keeps a watchful eye on each one. Although, if a man strive toward Him, there is realised the unity of Christ and man. But in general God does not rule within the world. The Kingdom of God is not in the world. He does not rule in cholera, in plague, in treason, in catastrophes. The world is full of evil! And in this regard Berdyaev is right. And it is difficult not to agree with him, that God hath not realised Himself, in an Armenian earthquake or an American earthquake. Certainly not! And herein it is profoundly true.

Christian theology investigates this from another angle: that freedom is given us for a belittling of the Divine. God has ceded to us a certain expanse within being, and in this expanse there act already (here Berdyaev was completely right) both the Will of God, and the human will, and the blind elements, and fate (fate or destiny not in the mystical sense, but in the sense of the foreordained, the physical, the psychological, the historical, the social).

Berdyaev was a philosopher of history. His book, "The Meaning of History", -- is one of the most remarkable. It came out when he was already in the emigration. For him history was a movement forward, but he emphasised the radical distinction of the Biblical world-view from that of antiquity, and from that of the ancient Indian. India and Greece did not know history as movement. Only the Bible tells us, that the world has a teleology, an end-purpose.

Berdyaev likewise wrote a book, which we have long regarded as extremely odious, -- "The Philosophy of Inequality". He wrote it during the revolutionary years, at the beginning of the 1920's, and here, in his Rodina native-land he wrote it for those representatives of the Intelligentsia, who like Blok were prepared to go encounter the dark destructive element. He called them betrayers of the spirit, betrayers of culture, desolators, collaborators of transgressive deeds. And we know today, that these deeds were transgressive, but Berdyaev raised his voice and shouted about it back then.

It mustneeds be said, that Berdyaev adopted, sort of, the general principles of socialism, and he was a despiser of the bourgeois. He considered that the bourgeois -- is a spiritual sickness. Even before the Revolution he had written about it, as concerning the abasement of consciousness, an abdicating of humanity. The spiritual bourgeoise -- is a primitivisation, a smugness, a residue of the spiritual current within man -- for him all this was just as contemptible as atheism.

The Person of Christ was for Berdyaev infinitely precious. It is because in Him there was realised the Divine in fulness, and in the fulness also of that before which He condescended Himself to come down, -- in front of the person of man... Christ hath revealed to us the humanness of God. Prior to this we would have thought, that there could be nothing human about God, but here through Christ we have come to recognise it. Berdyaev conceived of the mystery of the Trinity as something dynamic, for him the life within God was dynamic! Although, certainly, man is unable to penetrate into this mystery.

For Berdyaev the cognition of the world, the cognition of God, the cognition of mystery -- this is not simply a logical process, not simply the manipulation of a certain intellectual judgement. But rather it is an act, which involves the whole of the nature of man, the whole of his being! -- his intuition, his anguish, his senses, all bound up together. Only thus can we comprehend reality, wholly, and not merely in its separate aspects. And this intuitive, vital, wholistically integral approach was also a chief property of the philosophy of Berdyaev.

Many people have been surprised at the scope of this man, especially since in France there have been no few philosophers, historians, theologians, publicists, with each occupying their own little cubby-hole. But Berdyaev moved freely across all these worlds. His brief noticing of some knotty aspect of Christian theology could result sometimes in a precious whole tome. Well, let us say, he was speaking about Biblical criticism -- he would point out its purest significance. I shall not digress here further, but this phrase can reveal and show, how he could hit upon the chief things for us in the sphere of the knowledge of Scripture.

Life did not go so simply for him. Because there was both misfortune, and there were also difficulties. But he did not give up. He created the journal "Put'" ("The Way"), of which he was the editor from the 1920's up to the war years. This is not a journal, this is a treasure-trove of thought! Its sixty issues comprise a wealth, an inheritance, which we today are receiving, and God grant, that this should pass down to our descendants.

He gathered, he grouped around himself representatives of Christian thought. Such people as Frank, and Bulgakov, and Nikolai Lossky and Boris Vysheslavtsev, a remarkable thinker very little known here and who died in 1964, and there were many representatives of free philosophical thought, Protestants, Catholics, but basically the Orthodox.

It is interesting, the dramatic moments of history that Berdyaev lived through in the setting of the war, personally. What happened in the year 1917? -- He was about to be thrown into prison, but the February Revolution saved him. What happened with him on the eve of the Second World War? -- Everyone was attacking and cursing him. The first time, in 1917, he came out in defense of the monks of an Athos monastery, which the Synod persecuted. Nikolai Aleksandrovich wrote his article, "Gasiteli dukha" ("Quenchers of the Spirit"), for which they took him to criminal court. And before the Second World War there began attacks on his close friend, a professor from the Paris Theological Institute -- Georgii Petrovich Fedotov. And why did they attack him? -- for his activities. We shall speak with you later on separately about Fedotov.

Fedotov had the audacity to give an objective analysis of Soviet politics, for Stalin -- very serious stuff, very insightful. And they wrote him off as being a "red" (or "rosy", as they then said), although this was completely inaccurate. Ultimately they shoved him, they pushed him out, so to speak, out of the Theological Institute, wherein many of his colleagues, professors, knowing that he was not guilty of such things, they bandied about and signed petitions. This was a stiflingly oppressive moment. And then Berdyaev exploded with an article, which was entitled "Does There Exist Freedom of Thought and Conscience within

Orthodoxy?" And he, with the exceptional shrillness and pathos peculiar to his pen, pounced upon those craven cowards. He himself was fearless.

In 1937 he wrote a book, "The Sources and Meaning of Russian Communism".[1] This book provides a quite profound analysis of the situation. He does not come off in it as a rampant anti-Communist, he generally in no way was given to any sort of the "rampant", not some champion of the idea, but rather he attempts to show, how things came about.

Berdyaev was hostile to every sort of dictatorship, whether in the end it be the Nazi-ist, the Frankist, the Stalinist. And when the Germans occupied Paris, he as an already very well known figure was involved in all sorts of things, to show people, how much he disliked this Nazi-ist power. He wrote much against the Nazi ideology, coming out openly and sharply against it. He was swept up to be arrested, but people came forward even in the Gestapo, who knew his fame, and he was let go. He cautiously worked with collaborators for the front, the resistance. His soul was one together with the Red Army, together with Russia, he always wanted only that it be victorious, in spite of everything.

When the war ended, he began entertaining thoughts, whether or not he should return home. He began to mix in with people, who had journeyed from Soiuz, from the Soviet Union, he met with both soldiers and civilians and he was somewhat shocked and taken aback. "It would seem, that the materialism is still with us, -- he said jokingly, -- and here I had thought, that it would have been thrown out in the days of my youth". He said: "Revolutionaries, really indeed? These are now all dignitaries, in their decorations". These meetings for him were interesting, and also somewhat tragic. He could not return, perhaps, and amidst all the indecision he was already a man well up in years. But he worked to the end and died at his writing table.

Over the course of many years we had not a word about him, only some occasional histories, or very scant references in an encyclopedia. Then there appeared a critical work, and here now starts a whole new run of works. I so to speak, envy each of you, who now are just beginning to read Nikolai Aleksandrovich. This is a matter of profound delight for both thought and for the heart, when you get into the world of this free, this

---

[1] trans. note: published in English under title "The Origins of Russian Communism".

beautiful and lofty thought, into the world of this man, a philosopher of person and creativity and freedom who bears upon himself the seal of incomparable excellence.

Rather recently there seems to have opened a Museum in the name of Berdyaev, a museum which has files in Paris and also among us here. And again certainly, though only on paper, he actually consoles and agitates. Into this museum will be gathered both photographs of those times, and perhaps, photographs of those people, which were so bound up with that epoch, and its matters. I see here present the one managing the museum, and I think he will not be offended, if I turn to you with a request: if you stumble upon old discoveries from the 1910's, from the 1920's, any sort of things -- whatever, that might shed light upon this period, come forth with it. the museum is starting from nothing. The Paris files will be based, I hope, in that very room (it is empty at present), where Nikolai Aleksandrovich died.

His autobiographical book "Samopoznanie" has come out twice: it appeared first as a separate Paris edition, and then later it was republished as the first volume of the Paris collected works. This collection of works now comprises only three volumes.[1] But there is being readied a Soviet edition of this remarkable work, where the person, the image, the tragedy of this exceptional, this excellent, this contentious and fascinating man is to be given in all its stature. The edition is to be done first-hand from the original text, since the archive of Berdyaev at present in large part has been transferred to Moscow.

I have given you today only some rough points, some sketchings, trail lamps, which you can bring to bear for the knowing of the creativity of this great writer, thinker, critic.

And in conclusion, I want to quote for you some of his aphorisms, so that you can get a feel, as to how he tended to express his thoughts:
"The sovereign ruling power -- this is (he says about the genuine holding of power) an obligation, and not a right"; "Faith and knowledge -- are one selfsame thing", i.e. the possession of the fulness of real being (he often spoke in paradoxes); "The criterion of truth in the spirit is itself a manifestation of the spirit"; "The Gospel is the teaching about Christ, and not the teaching of Christ"; "Tolstoy did not know Christ, he knew only the teaching of Christ"; "Love is a sharing of life in God"; "The principle of

---

[1] trans. note: five volumes as of 1999.

evil manifests itself as non-realised good"; "Not only is there a maliciousness against good, but there is also a maliciousness against evil which despoils the spiritual world of man"; "The existence of evil is a proof for the existence of God, a proof of this, that this world is not the sole and ultimate one"; "Of necessity there is a fallen freedom"; "The moral consciousness begins with the question of God "Cain, where is thy brother Abel?" and it ends with the question of God "Abel, where is thy brother Cain?"; -- (I will not comment on this, instead I want, that you yourselves can sense the meaning of these expressions); "Religion ought not to be made moralistic, but rather morality made religious"; "Religion is the relationship to God of sinful mankind"; "Freedom is the freedom not only from masters, but also from slaves"; "There exists not one, but rather two freedoms: the first and the last -- the freedom of the choosing of good and evil and the freedom in good"; "The autocracy of the people -- is a very terrible autocracy, since the will of one or the will of several can no wise so extensively spread its pretensions, as does the will of all"; "It is not man that demands freedom from God, but rather God demands it from man"; "Being is begotten of freedom, and not freedom from being".

What is conscience according to Berdyaev? -- "This is a mindfulness about God", "Conscience is at a depth of person, where man comes in contact with God". What is humility according to Berdyaev? "Humility is the discovering of the soul in its reality"; "To regard one self the most terrible of sinners is suchlike a self-opinion, as to regard oneself holy"; "Humility is not the annihilation of the human will, but rather its enlightening and free submission to truth"; "Socialism is the ultimate truth and the ultimate justice of the bourgeoise" (a paradox!); "Suffering is the consequence of sin and the redemption of sin"; "The meaning of Golgotha is not the deification of suffering, but rather in the victory over death and suffering".

Such was Nikolai Aleksandrovich Berdyaev. I wanted, that you should get a feel of his soul and style. His books you still have to read. But we can regard today a special day of celebration of our culture, in that this man has returned to us. In life it seemed simply a matter of luck for me, that I could read him in my youthful years, but back then this was purely a matter of chance. But at present he stands before us in his full stature.

Translator's Postscriptum Comment (from back in the year 2000):

-- What a sweet delight to hear of one genius of Russian thought through the lips of another inspired genius of Russian thought! The stature of the one enhances the full stature of both not only for Russia, but for all the world! The understanding of the one helps explain the understanding of the other.

Fr Men's enthusiasm and love for Berdyaev shows likewise the dynamic depths at work in Fr Men's mind and heart, a living and engaging response. His prophetic vision of Berdyaev's return to Russia. His command, -- "I have given you only some rough sketchings, but now you must read for yourself...", and the "I envy you, just now beginning...". Yes, in times past, not only in Russia but also the West, it was a matter of chance and good fortune to find and to read Berdyaev. And now so much has changed...

A number of early Berdyaev texts, mentioned by Fr Men', such as "Philosophy of Freedom" and "Philosophy of Inequality", have not yet been translated in English. The future may remedy this. In the interim, much else in English does exist, and is newly appearing via the Internet.

Fr Aleksandr Men', and those others like him, are true evidence that Berdyaev's long-ago seemingly hopeless faith in Russia, his Rodina, -- was not in vain!

frsj

Father Sergei Bulgakov

There is an incident that occurred abroad during the XIX-XX Centuries. Along the hall of the Dresden Gallery, as always, tourists scampered, while before the pictures stand some of the more attentive and deeply absorbed, and among them was a young man -- in frock coat, dark wedged beard, a tremendous forehead, and knitted brows, -- he approaches, attentively gazes at the Sistine Madonna [by Raphael], heads away and as though under a spell again approaches it. And it becomes evident, that with him is occurring something unusual, that this is not some art-expert, not some aesthete, not simply some sentinel of art, but rather a man, who is experiencing the contemplation of this picture as some sort of an encounter, as a genuine, profound, inward encounter.

This man was neither a mystic, nor a visionary -- he was a Social Democrat, he was a political economist, he was a Russian Marxist of the legal sort. And he had journeyed to Germany for the purpose, not for contemplating the image of the Virgin Mary, but rather to study with other Social Democrats, to discuss with Karl Kautsky problems of the economic developement of the world, of the class struggle, of the coordination of markets amidst capitalist production. And suddenly something seized hold of this man, seized hold and remained there. It might be said, that from this moment began his turnabout towards childhood.

Each man to a certain degree is not only the result of his childhood, but everything best, everything precious, everything sacred, all those sparkles, which are there in the childhood for the majority of us, -- this is also that spiritual native-land, towards which we strive. True, we are already wise with experience, wounded by life -- but all the same the soul tends by affinity towards this primal experience and so too it happened with this man, whom they called Sergei Nikolaevich Bulgakov.

Actually, many of you now have already heard this name. When I began with this series of talks of these amazing persons, Bulgakov had not yet been republished for us, but now at present the first publications are appearing in journals, and all over the place has circulated a reproduction of the remarkable picture of Nesterov, "The Philosophers".

One of them, a young man, in white riasa, with a staff, -- is Father Paul Florensky (about whom we will, hopefully, later likewise speak of with you), and the second figure -- erudite, bare of head, filled tempestuously within his mind with ideas -- this is Sergei Nikolaevich Bulgakov.

Twenty-eight volumes of works, hundreds and hundreds of articles! The entirety of his creative work takes up twenty thousand printed pages. He was translated into almost all of the European languages. An economist, an historian, essayist, literary critic, philosopher, theologian, commentator on the Bible, a man extraordinarily many-sided, and finally, a priest, a professor at the Paris Theological Academy, -- all this was Sergei Nikolaevich Bulgakov. A man, born in the closing years of the XIX Century and dying in the closing years of WWII. The centennial of his birth in 1971 went by unnoticed for us. We would hope, that the next generation will have the ability to appreciate the worth of this man. And I want to help you better understand this amazing person.

Bulgakov was born at Orlovschina, into the family of a provincial priestly lineage. The extensive Bulgakov lineage, in descent from some sort of Tatar princes, was widely dispersed throughout Russia. Among the Bulgakovs were many churchly writers, historians, theologians, among them -- the noted writer Mikhail Bulgakov's father, Afanasii Bulgakov. The noteworthy metropolitan of Moscow from the past century, Makarii, likewise was from this lineage of the Bulgakovs. But Sergei Nikolaevich was born into the family of an impoverished priest, into a family, where it was difficult, and rough, and a struggle for them to get by. The family was large, and moreover, as Sergei Nikolaevich himself tended to remember, that his father feeling depressed with his work tended to frequently drink. But all the same the boy preserved a sort of organic, warm, vital and tender memories about this setting. His friends back then joked about him, that he was born in an epitrakhelion, the priestly neck-stole, in effect that he was born to be a priest. And he said of himself: "In me flows Levite blood" (the Levites were -- in the Old Testament -- an hereditary line, serving at the altar).

He starts in at the seminary, the clergy school. Very quickly his amazing abilities advance him along. But there, in the Orlov seminary, in him, it gets wrecked.

Back at the beginnings of the 1880's, the students are reading Pisarev, Dobroliubov, Chernyshevsky. They are having lively discussions about atheism as an extremely plausible hypothesis. Everyone is ready to go serve the people, but to serve God -- for them it is an empty and hollow word. And finally it is with Bulgakov, a man of exceptional sincerity, vulnerability, I would even say, sensitivity, all his religious awareness was rendered into dust, with only the moral consciousness remaining. For him the good old days, his existence, the theological school, theology -- all this blends together. And he sees, in general, the truth: that the conservative powers, including the churchly ones, are holding the people in a state of stagnation, of immobility. At present we sometimes tend to idealise the past, and the thinkers of the XIX Century too, as remote as they were from the people, also tended to idealise things, they spoke about the peasant commune, but irregardless of this, life in the small cities and villages of Russia was very harsh.

Remember what you have read in Ostrovsky, in Chekhov: Dobroliubov indeed not without reason termed this "the dark realm" (he himself was from a priestly lineage). Yes, the spiritual and intellectual catastrophes of our century had their preparation in the grievous negative processes of the past, which we now term "stagnation" -- a very appropriate word to describe that time. And the movement forward, towards a better lot, towards a better life, for the young Sergei Bulgakov was bound up with the liberation of the people from this stifling and unjust life.

As the son of a priest, he did not have the right to enter university -- then likewise there was discrimination. But the laws changed, and he enters university. And in what field? The legal, certainly, he wants to get involved in political economics. Why? Because it runs counter to the ideas of the Populists, as to the possibility of transforming the economic life of the people, and consequently, to render it happier a lot. But how to transform it? Here Marxism lights the way for him. What is it that attracted the student Sergei Bulgakov to Marxism? The pretensions of this teaching, that it has revealed and precisely knows the principles of developement for society; moreover, that it knows those principles, which will lead society to progress and enlightenment. It is not mere chaos in the world, not the clash of capricious forces, but rather a matter of certain objective laws, which apparently have been uncovered by Marx.

Bulgakov, a man with an extraordinary capacity for work, gets absorbed in "Kapital". It seems to him, that in this enormous book these laws for once have been discovered. And at the completion of university he devotes himself entirely to political economics in the Marxist field. This was a legal Marxism, not involved with the work in the sphere of the political opposition. And this too was a scientific attempt to understand developement, as the Marxists tended to say, as the "economic basis" of society.

Bulgakov then defends a dissertation, quite large a work, "Concerning Markets amidst Capitalistic Production", he teaches at a commerce school, and then he lectures at the university. Following his dissertation, "Capitalism and Agriculture" (he already is profoundly adept at Marxist literature), he made an attempt to work out those evident contradictions, which arose between agrarian problems and the Marxist approaches for dealing with them. And having attempted to demonstrate the correctness of Marxism, he all the more and more becomes convinced of the artificiality, the abstraction, the mere schematic aspect of his intellectual conception.

Bulgakov was not a fanatic for political myths, he was not "a believing Marxist" (you grasp what I am saying) -- he was a learned man! And when he subsequently and persistently had analysed it all, he perceived, that here it was moreso a myth, rather than authentic a science. And in the process of these searchings he begins to turn towards literature, to the problems of eternity. He writes a work, "The Inner Drama of Hertsen" -- of Hertsen, who saw the ideal to be in European progress, but who then suddenly perceived, that this is a Moloch, which leads nowhere.

Bulgakov then writes a small, but still profound a work, "Ivan Karamazov as Philosophic a Type", and he posits in it the problem of the suffering of innocents -- as this mystery is perhaps understood. And here during this period (he is then travelling in Germany) he feels, that someone is calling him. We would perhaps say, that it was his childhood calling out to him, that it was the mystery of life calling him, which had gotten hidden away from him during the time of his absorption with economic theories.

And here I just have to read you, very much so, some lines from his diary, from his reminiscences. "My 24th year, but for almost ten years already the faith has been undermined in my soul, and after stormy crises and doubts in it has reigned a religious emptiness. The soul had begun to forget the religious excitement, had extinguished the very possibility of a doubt, and from a bright childhood has remained but poetic fancies, a tender mist of remembrance, always ready to fade away. O, how terrible this dream of the soul. From it indeed one might not waken for an entire lifetime. Along with mental growth and scientific advancement, the soul irrepressibly and imperceptibly was immersed in a sticky slime of self-satisfaction, self-esteem, triteness. In it held sway a sort of grey-dull twilight, in measure of which all the childhood light faded. And then unexpectedly this came... Mysterious calls resounded within the soul and it rushed hence towards them to meet..."

During this time he was journeying to the Caucassus. "The dusk of evening. We had been journeying the Southern steppe, the windrows fragrant with sweet-scented grasses and hay, golden against the scarlet of a fine sunset. In the distance, the blue tint of the nearer Caucassus Mountains. The first I had seen of them. And, gazing with greedy glances into the opening vista of mountains, imbibing within myself the light and the air, I became heedful to the revelation of nature. The soul long ago had become accustomed, with a dull and silent aching, to see in nature only a dead desolation neathe a veiling of beauty, like under a deceptive mask; the soul unawares could not be at peace with a nature without God. And suddenly in that very hour my soul became agitated, filled with joy, it trembled: but if it indeed is so, if it is not desolation, not a lie, not a mask, not death, -- but rather He, the good and loving Father, His robe, His love... My heart was pounding amidst the clattering sounds from the train, and we were carried into the golden foot-hills and towards those slate-blue mountains...

But soon again it bespoke, now loudly, convincingly, powerfully. And again you, O Caucassus mountains! I behold your ice, gleaming from sea to sea, your snows, aglow neathe the morning dawn, with those peaks thrusting into the sky, and my soul melted in rapture. And that, which for a moment merely had flashed, and all at once had faded out amidst the evening steppe, now resounded and sang, interlaced into a wondrous solemn chorale. In front of me it was ablaze, the first day of the world-creation. All was lucid, all had become at peace, filled with a joyous twinkling".

Here thus in suchlike a moment of a profound experience was gradually demolished in his soul those barricades of rubbish, which the materialistic conception of things had heaped up. And in 1903 there came out a collection of his articles, already entitled as "From Marxism to Idealism". In it Bulgakov demonstrates, that over and beyond the economic problems there tend to exist spiritual problems, completely distinct from them. And it is impossible to disdainfully disregard them as some sort of overlying superstructure, in that they comprise also the essence and core of our life. And if in this spiritual sphere global transformations do not occur, then no sort of economic changes can be of help. There has to be a rebirth of spirit, without, social and economic renewal is impossible.

In 1911 appears his book, "Two Cities". From my point of view, subjectively, this is the most personal of his pre-war and pre-revolutionary books. Within it were gathered works of a striking intensity, for example, "Karl Marx as a Revolutionary Type", where Bulgakov points out that inner train of thought, that volitional intensity, that affective and passionate element, which lay hidden and concealed within the psychological composite of the founder of Marxism, that which was merely camouflaged over as a science in form, in objectivity, with the dialectical method. He showed the passion of this great man, a titanic passion. Titanism -- this is a revolt against the higher values, when man wants only to admit himself as God.

There is a noteworthy work about the significance of the spiritual person for culture, about the significance of Christianity for the history, the developement and revival of culture. There is a splendid work, which has not lost its freshness even today, -- concerning early Christianity. It indicates, that when Christianity went out into the world, it was a new power that had emerged -- but one that was not economic, nor political, nor social, -- rather instead, the power of the Spirit. And Bulgakov correctly asserts, that in the sphere of spiritual culture changes tend to occur within, and they often make their impact upon the surrounding world, they transform the visage of man, and around them occur all the major clashes.

In his work, "Apocalyptics and Socialism", Bulgakov indicates, that science does not know for sure the conception of a bright future. Science cannot accurately assert, that society and the world will develope in a positive direction. Moreover, historical experience tends to show, that mankind is apt to go around endlessly in circles: from democracy -- to tyranny, from tyranny -- to oligarchy, then again to despotism, then again to democracy. There has not been a continuous developement of society from a less just to a more just social order. And whoever thinks so (we, indeed, have been taught so in childhood, in the schools), well, such a person is totally failing to come to grips with the real historical facts.

And further on, Bulgakov points out, that the faith in progress, lodged within all the varied views of Socialism (not only the Marxist, but whichever), is not a matter of science, but rather a matter of faith, a faith-teaching. Such as with Christianity, which in distinction from all the other religious teachings, first reveals to the world the mystery, wherein the will of the Creator leads the creation and the crown of creation, man, towards perfection, leads to an higher life, to that, which in the Bible is called the Kingdom of God. But this -- is a matter of Revelation, and not of economics, not of politics, and not of philosophy in the abstract sense of the word. And when the faith in progress, which has entered into our flesh and blood, attempts to assert, that it is scientific -- this is a mistake, a self-deception. And actually, the teaching about a bright future is a secular variant of the Christian viewpoint -- on eschatology. Though the Bible says, that God will lead the world towards the light, -- science does not know this for a fact. And the social utopias, which have arisen since the time of Thomas More, Campanella, Owen, Fourier and others -- are unintentionally so to speak, a sort of contraband, snatched from the Christian idea of the perfecting of the world, and they then situated this idea into altogether different a content.

This theme even today for us is actual enough, and not only for our land. The thought, that mankind has to move unfailingly in the best possible direction, actually has been pilfered from Christianity into quite different concepts of progress. There was this French writer Condorcet, perishing during the terror times of the French Revolution, who developed this thought of progress into an entire harmonious theory -- that the world is moving without fail in a positive direction, from barbarity to enlightenment and civilisation. But here it was the XVIII Century, and enlightenment, and Condorcet, and quite much else, fell into the path of the guillotine.

And this issue is extremely disputable. Not for nothing did Stalin say: "To live has gotten better, to live has gotten happier". He exploited our hope, that life ought to get better. People, at the onset of the XX Century on the night of 31 December 1900 said: Here is coming a century of science, here is coming a century of progress! Who back then could foresee, that this would be a century of genocide, bitter wars, inhumanity, of widespread wickedness all over the world! This is a problem, absolutely so, connected with the growth of a spiritual culture, because no sort of history can prove to us, that everything automatically moves in a positive direction. Bulgakov devoted quite serious an investigation into this question, in writing, thus to say making it readily enough accessible; and for those interested he provides bibliographic a list.

Further on, in his article "Heroism and Asceticism" (From Considerations on the Religious Nature of the Russian Intelligentsia)", Bulgakov analyses the tragedy of the Russian Intelligentsia. Having lost its religious grounding, its faith, it nonetheless preserved the striving for good, for service to the people. And herein, this split between a speculative faith from life itself resulted in tragedy. "Heroism and Asceticism" is an article, which nowadays for us has been reprinted in several editions, but it first appeared in the anthology of articles, entitled "Vekhi" ["Landmarks"]. I think that all of you have heard about this book. It came out in 1909 and actually denoted a very important landmark or indicator in the spiritual and philosophic developement of Russia. Bulgakov, his friend Berdyaev, Frank and others had written this book -- as a forewarning, they said, that only a spiritual rebirth could lead the land onto other rail-tracks. Mere external outward changes would go nowhere.

The further path of Bulgakov becomes more complicated. He is an historian, and also an economist, but he is all more and more attracted to philosophy. In 1912 appears his book, "The Philosophy of Economics". From its title one might tend to think, that this is a text on economics. But no, this is the book of a contemplative, a seer and philosopher, one of his most interesting books (true though, not complete as such, for it was only the first volume that had come out, and for which the author received a doctoral degree). Economics, -- Bulgakov explains, -- is a great creative task allotted to man. In the Bible we read: "God created man in His own image and likeness, and gave him mastery of dominion over living things", -- man is proclaimed as a master of economy. The master in economy -- is not a tyrant, not a dictator, but rather a being, set within the creation, for the purpose of the humanising of it.

Bulgakov is the first to coin this term -- "humanification". Some years later, this term will be employed by Teilhard de Chardin: humanisation, the humanification of nature, the in-spiritising of nature. Here with Bulgakov in a sense first appears an idea of a spiritual core of the world; he called this the Wisdom of God, or in Greek, Sophia.

At the time he had become acquainted with Berdyaev. Their friendship closely became such, that their friends would joke and call them the Brothers Dioscuri, the Twins, or muddle it as Bergakov and Buldyaev -- for here they always seemed to figure in together, although their individual temperament in quite much was very different.

During this time at Moscow, not far from Volkhonka, there was the salon of the millionairess Margarita Morozova. This intelligent and beautiful woman was very fond of Prince Evgenii Trubetskoy, likewise marvelous a man, a thinker, writer, art-expert and philosopher. And her love impelled her to a great and noble step: out of her own financial means she established a publishing house and likewise financed religio-philosophic gatherings. And at her fine house gathered the likes of Bulgakov, Berdyaev, Frank and many others. Merezhkovsky too journeyed there from Peterburg. And by Morozova was created the publishing house "Put'" ("The Way"), which existed up until 1916.

The first books under the "Put'" imprint were published prior to the First World War. Among them also appeared the forgotten classical works of Russian philosophy. And first published there was the complete text of the book, "The Pillar and Foundation of Truth" by Florensky. First published there also was the complete (as of then) gathered works of Chaadaev under the redaction of Gershenson. First published too was Berdyaev's book, "The Philosophy of Freedom", which finally at present has come out in reprint for us (this is a brilliant book of still young a thinker -- Berdyaev was then about thirty years of age). And then too quite much else. Bulgakov worked at this publishing house, and under the "Put'" imprint appeared his books, "The Philosophy of Economics" and "Two Cities", and a whole series of other works, and in particular, a preface (a very important preface) to a book by Ignaz Seipel, an erudite Austrian Catholic, entitled "The Economic-Ethical Views of the Fathers of the Church". This book henceforth has become a classic text as such in the form of a chrestomathia, or reading anthology of sayings of all the Fathers of the Church, in the original and in translation, dealing with questions on labour, ownership, wealth, poverty and so forth; it is a book, which at present is still a reference text for all, who are concerned with these questions.

When Bulgakov was lecturing at university, at the Commerce Institute (on Greater Serpukhov Street)), he wrote an article, "An History of Economic Teachings". It is quite curious, in that he started it with the Old Testament, with the Biblical prophets, and from apocalyptic figures. He showed, that in the Bible are contained already the primal basic for the transformation of society. But in form these basics were most strongly bound up with the spiritual aspects of existence.

And finally, before the Revolution itself, there was completed a transitional book by Bulgakov, "Light Unfading" (it came out already during the time of the Revolution). The transition process occurs within the course of the book. The first half of it is as a philosopher, and one quite erudite, who is writing, and he posits a question in Kantian a manner: how possible is religion, how possible is the knowledge of higher worlds?" "On what can we have trust in?" -- as Kant said. The book's second half -- this is already a different Bulgakov, Bulgakov -- the contemplator of mysteries, which he works on himself, he does not give consideration about whom, about whose ever be the ancient or modern foreign thoughts, but rather it is that he himself fashions his own course of thought.

At this time he is already active in Church matters, as secretary of the All-Russian Church Sobor, compiling very important documents. This Sobor could not be convened before the Revolution, insofar as the old government and its over-prokurators prevented this, and because also over the course of many generations no Sobors had been convened. And then, in 1917, after the downfall of the autocracy, the Provisional Government decides to open the Sobor within the Kremlin. And at it they choose Patriarch Tikhon, now enumerated to the ranks of the saints. He highly esteems Sergei Nikolaevich Bulgakov, and when Bulgakov recourses to him with a petition for ordination to the priestly dignity, the saintly hierarch replies: "Sergei Nikolaevich, we need you more in suit-coat". He had in view, that the societal, political, scientific, publicist and philosophic activity of Bulgakov for him as patriarch was very important. But Sergei Nikolaevich continued to insist, and soon, during the very days of the {Bolshevik] Revolution, occurs the ordination of Bulgakov.

Upon the recommendation of Saint Tikhon, Bishop Feodor ordains him, and Bulgakov describes, how at first he went about, soaring with enthusiasm, after he had become a priest. This was as though a return to his primal vocation, to his proper nature.

But events turn stormy, they become all more and more tragic. Bulgakov with his family -- he had a wife and children (one small boy had died at an early age; this grieved Bulgakov terribly, and he found consolation at Optima Pustyn, whither he then loved to journey) -- set off to the Crimea. There he writes a philosophic drama, "At the Feast of the Gods": various people are seated round a table, and they discuss the fate of Russia. "At the feast of the Gods" -- is reminiscent of a verse [Cicero] by Tiutchev:

Blest is he, who hath visited this world,
In its fateful moments of destiny,
Him the all-blest hath invited,
At the feast to converse in company.

-- The gods have invited him to the feast, to see, what will happen with the world. And in the final end he happens to forsake Russia and sets off together with the emigres to Constantinople. It is the very same fate, which is familiar to all of you through the beautiful film "Fleeing Away", derived along the lines from the book by a different Bulgakov. Sergei Nikolaevich -- is at Constantinople. With quite abit of anguish, for a son has remained in Russia, and he does not know, what has become of him. His son remained here, having married a daughter of Mikhail Vasil'evich Nesterov, the reknown painter, and long survived, though essentially his life was nowise simple. And Nesterov too had written of Bulgakov while being here, at Sergiev Posad, which he frequented.

But at this later time -- a most grievous churchly crisis of the heart! First of all: the Russian Church leadership failed to cope with the revolutionary situation, and everything has gotten out of hand. Bulgakov has journeyed on to Constantinople, and meets with the Greek Church leadership: it is completely corrupt, entirely indifferent, and the very picture of total degradation. And in the private pages of his diary Bulgakov writes, that the East is perishing, that the sole remaining power in the Church remains but in the West. He is on the brink of going over into the Roman Catholic jurisdiction. But then in the final end his faith in the Church wins out: no, the Church is in a catastrophic crisis, but in the East nonetheless it has not perished. And with this renewed faith he makes his way to Western Europe.

At first he is in Berlin, and then -- at Paris. In Paris at this time is Metropolitan Evlogii -- a bishop, heading the emigration, who did not want to get aligned either with the Right, the monarchists, nor with the pro-Soviet groups, he wanted to keep neutral a line, and so he went under the Constantinople patriarch. The Evlogian Church group likewise founded the Ste. Sergius Institute in Paris. And it is there that Bulgakov serves the Church, he teaches, he holds the chairmanship of dogmatic theology, while creating his grandiose works, now quite in the theological sphere.

An artistic flair impels him onto an aesthetic path. His enormous books, written abroad, -- form as it were a sort of iconostas. And at the centre of this -- is a trilogy on God-manhood: comprising the three enormous volumes, -- ""The Lamb of God", "The Comforter" (on the Spirit of God), and "Bride of the Lamb" (on the Church). Along the sides -- a book about angels, and a personal mysterious book "Jacob's Ladder", another a book about the veneration of John the Baptist -- "Friend of the Bridegroom", another a book about the veneration of the Virgin Mary -- "The Unconsumed Burning Bush" ["Kupina Neopalimaya"], another a book about the Apostles -- "Peter and John -- the Foremost Apostles", and another a book about iconography. And he did not give up on philosophy, publishing then too "The tragedy of Philosophy" and "The Philosophy of the Name". Posthumously was published his commentary on the "Apocalypse" of John. And there were 80 written sermons, the greater part of which were published posthumously.

Bulgakov was a man, breaching the gap in the dialogue amongst Christians. When the first conferences, when the congresses of the World Council of Churches started up, Bulgakov represented the Orthodox Church there. I have read his diaries: how agitated he got, when he went -- for the first time! -- to these contacts, to which we now more or less have gotten accustomed. He provided a living testimony to the values and traditions of Orthodoxy, at Lausanne and other cities, where these conferences were held.

One of his students relates, that once of an evening he had gone about in Paris, in the Sacre-Cyr area -- where there were a lot of artists, noise, crowds -- and suddenly he saw a priest in riasa coming, one from Russia evidently, with long hair (in keeping with the old custom of his ancestral line, Bulgakov did not have his hair cut short). Bulgakov came, noticing nothing around, oblivious to everything, immersed in himself. And here this man suddenly sensed, had a feeling of the convoluted spirit of Father Sergei...

He had many a student. It was my good fortune to know many of them, people, who mentioned about his extraordinary warmth, his emotion, wisdom, and amazing erudition. And in particular, Bulgakov at his home gathered seminars for discussion of the most important kind of churchly and theological questions. Anyone could approach him. He was not the aloof professor; the problems, about which he wrote, agitated him to the depths of his soul -- this was his life, and he entirely devoted himself to this!

In the decade of the 30's a tragedy was to play out. It involved this, that the churchly Rightists, monarchists, having split themself off from our Church by their regarding the Russian Orthodox Church in Russia -- as all a bunch of "NKVD-ists", tended to hate Bulgakov, because he had not come over to their camp. Pro-Soviet groups likewise tended to regard him negatively, and for much the same reason -- he was not receptive towards them (though the politics during this time already did not get him especially perturbed). And so they begin trying to undermine him dogmatically, so as to accuse Bulgakov of heresy, attempting to render him into a creator of false-teachings. Such a giant of a mind, absolutely, and he had tackled a mass of debatable questions. He was vulnerable, as any great man would be. Lacking in such vulnerability is only someone stupid, given to muttering simple truisms: twice two is four -- how can one be vulnerable in this? But one who indeed tackles the problems, certainly, -- is vulnerable!

And so there pours a flood of criticism upon Bulgakov. A Karlovtsi Synod Abroad monarchist writes a thick tome on the Sophiology of Bulgakov (the teaching about Sophia -- the Wisdom of God). I myself do not adhere to this teaching, and have never accepted it, but I am aware of the fact, that this conception of thought has its own proper place as a theological opinion, a theologoumenon.

And so, the Karlovtsi people pounced upon Bulgakov and accused him of heresy. The Moscow Patriarchate was then situated under the assault of Stalinist repressions, but it too, under such dire a condition, managed to publish a document against Bulgakov. This was on the eve of 1937. Even the Paris theologian Vladimir Lossky, then still a young man, quite sincere and always faithful to our Moscow Patriarchate, got involved in these polemics and wrote a denunciatory book about the Sophiology of Bulgakov. Lossky himself later became ashamed of this book. And this was because there had occurred an one-sided, unjust, fierce and aggressive assault upon a man, who nowise had expressed new dogmas, but merely tended to think aloud. With him one might disagree, but to pounce on him as an heretic was unjust.

At the present time, happily, the attitude towards Bulgakov has changed, and we have in the "Theological Works" a first printing of his biography, quite detailed, with a bibliography of his writings (besides which, abroad it comprises an entire volume). And while therein, true, it was pointed out, that his opinion concerning Sophia -- the Wisdom of God -- evoked criticism, but nowadays on this aspect it does not dwell.

Nonetheless, I have two things to say on this. Bulgakov conceived, that the creation of the world has to have at its foundation a certain spiritual principle: God created the Soul of the World (as thus we term it). But this Soul of the world is very closely connected with the Divine principle itself, it -- is as if it were the thought of God, pervading the creation (I am explaining in very simple terms). But along the same lines, this can sometimes be conceived such, that between the world and God there is no abyss, that the Absolute and the created as it were constantly pass over each into the other. Wherefore it obtains, that the creation -- is not the result of an act, a miracle, when from nothingness is begotten being, but the rather obtains, that from thought which is situated within God, from the heavenly Sophia, from the Wisdom of God, -- is begotten the spiritual foundation of the world, and from it -- the world. This is a world, more bound up in connection with God, than Christian theology always has generally reckoned. And herein lies many a temptation for straying, as for example, a tendency towards Pantheism. But Bulgakov never advanced this as dogmatic, this was only theological an opinion, a theologoumenon. Theologoumena, theological opinions, are permissible in the Church -- always they are permissible, -- if they do not make pretense to being absolute truth.

Bulgakov in his final years was afflicted with cancer of the throat, for which he had an operation, and he could no longer lecture nor serve. Only close associates understood his whispers. But he continued to work, incessantly to work, and at present his unpublished materials are being published.

The impressions, which this person left on people, those that knew him, were indelible and lasting. And I was told by a man, who was present at his death, that this was not a death, but rather a transformation. And even Sergei Nikolaevich had said concerning himself: "I shall not die, but rather be transformed". Over the course of several hours from his face shone an extraordinary light, and they all saw this. This was not an agony, but rather an ascent of spirit... He as it were passed over, he had contemplated those worlds, in which always he inwardly lived, and in this contemplation he passed over the boundary line, separating this world from that world.

For many decades after his death his name went without mention among us. In the philosophic dictionary, say, that came out in 1952-1953, you would not find the name Bulgakov. It first appeared in the philosophic encyclopedia of the 1960's -- a brief mention. Yet here at present is happening his return to us. True, the return is rather slower, than the return of Vladimir Solov'ev, Nikolai Berdyaev and other philosophers. And this is because that in the second half of his life Bulgakov devoted greater attentions to problems specifically theological, rather than philosophic. And therefore the publishing of his works, actually, had to be a matter of churchly academic initiatives and adjucations. But, somehow or other, the grandiose and luminous figure of this gentle, wise, enlightened man with giant a mind, of enormous faith, a man, whose life was a searching, and not only a searching, but also a discovery, full of discovery -- is with us again today.

Many regard him as a saint. I carefully keep, like a relic, certain objects, which lay upon his table, which he used, and it seems to me, that the spiritual rebirth of the present times occurs not only through the influence of the works, which he and his co-workers have left us, but also through the direct influence of his person. For suchlike is the privilege of great souls -- having departed this world, they yet continue to act upon it, continue to participate in the establishing of the Kingdom of God upon earth.

Father Pavel Florensky

To speak at length, and in detail, about the literary, the scientific and philosophic work of such a man, as Pavel Aleksandrovich Florensky, can hardly be possible in ten sessions, let alone one. But my task will be simple. Just as in our previous meetings, I should want, that you will have sensed, and will have caught an image of this man, the style of his thinking, and might then too get a glance at his creative path in life.

This is peculiar a figure. Peculiar as regards his fate. Because the majority of Russian religious thinkers, about whom we have spoken with you, were either banished into exile or else they voluntarily quit their fatherland, and their fate was then connected with the Russian emigration. Florensky was one of the few, who remained here. And moreover, Florensky -- is a man, whom it is nowise possible to characterise in any one particular an area. An engineer? -- yes, with thirty patents for inventions during Soviet times. A philosopher? -- yes, one of the most brilliant interprets of Platonism, one of the most incisive of Russian Platonists. A poet? -- yes, though perhaps not of the major sort, but all the same writing poetry and putting out a book of verse, a friend of Andrei Bely, raised in the atmosphere of the Symbolists. A mathematician? -- yes, a student of the reknown professor Bugaev (the father of Andrei Bely), and creating very interesting concepts in this field; a man, who at the same time as the now reknown Petrograd scholar Aleksandr Friedman and independently of him arrived at the idea of the curvature of space. Friedman -- is the father of the theory of the expanding universe, a theory which he constructed on the basis of the equations of Einstein. And Florensky came very close to this theory precisely at the same time, in 1922, working in quite different an area.

The thought of Florensky extends likewise into the history of art, which was, perhaps, his second profession (or third, or tenth even). Florensky was erudite. Archpriest Vasily Zenkovsky, author of a monumental "History of Russian Philosophy", speaks about his imposing erudition. People, who knew Florensky, have told me, that it was possible to receive from him a thoroughly detailed answer on whatever the question in very disparate areas of the humanitarian and technical sciences. Florensky was a refined theologian. Florensky -- was an historian; although historical themes are little present in his works, he was nonetheless an archeological historian, he was the author of numerous small monographs, articles on the investigation of ancient Russian and medieval creativity, iconography, the fine arts. A tireless toiler, a man, respected and valued by Vernadsky. They went the same path of scientific investigations. Vernadsky took as it were the path from above, from the total and global view; Florensky went the lower path, in searches for this global view.

Regretably, not all of the works of Florensky have yet been published. But today it is possible to say, that here was a figure, of absolutely enormous a stature, both having evoked and at present still evoking disputes. And they all even have had disputes -- Pushkin too, and Leonardo da Vinci. The man, over whom there is no dispute, is of interest to no one.

Florensky was connected with Moscow University, with the plans and institutions for the electrification of the land; Florensky -- was a teacher of the Moscow Theological Academy, professor of the history of philosophy; and at the same time he was editor of the journal, "The Theological Messenger". The manifold scope of his interests had arisen already back in his childhood. And they called him a Russian Leonardo da Vinci. But when we speak about "Leonardo da Vinci", we have in mind the grandiose old man, as though from the loftiness of his years gazing upon mankind. But Florensky died young. He simply vanished. Arrested in 1933, he simply vanished, and his family (wife and five children) did not know, where he was or what had become of him, for a very long time they did not know, insofar as that in 1937 they had deprived him of the right of correspondence. I remember, when we had gone with my mother to Zagorsk during the time of the war, and she exchanged greetings with Florensky's wife and said: "This woman bears difficult a cross". And she further explained to me, that the woman did not know, what had become of her husband (my father during this time had only just been set free from imprisonment, and I, though still quite young, understood, what this meant). And in actual fact at this time Florensky was no longer among the living. Under Khrushchev in 1958 his wife had recourse to the rehabilitation and received the information, that he had died in 1943 -- which was when his 10 year sentence was to have ended (in 1933 they gave him 10 years imprisonment, as a major criminal -- such a sentence was given for a major crime). But now everything has become clear. When we had spoken with my mother about his fate, he was already no longer among the living. Here is an account about his death, received by relatives only recently, in November of last year:

"Account of death. Citizen Florensky, Pavel Aleksandrovich, died 8 December 1937. Age -- 55 years (roughly -- 56). Cause of death -- shot. Place of death -- Leningrad oblast'".

Fifty-six years. A man, who for several months prior to these events, was situated in hellish convict conditions, and had continued active scientific work; a man, who lived a deep spiritual and mental life, who bestowed to his children his riches of knowledge (prior to 1937 he was permitted to write, and there were even moments, when his family could come to see him), -- of such a man any civilisation could be proud. He stands on the same level with Pascal, with Teilhard de Chardin, with many of the erudite thinkers from all times and peoples. And he was shot ultimately as a criminal -- he, that was absolutely guiltless a man!

Among Russian philosophers, Florensky was the most apolitical. All wrapped up in the world of his thoughts, immersed in work, he always stood somewhat on the sidelines of the societal aspect. Even his attempts to get more involved in it ended up nowhere. He was politically uninvolved and hence guiltless and he was a man his land needed -- as an engineer, as a scholar, as ungreedy a worker. But they preferred instead simply to shoot him. Together with this accounting by the Committee for State Security, there was handed over to the relatives a copy of the act: "Sentence by a Troika-Panel of the ONKVD on Protocol No. 199 of 25 November 1937, in this regard is adjudged to V.M.N. (i.e. the highest measure of punishment) of Florensky Pavel Aleksandrovich, set for carrying out on 8 December 1937, as comprised by the present act". And undersigned, as in all official papers. And a photograph was attached -- a man with traces of beatings on the face, a man, totally withdrawn inwards, because they had tormented and tortured him. Here suchlike has been our era.

And here before you is a reproduction of the canvas, "The Philosophers", now familiar throughout all Moscow. The artist Nesterov painted it for us at Sergiev Posad, in a garden area, of Father Pavel, conversing with Bulgakov. They were strolling through the garden, and Nesterov then painted the picture.

Several words about his life. He was born, NS -- 22 January 1882 [trans. note: the correct day is 21 January, a minor error by Fr. Men', whose own birthday is 22 January]. Born in the territory of modern day Azerbaizhan, near the locale Evlakh. His own father, Aleksandr Ivanovich Florensky, came from a priestly line, and was an engineer by profession, an educated and cultured man, but one who had lost his connections with the Church, with the religious life. Fr Florensky's mother, nee Safarova, belonged to a cultured Armenian family, living at Tiflis (Tbilisi). Florensky had studied at the Tiflis gymnasium-school together with two afterwards outstanding figures of the Russian religious renaissance -- Elchaninov and Ern. Ern died in 1917 of tuberculosis, and Elchaninov went abroad, became a priest, served in Paris, and died in 1934. Throughout the world is known his book, "Zapisi/Notes" [published in English under the title, "Diary of a Russian Priest"] -- is a collection of small aphorisms, compiled shortly after his death.

They were great friends. Nonetheless, according to the reminiscences of Florensky, which we now have in partially published form -- in the journal "Literary Studies", and the almanac "Prometheus" -- we see, that he lived as it were upon his own special island. He was more interested in nature, than in people. He had a special love for stones, for plants, for colours; in this regard he was very akin to Teilhard de Chardin, who likewise in childhood had a close maternal bond, and I would say, -- a great fondness from the mother. With Florensky this had all existed since childhood. And even the world of people, perhaps, was for him strange and at times vexing. There was a certain doctor, Buchholtz, a man earnestly Orthodox, who with Florensky had begun to compile a dictionary of symbols, and someone asked Buchholtz, "What is it that you have in common with this man?" "We both dislike people", -- said Buchholtz. Well, he was certainly speaking for himself -- although this hardly can be said for Florensky. Today, reading his letters to his friends, to his wife, his children, we tend to see, what an enormous amount of tenderness, of attention, of a genuine and amazing love lay hidden within his heart. But this was an heart not gushingly open, on the contrary, it was moreso one shut off from view, through which at times there issued feeble bursts.

No less than three profound emotional crises shook the life of Pavel Aleksandrovich. The first was a beneficial crisis during the period of his youth, when he was growing up in the midst of the non-religious, remote from the Church, and he at one point perceived the non-viability of the materialistic world-view, and thus he began passionately to search for a way out from this.

A second intense personal crisis occurred, when he attempted to set himself aright. For such a man to deal with his own personal burden, the burden of him himself, was quite far from simple. One man, who had known him, told me, how Florensky jokingly had said to him, that logically he was capable of demonstrating, and very persuasively so, things completely contradictory. His intellect was a colossal machine, but together with this, here was not only a man of abstractions, a theoretician, but also a man deeply passionate. Berdyaev recollects, how at the monastery of one of the startsi/elders, whither he had gone with pious friends, he caught sight of the young Florensky: standing in church and crying, wailing... This was nowise simple a life.

And yet another crisis, somewhat before the Revolution, yet little noted in the biographies. This was in 1916, when Florensky had written a book, "Concerning Khomyakov", -- a critical investigation. And in it he put forward an entire series of points, which evoked a strong reaction on the part of his ultra-Orthodox friends, in particular from Novoselov (a former Tolstoyan, who then became Orthodox, a man very good and very brunt, but certainly not of philosophic a frame of mind, but who very highly esteemed Khomyakov). The criticism of Khomyakov evoked in him such a turbulence of soul, that he sped off to Sergiev Posad to Florensky and all night long badgered him there, with Fr Pavel refusing to give in and finally he said: "On theology nothing more will I write!" To provoke such a statement out of such a man, the author of so noteworthy a book as "The Pillar and Affirmation of Truth", -- had to be not in the least simple a matter. And in actual fact, after this, Florensky did not work further on the creation of an entire religio-philosophic system. His final work in this area, as though redoubled a departure from the theological field, -- was his lectures on the philosophy of the cult. They were published only many years afterwards, posthumously, and it also seems, have evoked quite strong criticism.

Father Pavel was a complex and contradictory man. He finished Moscow University as a brilliant mathematician, and they offered him a seat. Mathematics for him was uniquely a basis to the world edifice. In the final end, he ultimately came towards thinking, that the entirety of visible nature in sum total might be reduced to certain unseen residually basic points. And here is why he so loved Plato, since for Plato the unseen was the source of the seen. Pavel Florensky all his life loved Plato, he studied Plato, he commented on Plato. And it mustneeds be said, that the whole of world philosophy represents but a scribbling of footnotes on Plato. Platonic thought for once and always has defined the chief currents for the human spirit and human thought.

Vladimir Solov'ev exerted no little influence upon Florensky in his student years. It must be mentioned, that they were both Platonists, both were concerned with the problem of the spiritual grounds of being and the theme of the mysteried Sophia -- the Wisdom of God. And perhaps, because Florensky attempted to distance himself from Solov'ev, for he hardly refers to him, and indeed if he does refer to him -- then he does so critically. Still, between them, in the history of thought they stand very close, closer indeed, than Florensky himself suspected.

But mathematics did not become his mainstay all his life. He forsakes the scientific pursuits, resettles at Sergiev Posad, and enters the Theological Academy. Andrei Bely, who knew him during these years, speaks fondly and ironically about this youth with long hair, and remembers, that they used to call him "the nose in the curls", because Florensky's face was swarthy in complexion, the result of his Armenian mother, with Gogol-like a nose and long curly hair. He was not overly tall, and was delicate of condition. He spoke softly -- particularly after he moved to the monastery, and as such was adopting for himself a monastic style of mannerisms. In 1909 when they unveiled the memorial to Gogol (the present memorial to Gogol -- is not the statue, which presently stands on the boulevard, but rather the one which now is in the courtyard), and they removed the cover, and one man exclaimed: "O, tis Pavlik himself!" Actually, both this stooped figure, and these noses, and this nose -- this was all in an amazing resemblance.

Sergei Iosifovich Fudel', a church writer, who died about 15 years back, a resident of Sergiev Posad, a shop-attendant, and son of the reknown archpriest Iosif Fudel' (who had been friends with Konstantin Leont'ev), in his youth was acquainted with Florensky. He described to me his outward appearance and gestures, and he said, that most of all he walked like an Egyptian fresco. Listening to the quiet conversation with his father could run quite awhile, he said; and it was not always clear, what they were talking about, but everything got mixed up in it: be it women's fashions, which serve as a precise indicator, definitive of the style of a given civilisation; or perhaps some occult experiences; or the mystery of the colours of an icon; or perhaps some deep and mysterious meanings of words -- Florensky all his life had philological and philosophic an interest in the meaning of this or that other word.

He had another friend -- Sergei Troitsky, with whom Florensky in his youth was very close. The loss of this friend pained him very deeply: Troitsky had journeyed off to Tiflis and there after a few years had tragically perished. And it was to him that Florensky had dedicated his as then chief published book, "The Pillar and Affirmation of Truth".

The book came out in 1914, but it had quite an history of preparation behind it. When he was studying at the Theological Academy, everything tended to interest him. He immersed himself in the library, he studied ancient manuscripts, and symbols. Andrei Bely relates, that Valery Briusov attentively listened to his explanations, when he would interpret for him whatever sort emblems and monograms. Florensky was quite fond of genealogy. Vladimir Favorsky, the reknown artist (you all know him, I think) afterwards sketched for Florensky an ex-libris bookplate: on it was depicted a knight, pierced with an arrow, and in hand holding -- a scroll of genealogy. To understand this, one can think what one will, but a knight always is symbolic of aristocratism and with attentive a regard towards ancestry.

In his creativity Florensky wanted only to be an interpreter of enormous a legacy -- liturgical, literary, philosophic, theological. In the "Pillar" he simply hides himself behind this. But this is only a mere method, a special method, -- as we might term it, say, a "literary-scientific fathoming". He had his own thoughts, his own approaches, and what is needed, is to be able to find and to read, what lies concealed behind the abundance of materials, which he gives.

Florensky was quite attracted to everything mysterious. According to certain accounts, in his youth he became involved with spiritism, and all sort of occult things; later on, he essentially moved away from this. But it remained a problem for him how to regard occult things, things not tangible for him in experience. This was always a stumbling block for him and a peculiar problem.

At Sergiev Posad he becomes a teacher of the history of philosophy -- for one simple reason: I suggest, that his teachers could not but take note of the originality of his thought and hence they were afraid, that if he were to begin teaching theology, he might include too much of his own thinking. And therefore he was (true, and very correctly) consigned to teaching the history of philosophy.

It has to be mentioned, that there was a myth, that there were certain illustrious hierarchs of the time who regarded his theories with hostile a view, but there is little basis for this. First of all, the rector of our Academy, Bishop Feodor -- a man exceedingly Orthodox -- highly esteemed Florensky's chief work, "The Pillar and Affirmation of Truth" (this work became his dissertation). It is actually filled with a multitude of debatable concepts, unexpected conclusions, non-trivial approaches. But Bishop Feodor pointed out herein to its breadth of scope. They have said, that the illustrious Antonii Khrapovitsky, the metropolitan, a man with very sharp a tongue, exclaimed that when he had read through the "Pillar", that it had the smell of heresy or Khlysty-like ravings. Precisely on what this is based is unknown, but according both to documents and letters it is known, that later on Metropolitan Antonii regarded Florensky with great esteem, as did many of the erudite, and the theologians, and the philosophers. Bulgakov -- was quite warmly fond of him. Vasily Vasil'evich Rozanov, a man of tremendous talent and mind, but with quite ungoverned a pen, from a profound anti-Christianity having shifted over to a deep love as regards the Church, literally grabbed hold of Florensky. Rozanov lived at Sergiev Posad (and died there of starvation in 1919). Florensky often visited with him.

But, not all were such. Heading the chair of moral theology was professor Mikhail Mikhailovich Tareev (likewise similarly imposing a figure in the Russian Religious Renaissance), and he regarded all the directions undertaken by the young Florensky, as utter nonsense. And take notice, how broad a scope of theological thought existed here: under the same roof of the Academy two professors managed their chairmanships, side by side, nothing separating their glances at each other. Certainly, they were both Christians, both were Orthodox, both were talented. But in spirit they were not acceptive of each other! Florensky belonged to the world of the Romantics of the beginning of the century, he was close in affinity to Nesterov, and to that romanticised image of Orthodoxy, which only then had begun to arise within the awareness of the Intelligentsia; he was an aesthete and a valuer and lover of things old, a lover of ancient emblems and symbols. Tareev regarded all this as Gnosticism, as rubbish within the setting of Christianity, and he acknowledged only the Gospel and chiefly -- its moral grounds. For him the "Pillar" -- was all nonsense. Between them there was strife. (Tareev was somewhat the older, and he died in 1934). But this struggle, however, was always waged within gentlemanly bounds.

In any case, prior to the Revolution they continued to work side by side, though this was very difficult an arrangement. And yet it has to be mentioned, that at the time of the Revolution, Tareev won out. Florensky was sacked from his post as editor of the journal, "Theological Messenger", and Tareev took his place; but the journal already had not long to exist: all these discussions were halted by the deadly malaise, which beset the whole of culture (but halted only for this moment, and then all arose anew).

When Florensky studied and later worked at the Academy, two spiritual personages exerted an influence upon him: Serapion Mashkin, a monk barely known by anyone, and so to speak an home-grown philosopher, and secondly the starets/elder Isidor of the Gethsemane skete-monastery near Sergiev Posad. In a short while they were both to die. But their thoughts and spirit in some manner were reflected in the book, "The Pillar and Affirmation of Truth". Such was the title given his book by a man, who had passed through a stormy tempest of doubt. This storm had left its mark on him. The sub-title is -- "An Essay on Orthodox Theodicy" ("theodicy" -- this is an old word, coined by Leibnitz in the XVII Century, meaning "God-justification": i.e. how to reconcile a good God and the existence of evil in the world). If you think that this is a tract, consistently and systematically expounding a particular conception of things, then you are mistaken. Here it is not a matter of chapters, but rather of letters, addressed to a friend. And this was a deliberate device. (And this, moreover, evoked great dissatisfaction in academic circles.) Prior to the publication of the book Florensky demanded, that it should be printed in a special font-type. In each chapter there were vignette images, taken from a Latin tract of the XVII Century, vignettes with under-writings, very expressive and affective. Nearly each chapter begins with a lyrical prelude. Very erudite a book, scientific commentaries occupy nearly half the text, with thousands upon thousands of extracts from authors ancient and modern, written as though in the form of a lyrical diary. A matter of caprice? No, not caprice, but rather what shortly in Europe will be called existential philosophy. This is not a philosophy of theories, but rather a philosophy of man -- of a living man.

This is very personal a book. A book, with writing indicative of the person of the author, accompanied as it were with a mass of notes. We find here excerpts from works ancient and modern, from saints, ascetics, poets; all with complex a logical arrangement. A lyrical overture of sorts to play a special role: to introduce readers to the condition of soul, experienced by the author, when he was creating the book. And we have to remember, that this enormous work, "The Pillar and Affirmation of Truth", was created by Florensky at age twenty-six (the first edition of the book appeared in 1908).

Florensky arrives at the conclusion, that truth is intuitively cognitive, but with reality simultaneously being rationally intelligible. Which is to say, in his terminology, truth is intuition-discourse, that, which is known intuitively and rationally.

But suddenly he sees, that in everything, knowable to him, in the final reckoning has hidden within it a contradiction. He might be considering, let us say, imaginary numbers in mathematics. The mass of facets within nature is indicative of the insufficiency of formal logic, it leads man to thoughts of this, that the paradox, or antinomy, is something characteristic to being (antinomy -- this is profoundly deep a contradiction, with these, quite exclusive of each other).

A special chapter, "Contradictions", was written with a power of genius. As present-day physics has asserted (in the conceptions of Niels Bohr and other physicists): within the fundamental peculiarities of nature we find logically irremovable contradictions. And herein arises the principle of complementarity, which allows for the describing of a phenomenon from two sides, so as not to give it but one single interpretation. This does not mean, however, that Florensky regarded truth as something not existing as a whole, as an entirety. He vividly expressed it thus: the whole-entirety of truth, falling from heaven, shatters apart down here into contrary elements, and a man can grasp the whole, but for this is needed a sort of penetration into reality. And this penetration does occur via the perceptions of the mysteried experience of the Church.

The perceptive knowledge of the dogmas of the Church, according to Florensky, -- is not simply the intellectual knowing of a certain system of views, but rather the entering into a certain mystical experience, through which one then approaches from within towards knowledge of the mystery of the Church. The Church -- is not simply an organisation, not some sort of institution, it is the mysteried uniting of people with God and with each other. And in this unification, when the "I" and the "thou" open themself each to the other and ultimately to the utmost "Thou", Love is begotten.

Many, and among them Berdyaev, Tareev and other religious philosophers of the time, subjected the "Pillar" to harsh criticism. But the harshest article against Florensky was that written by Berdyaev, entitled "Stylised Orthodoxy". Florensky -- was a man, raised outside the religious tradition, -- and he wants to enter into it all the way totally, to the very end. Students of Florensky at the Academy have remarked to me, that he always had given them a moment's pause, when in going along the corridor he would bow low in monk-like greeting to all the students: he wanted to adopt the traditional form in everything. Berdyaev was different -- for him the dignity of man was utmost a thing, and having become a Christian, he remained simultaneously likewise a democrat and an aristocrat, and he never occasioned to conduct himself in so awkward a manner. They were different people, and it is impossible to judge either the one or the other, it is necessary instead to understand, that multiplicity -- reflects the richness of life. There was Florensky -- quiet, modest, with downcast gaze, as Berdyaev venomously remarks, "speaking with phony a voice"; and there was Berdyaev, who could roar, a tremendous man, with his nervous tic, -- these were both different people, part of the total richness, a richness we ought not to lose.

What is it there in this book -- "The Pillar and Affirmation of Truth" -- what is the major and specifically chief thing? The attempt to find God (to put it crudely) -- here in this flower. He later on termed this a concrete idealism. Florensky all more and more became convinced, that theories do not float about up in the clouds, but rather, that everything is inter-connected and inter-pervasive, that the Divine Spirit is right alongside everything, in the ordinary, in the trivial minutiae.

Essentially, what Florensky apparently had a poor grasp of, was the historical view of things. He was a man as it were external to history and they called him an Alexandrian at heart, he belonged to the past, and as it were had come from the past: however, as our reknown modern historian of philosophy R. Gal'tseva tends to note, he belonged to the avant-garde, even though he had come from the past. A man, who in his soul better understood Andrei Bely, than did some of his friends, certainly, for he belonged to that Russian avant-garde, which gave birth to Symbolism, and to all that curiously eager half-mystical movement with its overtones of a sort of mysterious eroticism.

The 1910 decade had within it its own quite definite an imprint. We have to perceive it as sort of an amazing phenomenon. And these were not people, as it were misfits and weaklings, as some have sought to portray them. They were essentially susceptible to the current of the times, to a sort of the dust of a subtle decay, which then wafted about through the air. This was a trait common to Blok, and to Briusov, who played into all the devilry, and to Sologub, and to the artists, who worked round about. This was peculiar and definitive a medium. But Florensky did not belong to it entirely, he belonged also to another medium -- to the theologians of Sergiev Posad, where he was accepted, loved and esteemed, in spite of the mischief of Tareev and his party.

One of Florensky's students remarks, how the student auditorium filled up, when Florensky gave his lectures on the history of philosophy, how he entered from the side, stood at a table (he was never on a chair) and in a soft voice, often with downcast eyes, he spoke. And all listened. True, some do say, that they did not understand. "Do you understand?" -- Florensky would ask. "Honestly speaking, Pavel Aleksandrovich, not a word". But for myself I tell you, that this was not because of the complexity of Florensky's thought. Yes, it was complex, but also sufficiently clear, so that it could be understood by any man, seriously pondering it. (In the postscript of the "Pillar" was written, that the book should prove understandable to everyone -- said with a certain twist of erudite humour.)

And people did understand it. Sergei Iosifovich Fudel' mentioned to me, that in 1914 when he read this book, he was inwardly brought back to the Church. Prior to this he was living emotionally as a symbolist bohemian, and the churchly world seemed to him a world stale and obsolete, done for, sclerotic -- something right out of Ostrovsky. But suddenly he saw, that it was possible to write about the Church in the same refined manner, used by the Symbolists in writing, used by Andrei Bely in writing. And I can confirm this with an example of my own. I was a student in the first course level, when I first read "The Pillar and Affirmation of Truth" (this was the year Stalin died), and the book made an impression on me, but it made an impression on me namely, because like Solov'ev, Florensky emerged as a man, standing atop the summits of culture, and not merely coming into it from the sidelines somewhat, to swipe its fruits only for his own benefit, rather, he was actually himself someone cultural. Both Florensky, and Solov'ev -- these were the very embodiment of culture! And they spoke in witness concerning the Church, concerning Christ, concerning Christianity.

When the train of thought in the "Pillar" arrives at this, that truth is paradoxical and antinomic -- we are brought to the chief mystery underlying dogma. I think, that many of you are familiar with the basic Christian dogmas. And you will note at once, that namely it is a sense of paradox that pervades them all: God is one -- but He is also Three Persons, Christ is a man -- but He is also God, authentically genuine a man -- and true God. And so on. Well, let us say, man is free, but at the same time God foresees everything. It all involves paradoxes. Truth tends to be paradoxical the same, as the reality of being tends to be paradoxical. And the great merit of Florensky -- consists in this, that he, while still young a man, was able to demonstrate this.

He accepted the priestly dignity in 1911. Simply to serve in a parish held little attraction for him. One of his contemporaries relates, that Florensky was not fond of the churchly lifestyle, and as a man profoundly intelligent, refinedly intelligent, he would have actually found it wearisome had they sent him off to a parish somewhere. But his fate was already pre-decided. He was a scholar, a professor of the Academy. Prior to the Revolution he served at Sergiev Posad. During the time of the First World War, for a certain while he was dispatched to the front as army chaplain, and he very vividly describes his experiences.

Shortly before Florensky became a priest, he had married the sister of his friend, Giatsintova, a young rural school-teacher. I dimly remember her (from my childhood), but I well remember her niece, who was a close friend of my mother. Anna Mikhailovna Giatsintova actually took on heavy a cross, in marrying a genius (they all then already understood, that this man -- was a genius). A difficult life, and afterwards a bitter fate. Anna Mikhailovna died already back in the 1970's. And then too another relevant point to mention, -- it was not only the house, where they lived, that happened to be preserved. If you go along Pioneer Street, beyond the movie theater you will see the number of the house and an old, twenties style inscription: "Owner P. A. Florensky". This inscription in some miraculous manner managed to survive and outlast its owner. The children and grandchildren of Florensky became scholars, and one of the grandsons -- the noted scholar Pavel Vasil'evich Florensky, and another -- the monk, hegumen Andronik (Trubachev), the biographer and researcher into the creativity of P. A. Florensky.

In the "Theological Messenger" Florensky also published a series of interesting works on idealism, likewise arguable. Magic had always interested him. He spoke about the magical origins of Platonic philosophy, about the influence of man upon the earth. This theme extremely fascinated him. And he therefore became passionately interested in old popular beliefs and customs. Why? Because the central intuition in the philosophy of Florensky (I stress this, so try to grasp it) -- was all-unity, the same, as with Solov'ev. All is inter-connected, the whole world is pervaded by unitary forces. The Divine power enters into the world edifice and nothing is apart from it, all is interwoven, in one place it aches -- in another is a reaction.

On this basis he attempts to construct his philosophy of the cult. For him the cult was not simply a sign of our inner condition (usually we understand the cult as an external sign, a sign psychological, aesthetic a ritual sign of my faith, of my encounter with God), but the cult for Florensky -- was something rather more, the cult -- is something, connecting reality with the symbol. And he constructed extraordinarily complex a system. Already after the Revolution he conducted a series of lectures on "The Philosophy of the Cult", where he dealt with a number of mysteries inferred from nature. But in these lectures there was much of the debatable.

With the onset of the Revolution, Florensky attempted to get involved in the social movement. Still back at the time of the 1905 Revolution together with his friends he formed the "Christian Brotherhood for the Struggle" -- a religio-revolutionary movement. And when Florensky was already at the Academy, he gave a sermon (students were not allowed to give sermons), and it was entitled "The Crying-Out of Blood", and it was published. This denunciatory speech was on account of the execution of a Lieutenant Shmidt, and for this Florensky was arrested.

After the Revolution, Fr Pavel did not emigrate and he never openly expressed his attitude towards the authorities. He merely continued to work. he considered himself a scholar, one who should toil in behalf of his fatherland. And the Lavra-monastery was not closed down in a single day: at first they wanted to make a museum of it, and Florensky became involved in a commission, he attempted to point out, that the overall aesthetics of the Lavra could not exist without monks, and without divine-services. If they wanted to make a museum of it -- let them do so, but in a manner leaving there the divine-services. This was certainly a naive proposal, no one still remained there making services, and both the Lavra, and the Academy, were closed. But until the end of the 1920's he read his own separate lectures to students, who were clustered then outside Sergiev Posad, at a certain skete-monastery.

One of the outstanding works of Florensky was devoted to the field of dielectrics, and one of his final philosophic scientific works -- was "Imagination in Geometry". And later appeared investigations in the field of engineering. He gave lectures on aesthetics and on quite a range of engineering problems. To serve as a priest he could not, because a man engaged in Soviet work, even if he were a religious, did not have the right of priestly service. But in order to prove, and to show people, that he had not relented, had not given it up, he arrived at lectures in a riasa.

My father studied under him and remembers, what a strange spectacle it presented: the end of the 1920's, the Technological Institute, and here comes a diminutive man in riasa, with long hair. But everyone held him in quite high a regard. There was even an instance, when Lev Trotsky asked, why he walked about in riasa. Florensky replied: "I have not reneged the priestly dignity, and therefore I cannot do otherwise". Trotsky answered: "well then, go ahead". And what's more, they even rode together in an automobile. Trotsky took him along in an open car, and Muscovites aghast beheld this strange sight: Trotsky, this veritable Mephistopheles, in his pince-nez eyeglasses, and alongside him Florensky in his cassock and skull-cap, as they rode through Moscow... The Kamenevs likewise were well disposed towards him. Florensky was widely known in the highest "Soviet" circles, but this did not help him.

In the Summer of 1928 they exiled Florensky to Nizhny-Novgorod, and in 1933 they arrested him, and sent him off to BAM (BAM -- the Baikal-Amur Rail-line -- has indeed long been under construction, and they were working on it even back then), where he was stripped down, and lived in very difficult conditions. His wife carefully kept his letters. Then they sent Florensky to a camp, an horrid place, where he worked in the eternal permafrost, and afterwards he was transferred to Solovki, where he worked on problems in the extraction of iodine. In those grievous conditions of the Solovetsk region, so as to lighten the monstrous toil of the workers, he constructed a machine, an apparatus, which helped extract the iodine. From Florensky's letters to his wife, and to his children, it is evident that he was involved totally in science. In these unbelievable conditions he was involved in research! Florensky wrote about Mozart; he, who earlier was rather moreso the melancholy pessimist, suddenly he approves of the joyful Mozart! He became enraptured with the plays of Racine. In his letters (published in the journal "Our Legacy" he sent sketches of the sea-weed, which he was studying.

Effectively, and with great interest, Florensky describes the life of the inhabitants on the Solovetsk frontier region; to his children he writes about porpoises being born, and how he himself had held a grey fox. On 24 January 1935 he wrote, that the day before yesterday he had celebrated his birthday, 54 years in all. In one of his letters soon after this he outlines an inventory of what he has done in various directions in the advance of science. To enumerate them all at present would perhaps prove tiring, since the list is very long: twelve articles just on mathematics and electronics. And he was even himself very discrete, since a censor was watching everything, and he could not write about theology, he could only write about such things as: "The cultic roots at the inception of philosophy... antinomies of judgement... historico-philosophic investigations of terminology... The material basis of anthropodicy (i.e. the theological teaching about man)...", -- all which needed to be deciphered.

And here too -- bitter words, which we read in these letters. Florensky writes: "Society seems not to need my knowledge. Well then, all the worse for society". And this was the truth, for our society has suffered. "Factually, -- he writes, -- the denigration of experience across the whole of life, which now only is at its maturity, could have produced genuine real fruit. On this I would not be upset, so neither should you be. If society has no need of the fruits of my life and my work -- let it remain without them. There is still the question, who gets punished more by this -- society or me -- in that I did not bring forth, what I might have. But it grieves me, that I cannot share and pass on to you my experience, and the chief thing -- that I cannot hug you, as always in my thoughts I want to hug you". Two more years will pass, and the bullet of the killer-executioner will cut short this noble life.

A particular theme -- was Florensky's interpretation of the problem of East and West. He sensed, that the developement of western civilisation bears within it not a few dangerous tendencies. And that deviation, which took hold in Russia as a part of Europe, began with the era of the Renaissance, towards which he was sharply negative (though, as a philosopher, with his idea of the all-unity he was very close to Renaissance thinkers of a type such as Paracelsus, Boehme and others).

In his book, "Iconostas", he attempted to contrast East and West. But what he did was not altogether precise, since he contrasted the Renaissance West and the Medieval East -- that of Rus' and Byzantium. And although in the Middle Ages in the West there was likewise a symbolic art, there was likewise a different world-view. And when the Renaissance had penetrated to us in the East, it likewise had its own crudity, sensuality, and this-worldliness. Florensky in mindset was always anti-Western, and in this sense too he was anti-ecumenical. And it was only when he realised, that the hostility among Christians, their wont for confrontation was bringing colossal a catastrophe for the Russian Church, which remained alone and isolated and in shambles, with no one to help it, -- and he then began to rethink his views.

Some final evidence on this matter. In 1923 he writes some small pieces on Orthodoxy. One of these is entitled "Notes on Christianity and Culture". Father Pavel writes, that the divisions between Christians occurs, not because there are different dogmas, rites and customs, but the rather because of the absence of a genuinely authentic faith, of genuine love. "The Christian world, -- he writes, -- is filled with mutual contemptuous suspicion, malicious feelings and hostility. It has become rotted down to its very foundations, since it has not the activeness of faith in Christ and moreover lacks the bravery and sincerity of heart to admit the existence of the rot infecting its faith <...> neither any issues of churchly calendar, nor any sort of bureaucracy, nor any sort of diplomacy, can inspire an unified oneness of faith and of love there, where it is not, where it does not actually exist. All the external patchwork efforts not only do not reunite the Christian world, but on the contrary, tend to further evidence the isolation between confessions. We have to realise, that it was not these or some other differences of teaching, of ritual or ecclesial arrangement that serves as the true reason for the disintegration of the Christian world, but rather a deep mutual mistrust in what is basic, the faith in Christ, the Son of God, manifest in the flesh". And in conclusion Florensky says, that the search for unity of oneness is necessary and "it is necessary to work out special theses, of moreso particular a character, for reunification with the Roman Catholic Church; the chief thing here having to be formulated is the primacy of honour and of an all-Christian initiative, as to the right accorded the Roman Bishop". This was written in the Summer of 1923. And in the camps he happened to sit together with numerous Christians from all the confessions, with believers and with non-believers. The experience was bitter, and difficult. How he actually viewed things, we cannot always understand, since his letters were obviously subject to internal censorship. But I think, that Aleksei Feodorovich Losev, a younger contemporary and in much a student of Florensky, -- was right, when he said, that Florensky had never betrayed his convictions, and that in having conceived a sort of primal intuition of a Christian Platonism, he continued on with it right down to the very end of his days, with his martyr's death.

As one forcibly purged from the annals of our country's culture, a philosopher, a great theologian, a great scholar, a great engineer, a great cultural figure is today again being revived. And you know, that at TsDL [Central Literary House] was an exhibit of documents, and formerly a multitude of symposiums, of conferences, devoted to him, both here and abroad. I think, that the acquaintance with such a man through his books, which are soon coming out, will be for those who love philosophy (and philosophy is the love for wisdom) -- will be great an occasion and a source of insight. Even those, not in agreement with many of the ideas of Florensky (and agreement is quite unnecessary, nor did he insist on this), will nonetheless still be enriched by the process of reading and pondering over the pages of his books.

Semeon Ludvigovich Frank

Semeon Ludvigovich Frank resembled an ancient seer, an ancient wise-man, who appeared out of some remote age. Here, in the photograph, you see him as quite an old man. But he was already a seer in youth. Slow in approach, not quick with words, solid in his judgements and opinions, absolutely imperturbable, and it is only, as his friend Struve notes -- the special radiant eyes, from which as it were there flows forth light, there pours forth wisdom, joy and warmth. All who knew Semeon Ludvigovich Frank -- remember these eyes.

Archpriest Vasily Zenkovsky, an historian of Russian philosophy and who died in Paris, wrote, that amongst the thinkers of that generation, Frank was the most philosophic -- in the actual sense of this word. His was mighty a philosophical intellect. He was not a publicist in writing articles, he was not a theologian, although certainly, he also happened to write sharp publicist-type articles, and in the sequence of his books he directly touched upon theological themes. Here was a man of thought, like many of the colossal figures of world philosophy. He himself even jokingly said, concerning himself: "I have mused away all my life". This, certainly, was no idle daydreaming, but rather a profound contemplation. He had plunged as it were into the ocean of thought, into the ocean of the abstract schemae of all the deeper down, and finally, he reached the day of reality.

Semeon Ludvigovich was born in 1877 at Moscow, on Pyatnitsk Street, and his childhood was spent near the alleyways of Maroseika and Pokrovka. His father had been an army doctor and had lived at Vilnius; as a military physician he had participated in the defense of Sebastopol', and was awarded the Order of Stanislas. He died early, and Semeon Frank did not remember him. His mother was an intellectually refined woman, but it was his grandfather who had an especial influence upon him. His family was Jewish by origin, from the Baltic region. His grandfather was a deeply religious and self-educated man. He excellently knew the ancient Hebrew language, the Bible, the old sacred literature; when he died (Semeon was then age 14), Semeon carried away with him his words: always study the Scriptures, the old Hebrew tongue and theology. And Frank the philosopher afterwards recollects: "In a formal sense I did not fulfill his command, but that, to which was the striving of my heart, my reason, my spiritual searchings and, ultimately, my Christianity (he accepted Orthodoxy in 1912), -- all this was essentially and organically a continuation of those lessons, which I learned from my grandfather".

Since his father died early, his mother remarried, and his stepfather was a man of Populist views. This was still another element in his upbringing. He completed the juridical course of study. Back then the juridical course of study prepared not only those involved in jurisprudence, in law, but was instead a broad humanities course of study, under which studied half of the noteworthy people of the late XIX and early XX Centuries.

In his youth, just like with Berdyaev, Bulgakov, the brothers Trubetskoy, he became attracted to Social Democratic ideas. While still in lower level gymnasium-school and later as a student, he became interested in Marxism, since they seemed to assure him, that Marxism ultimately provides a scientific explanation of social processes. These promises of Marxism tempted not only Frank, but indeed quite many others, and therefore we ought not to be amazed, that the majority of the representatives of Russian religious philosophy had passed through Marxism in their youth. Frank with eagerness studied "Kapital" (back then only the first volume had come out); and just like any youth with a developing intellect, it attracted him, in that here was this enormous book, written in a ponderous Hegelian language requiring serious effort to get into it, and whoever managed indeed to devour it, would have reached some sort of a supreme accomplishment. I have to stress, that afterwards, having become sufficiently adept a sociologist, Frank totally parted company with this philosophy and this sociology, having exposed their incapacity, their scientific lacking -- that these were all just words, bandied about by writers, and these thick tomes in actual fact were just a bunch of "giving birth to mice".

The social problem and the social theme long remained in the thoughts and the creativity of Frank, and possibly might even be said, even up to the end of his days (he died in London in 1950).

In his youth he becomes involved in Marxist circles, he studies problems of Social Democracy, he even gets arrested, he spends a certain while in prison, and then is exiled. But finally, in the 1890's he is severing his connection with the revolutionaries (these are basically the SR's and

Populists), since his basic scientific thinking becomes devoted already back then to knowing about oneself. And suddenly he realised, that within Marxism there is a lack of this fundamental approach to actuality, a lack within its seeming appeal.

Frank during this time (he had an excellent grasp of the German language) begins to study the multi-volumed work of Kuno Fisher, "The History of Modern Philosophy" (and moreover, this work was almost entirely translated into the Russian language). Each volume of this enormous and grandiose effort is devoted to a particular philosophy. This is very immensely significant a series, which we have at present in the Russian language; it came out at the beginning of our century.

Having broken with Marxism, Frank seeks for something other to serve in the capacity of a basis for his world-concept. And herein a strange thing. His break-through into a sort of different way at looking at things occurred under the influence of Nietzsche -- a man, who in having confessed materialism, already then seemed suspect to Frank. But the clarion call of Friedrich Nietzsche, his revolt against mortality, against herd-like philistinism, against the denigration of the world, -- all this in some mysterious manner acted upon the young student, and within him occurred something on the order of a turnabout, a metamorphosis, an orientation towards the realm of spirit.

In a single moment he suddenly sensed, that there is another reality, which the intellect cannot fully encompass and exhaust, and which in so doing tends to decompose and dismember everything. And here in this primal intuition -- is the whole philosophy of Frank. Not without reason was one of his books, written right before the war, given the title, "The Unfathomable". This is very characteristic a title. The genuinely authentic reality, -- he says, -- is something unfathomable, in the sense, that man can sense and always comprehend, but can never comprehend completely. Man is never able to grasp totally the unfathomable.

In 1900, when he was slightly over 20 years of age, he was already the author of several works, and he writes a critical work on Marxism, "Marx's Theory of Values", and a short while afterwards he totally forsakes his original enthusiasms and seeks out other paths.

In 1908 he marries, and he works on a dissertation, in which he raises very important questions on the theory of cognition. And when Frank gets to be republished, and you happen to read him, remember however one thing. If it is possible in Berdyaev to peruse a single page and each phrase of his becomes an organism in itself, a whole complete world, and if in Bulgakov it is possible to read individual themes, individual paragraphs, and transpose them, then in Frank everything is set up differently. He was a faithful disciple of Vladimir Solov'ev, and moreover, there was no one was so close (from a philosophical point of view) to Solov'ev, as was this his direct continuator in the XX Century -- Frank. If you want to begin to catch the drift of his thought, you cannot jump into it in the middle -- with him everything is strict and orderly, logically connected, where one thing derives from the other. These are unhurried, attentive observations, and observations of a sort over very profound a process of thought.

In 1915 was published "The Object of Knowledge". For this work Frank received the degree of magister.

For the Western philosophy of the time, the problem of subjective idealism played tremendous a role. You know, that Lenin launched an attack against it within his "Materialism and Empirocriticism". And especially on account of this was very hastily written also this booklet. Subjective idealism at the time had developed along various lines, but primarily so the Kantian. Lenin wrote, that this point of view cannot be refuted, but insofar as it is totally stupid, it has to be cast aside. Frank regarded it otherwise. He felt, that there are serious philosophic and logical arguments to be made against subjective idealism. Subjective idealism issues from the "I", which stands at the centre of the world-edifice. Amidst the interaction of dialogue with the world, man within himself reveals something -- that, what can be termed the "thou". But there is also something else -- that, what we term as the "we".

Like his predecessors, Sergei Trubetskoy and Solov'ev, Frank stressed, that human consciousness, the "I" in the human plural is not cut off each from the other. Real cognition, real being is possible only then, when between people there arises a point of contact, a point of unity. We live as it were not on isolated islands, but rather upon a single continent. And this sort of continent, which unites us all, is also the ultimate and authentic object of cognition. In cognition man knows not only the reflection of his own particular senses, he has knowledge via a certain substrate, at depth. The German philosopher Paul Tillich later on wrote, that God -- is not way up in the heavens above us, but rather in the depths of being. But Frank expressed this earlier.

In 1917 he publishes a remarkable book, "The Soul of Man", which then appeared more than once in foreign languages. Frank was translated into many languages, including Japanese, Czech, Polish, German, English -- he essentially also wrote books in these latter two languages. In this book he brilliantly analyses the question about the unity of the spiritual life, which it is impossible to resolve, impossible to sever off. This unity involves not only our own "I", but also of that other, in which are situated those other "I's" in the plural, towards which we are oriented. This is the "I", then the "we", and finally, a certain mysterious substrate, which also is unfathomable.

The revolutionary period begins. Frank already has a family, he becomes a professor of Moscow University, but herein -- was hunger, and ruin. I knew people, who attended his lectures. Students of philosophy and philology listened spellbound to his slow speaking when, as they described it, one moment clearly followed after the other, and the other -- from a third. But the times were severe; the exams were quickly given, prematurely early, and everyone dispersed. And Frank was offered to become the dean of the philosophy faculty at Saratov University.

This was the final outpost of intellectual freedom. Fedotov and certain other outstanding figures had been invited there. But then Semeon Ludvigovich returns to Moscow. In 1922 he lived with his family -- his wife and three children -- in a dacha cottage at Pushkino. (His son Viktor Frank became a reknown historian and writer abroad). One day he happened to journey to Moscow, and here they arrested him and together with his family he was deported from Russia. He sailed on the very same steamship, on which sailed Berdyaev, Stepun and two hundred suchlike men, who comprised the flourish and pride of Russian culture and thought.

The European world for Frank was sufficiently his own, since he spoke freely in several languages. He gave lectures at Berlin, at Paris, and worked much. He wrote a remarkable book, "The Meaning of Life", oriented towards the youth; also a book, "The Collapse of the Idols", in which he decrowned the halo off Marxism and the false old conceptions. He wrote a book, "Light in the Darkness". Especially important was a book, "The Spiritual Foundations of Society", with its theme at present very relevant for us. Frank indicated, that a society which is healthy can exist only then, when it possesses a spiritual substrate. A society of people -- is not simply a phenomenon of the material world, but simultaneously also a phenomenon of the spiritual world.

In the 1930's, under the Nazis, he was deprived of his teaching chair in Germany, after which he moved on to France and finally, after the German occupation of France, he was compelled to emigrate to England, to London, where he spent the final postwar years right up to his death. Among us here, essentially, nothing was written about his death, and as I have already said, they reprinted no books nor articles of his here. Soon it will be forty years from the day of his death, and the first reprints are appearing.

For those people, who have the capacity to love and to appreciate the sphere of pure thought, reading the books of Frank will be a pure delight. Just the same as in youth he had been contemplative, stolid and steady, so also he remained to the end of his days. If Nikolai Aleksandrovich Berdyaev was a man extremely subjective, who always wrote about his own perceptions, who spoke passionately as his own person and who could in a philosophic book offer insights from the moments of his own personal life, well then, -- Frank in this regard was totally different a man. He was hesitant to speak about himself and always spoke only about the outward trifles, and even in his autobiographical notes, compiled in the final years of his life, he all with equal a modesty guarded his own inner spiritual life. And one can only but guess, what tempests may have occurred within him.

Very important for Frank was the correlation of science and religion. This was because he was not only a philosopher, but also a sociologist, and religiously knowledgeable. There is a book of his, not large, but quite important, entitled "Religion and Science". It was published a number of times in the west and came out in those years, when a fierce anti-religious propaganda was being waged. "We assert, -- he said, -- in opposition to the prevailing opinion, that religion and science do not and cannot contradict each other on the simple principle, that they speak about totally different things, and contradiction however is possible only there, where two opposing assertions are expressed about one and the same object". Rather a bit abstract, but if you think it through, what is said goes right to the point. He elucidates his thought with a series of concrete examples. A man is sitting in a railway car, he sits there motionless; his neighbour turns to him and says: "But can you actually be sitting motionless?" He replies: "Pardon, but I am thus indeed sitting motionless". Which of them is right? The man who says that he is sitting motionless, certainly, is right. But the other one too, who reproached him, is also right, since he is being carried along at high speed -- on the train. They are talking from different perspectives, different levels. Approaches to one and the same phenomenon can be so very different, that it becomes impossible to consider them from only one perspective.

The same also in regards to science and religion. In his words: "...science regards the world as a self-contained system of phenomena and it studies the correlation between these phenomena without regard for the world as an integral whole, and consequently, without regard for each, even the smallest part towards its supreme grounding, its first principle, its absolute principle, from which it issued and to which it reposes". Science considers it a working hypothesis, that the world -- is a ready made self-contained system. "Religion namely however conceives of a relationship of the world, and consequently, also of man, to this absolute and primal basis of being, to God, and from this knowledge it derives explanation of the general meaning of being, which lies outside the scope of vision of science.

Science as it were studies an aspective medium, the spatial level or a particle of being in its inner structure, whereas religion has cognition of this selfsame medium in its relationship to beginning and end, to the totality of being or to its integral initial-basis".

Further on, he raises the question of miracles, which customarily has evoked sharp criticism from the point of anti-religious propaganda. Frank says it thus: when a man denies a phenomenon, ungraspable for him, he already beforehand is attempting to construct for himself a model of the world. But is there a proper basis to assert, that his model -- is in precise correspondence to actuality? Semeon Ludvigovich Frank resorts to the words of St Augustine, who wrote, that religion does not contradict the laws of nature, but rather only the laws seemingly known to us. And by a far shot not all the laws are known to us.

As I have already said, Frank devoted an especially great attention to the social sciences. And this nowise signified, that the physical sciences for him were something second rate, but simply rather that for him the scientific approach was merely a partial approach. Frank writes: "One is not learnedly erudite, not a man of science, if for him all the world consists of the unmediatedly visible, to whom it seems, that he is catching sight of the whole of reality, that it is laying there right before him as though in the palm of his hand and that it is very easy and simple a thing to know everything. On the contrary, only that one is learnedly erudite, who has a sense of the mysterious depths of being, who with an immediacy together with Shakespeare knows: "There is much under the light, friend Horatio, not grasped by our wise" [actual quote from Hamlet is: "There are more things in heaven and earth, Horatio, than are dreamt of in your philosophy"]. The knowledge of one's ignorance, as expressed in the words of Socrates: "I know only this, that I know nothing", -- is the beginning and continuing basis of a scientific awareness. The great Newton, penetrating into the structure and dynamics of the Universe, said of himself: "I do not know, what posterity will think of me, but I imagine myself to be like a little boy, who on the shores of a boundless ocean gathers up exposed sea shells, cast by the waves onto shore, all the while that the ocean itself and its depths remain as before for me unfathomable".

In 1939 is published his book, "The Unfathomable, or an Ontological Introduction to the Philosophy of Religion". Several books, along this same theme, also came out posthumously: "Reality and Man"; the theological ponderings in "God is With Us" -- is a profound and brilliant discourse on Christian hope and faith. Besides this, there also appeared a number of his smaller works. One of them was devoted to an ontological proof for the existence of God, to wit, that man possesses in his own immediate experience a connective bond with this great mystery of existence.

Frank also had political works: ""Beyond Right and Left". He was one of the first Christian thinkers to indicate the value of Freudian psychoanalysis, but he stressed that Freud, in having explored the subconsciousness, did not know totally what to do with it. Freud was not governed by any sort of rational theory, he merely made use of remnants of the old vulgar materialism -- this hindered him also from creating an authentic and genuine theory of culture.

Hence, various themes pervade the creativity of Frank. I do not know for sure, whether in Russia there will be reprinted his book, "The Meaning of Life" (very important for youth); this is very much to be desired, but at any rate they have reprinted it in Belgium, at the Centre for Eastern Christianity.

His political position was always based upon principle. At the end of the war, when Berdyaev, in a sign of solidarity with the Russian war effort, wanted to accept Soviet citizenship and was involuntarily drawn along by the appeals of those, who had journeyed from the Soviet Union saying, that now we are beginning to have freedom, now all is going to be fine for us, Frank became annoyed at this. I have known people, who were given the task of enticing the emigrants. A certain hierarch, whom I know, in general a decent man, journeyed to Paris with a whole sack of Russian earth: he flung it from the balcony, and with tears the emigrants kissed it and took the Soviet passports, and they departed right straight off, into the camps. This was a tragedy happening for many people. Some wanted to believe, others did not want to believe -- it was all suspicious: those who had gone had disappeared, as though in the water of a canal, and any news of them had ceased to come. But the moment was joyous -- victory was near. Because of all this Frank had a sharp disagreement with Berdyaev: Frank wrote to Berdyaev, saying that Berdyaev had been swayed into thinking that there beyond the border, everything was fine, but he, Frank, does not believe this, and he reckons, that the tyranny is continuing its activity, despite the victory of the people. And we know, that Frank was proven right.

Besides Berdyaev, Frank was very close with Petr Bernardovich Struve -- one of the prominent political and social activists of Russia in those years. Struve edited a journal, "Russian Thought", quite brilliant and rich in content, but which was, essentially, shut down in 1917. Frank handled the philosophic section of it. At present issues of this journal are appearing in the second-hand bookstores, and I think, that this will make for remarkable reading.

And now several extracts from the works of Frank, so that you may form for yourself a concept about his style of thinking. Here is what he says about the relationship within society towards freedom, and about how we ought to benefit from the fruits of civilisation: "There have existed societies, based upon the toiling of slaves, and in fact in any society there are people, consigned to a slave's condition; but then too they do not become participants and active figures of societal life, and in their eyes society constitutes in itself but a certain type of deadening drudgery. No sort of disciplinary, no sort of the fiercest pressure can properly substitute for the spontaneous wellspring of powers, issuing forth from the depths of the human spirit. A verymost severe military and state discipline can only regulate and direct a societal unity, but cannot create it: the free will creates it. Every attempt to paralyse the individual will, insofar as in general it may be possible, leading to the loss by man of his existence in the image of God, by this also leads to the paralysis and deadening of life, to the dissociation and destruction of society. Every despotism can in general exist, only insofar as it is partialised and, on its end, buttressed upon freedom. Every dictatorship is empowered and given to exist... only insofar as it, on its end, is created as such by the free moral will... Here is why socialism in its basic socio-philosophic intent -- totally substitutes in place of the individual will rather the collective will... having posited in its place the being of the "collective", as though to mash or meld together the monads into one continuous lump of the "masses", which is an absurd idea, destructive of the basic ineradicable principle of the societal aspect and capable only of leading to the paralysis and dissolution of society. It is based upon the crazy and blasphemous dream, that man on account of his measure of planning and the regulative ability of his ownership and the just distribution of the goods of ownership -- that he is capable of renouncing his own freedom, repudiating his own "I" and thereby to become totally and without residue a mere screw within the societal machine, an impersonal medium of activity of general forces. It can in fact lead to nothing other, than the unbridled resiliency of the despotic power and a dull passivity or a beastly revolt of the oppressed". Thus wrote Frank about an half century back.

And on a final note, Frank showed in his philosophy, that a religious world-outlook, and Christianity, is by no means merely something irrational. At present it often happens, that a man in turning to the Christian faith, tends to think, that on account of this he has to consign to the devil his ability to think, his logical and reasoning ability. But instead there are here such people, as Vladimir Solov'ev, Sergei Trubetskoy or Semeon Frank, and they demonstrate, that the mighty workings of reason not only do not undermine the groundings of the religious world-outlook, but on the contrary, they give it meaning, and at times even a foundation. Certainly, the fundamental grounding for Frank was in his experience, a profound experience of the grasping of reality as an integral and deep experience tangential with the Divine as with something, nowise ever definable in human language. But this experience, in common for all mankind, for all Christianity, he tended to filter through the crystalising gateway of the reason and he had to tell about it not only in the language of poetry, in the language of mysticism, but also in the lucidly vivid language of the philosopher-seer. And Frank remained a seer not only in the pages of his books, but also in his appearance -- a man tranquil, bright, imperturbable, happy, despite the sorrowful pages of his life (exile, wandering through Europe), and despite all the grief of our century. He went through it and was like a blazing candle, unshaken by the wind.

He was always direct. And his wife mentioned (I still remember the time, when she was alive and spoke on Western radio) that in youth, when they met, Frank impressed her with this enlightened sort of wisdom. And when you turn to his collected works, I would hope, that behind these polished and unhasty constructions you get to sense the spirit of an enlightened wisdom. It was characteristic not only of Semeon Ludvigovich Frank himself, it was characteristic in general to this whole torrent of thought, which we term as the Russian Religio-Philosophic Renaissance. And it mustneeds be said, that this torrential current was not merely something derivative of Western searchings in this direction, but rather in much surpassed them. All these persons, about whom we have spoken with you, and many also unintentionally remaining outside the scope of vision, were immense figures. They were not simply university professors, scribbling out papers, these were figures, as though chiseled out of stone, figures, that any civilisation in any age would be proud of.

Georgii Petrovich Fedotov

We are meeting with you today regarding still another remarkable man, whom we are as it were discovering anew, -- Georgii Petrovich Fedotov. In the journal, "Our Legacy", which in bits is gathering up that, which had been dispersed, scattered and neglected, has had quite recently in it appear an excerpt from his book, "The Saints of Ancient Rus'", with a forward by our noted historian of culture, Vladimir Toporov. It is almost seventy years from when the work of Fedotov was last published in Russia (it came out in 1925).

Fedotov often has been compared to Hertsen. And actually, he did happen to set historical, historico-philosophic problems into vividly publicist a format. But he did not become a living legend, as did Hertsen, though he also was an emigre and died abroad. And unlike Berdyaev or Father Sergei Bulgakov, he was not sufficiently well-known in Russia prior to emigration. Quite recently indeed, in 1986, was the hundred years anniversary of his birth.

The origins of Georgii Petrovich -- are from the Volga. He was born in the Saratov gubernia into the family of a civil servant, serving under the city administrator, and he was born into the same sort of situation and setting, as described by Ostrovsky. His mother, a delicate and refined woman (she was a music teacher), suffered much from the poverty, which beset their home soon after the death of her husband, Petr Fedotov. They were helped by a grandfather, who was a chief of police. She survived by giving music lessons.

Fedotov was frail, short of stature, rather delicate as a boy. Such people often tend towards an inferiority complex, they often tend towards a "Napoleonic complex", and they want to show all the world how important they are. As though refuting this sweeping generalisation, Fedotov from his childhood years demonstrated a remarkable harmony of character, being both observant and just. And in this regard it is impossible to compare him in his nature with any of the great thinkers, whom recently we have spoken on. Whether the tempestuous and haughty Berdyaev, or the brooding, at times restless, but aspiring and passionate Father Sergei Bulgakov, or

171

Merezhkovsky with his contradictions: "God -- beast -- abyss", or Tolstoy with his titanic attempts to found a new religion -- these were not such as Fedotov. Georgii Petrovich, according to the recollections of his school chums, struck everyone with his affability, his gentleness and warmth, and everyone said: "Our Georgie, he was so very good". And along with this -- a colossal intellect! He grasped it all in a mere instant! And essentially, this typical Volga lifestyle was tedious for him. From the very beginning it was there all a matter of black and white, but never proved to be such. And quite simply in his harmony of soul there matured the tranquil and assured thought: it is impossible to go on living thus, this needs radically to change.

Fedotov studies at Voronezh, and later returns to Saratov. During this time, as a youth, he has already gotten filled with the ideas of Pisarev, Chernyshevsky and Dobroliubov. And why was this? Why was he, considering that later on he was to make quite devastating, but nonetheless objective and cold-blooded a critique of their ideas, yet why was he initially so attracted to them? Precisely because, that he was honest and sincere, and in his mind and heart he perceived, that to go on living thus was impossible, and they were the ones calling for a change, for a transformation.

Fedotov wants to serve the people, but not like Bulgakov, who got involved in political economics. At first he wanted to go into engineering, in order to raise the industrial level of the backward regions. But before actually getting involved with science, like many of the young of his generation, he starts going to gatherings of revolutionaries, Populists, Marxists, and keeping illegal literature, and it all ends up, that he happens to get arrested, and the policeman whispers: "Keep quiet, quiet", so as not to waken the grandfather (his grandfather -- the police chief). And so, not having roused the grandfather, all nice and quietly they go off with Georgie in tow.

But all the fuss over the grandfather led to favourable results. For his illegal subversive activity he received not very severe a sentence -- they sent him off to Germany, where he lived at Jena and other cities, attending courses at the universities (imagine being exiled to this!), where he first begins his interest in history. And suddenly Fedotov, with his mighty and astute mind, already back then, at the turn of the century, realised, that the slogans, the utopias, the political myths -- all this would lead nowhere, all this could not transform the world nor bring it the results, about which he dreamt.

He explores the works of German historians, the medievalists chiefly, the specialists on the Middle Ages. He finds this era interesting, since he already then understood, that to make sense of the present-day situation is possible only by having traced out all the stages that gave rise to it. The European situation, just like the Russian also, has its roots extending back into the medieval models -- political, social, cultural and even economic. And having returned to Peterburg after the finish of his exile, he pursues historical a course of studies.

And the result: his professor was the noted Peterburg historian Grevs [Ivan Mikhailovich, 1860-1941], and he learned quite much from Vladimir Ivanovich Ger'e -- these were major specialists, brilliant pedagogues, masters in their field. They helped Fedotov not only to research the actual realities in the Middle Ages, but also to fall in love with this era, and they helped him become a first class specialist. But when he completed Peterburg University, the First World War had broken out, and medievalists had become superfluous.

He manages to get employed at a library, and all the time he is thinking, he is studying, he is mulling over things. During this time -- transpired the years of his learning in the utmost and Goethean sense. And when the February Revolution begins, and later on the October Revolution, Georgii Petrovich, a young man, still a bachelor, meets it with a full understanding of the situation, like a genuine historian. Subjecting it afterwards to a profound comparative-historical analysis, he said concerning it, that violent actions -- are not the path to freedom. Having analysed the situation with the French Revolution, Fedotov was one of the first to point out, that the French Revolution was not a cradle of freedom: it created a centralised empire, and only the military collapse of Napoleon's empire saved Europe from totalitarianism in the XIX Century.

Further on he noted, that in the preceeding formats (being well acquainted with Marxism, Fedotov loved to employ these terms, and he had a fine orientation with Marxist historiography), the medieval and the capitalistic, there already were comprised of many elements involving the free developement of social structures, as well as economic and political. The medieval times had forged the autonomy and independence of the city communes, and the capitalistic developement in the times prior to the French Revolution had made for freedom quite moreso, than all the bloodshed, initiated by Robespierre, Danton and their minions. On the contrary, these events, the 200th anniversary of which was recently celebrated, had thrown the land backwards, and this would have ended very tragically for France, had it not been cut short by the liquidation of Robespierre, and later on also of Napoleon.

One ought not to think, that Thermidor [the coup of 9 Thermidor (27 July 1794)], when Robespierre was overthrown, -- represented the path to freedom; no, "the death of Robespierre", -- says Fedotov, -- cleared the path for "the Little Corporal", -- Napoleon". Gone was the bloody romantic-dictator of the XVIII Century, and in his stead came the new dictator of the XIX Century -- they always tend to appear, when society has come into a condition of destabilisation.

The Russian Revolution in its totality (the February and October Revolutions) Fedotov termed as being large scale, and he compared it with the French Revolution. And with an extraordinary astuteness of perspective, he evaluated the "from whence" of things. That which he described about in the French Revolution, enabled him to foresee as also arising in the impending future, that which we at present term the administrative-command system. He foresaw all this already back in those years! History taught him, it enabled him to come up with the prognosis (actually, not history itself, but rather an attentive and objective approach to events).

During this period Fedotov marries, and he has to feed a family. There is disorder, and famine is beginning, and from Peterburg he travels again to Saratov -- there it was still possible to have some sort of a life during these times. And here -- a problem! The thing, it would seem, was innocent a matter: the universities in those years (the beginning of the 1920's) entered into an associate relationship with various peasant and workers unions -- basically were taken under their protection and apportioned food, and in turn lectures were provided. (Fantastically strange things! By way of an example, Merezhkovsky, when he fled Russia in 1920, had in hand a certificate to read, within units of the Red Army, lectures on ancient Egypt -- one can only wonder why!) A similar sort of giving lectures and relationship arose between the Saratov University and the workers unions. And with this occurred meetings, at which all the professors had to come out and be trained in those loyalty speeches and suchlike various aspects, but which they were totally unable to prevail upon Fedotov to do. He said, that he would not compromise -- not even for a crust of bread. In him, in this small, diminutive man, was something nobly knight-like in attitude. This continues to be a surprising trait in him;

with Berdyaev it was another matter, in being actually a descendent of knights, and a mighty man moreover, but here in contrast -- is a quiet and modest sort Intelligentsia person -- and he declared: No! He gives up on the Saratov University and with his family he journeys back to Peterburg, the poor and starving Peterburg of the 1920's.

Fedotov attempts to publish. And here he meets up with a remarkable and interesting person -- Aleksandr Meier. He is a man of philosophic a frame of mind, insightful, with broad views; still not a Christian (though by birth a Protestant, of German descent), but very close to Christianity. Meier perceived himself as a preserver of cultural traditions. At present this may seem to us a Don Quixote sort of venture. When all around there was famine, chaos, madness, executions, Meier gathered around him a small handful of people, basically Intelligentsia people, who systematically read reports, had discussions, got together on spiritual a basis. Among them were Christians, and also non-believers, though being nigh close to Christianity, -- this was not some sort of churchly gathering, but rather a small outpost of culture. Initially they even attempted to publish a newspaper (I think it came out in 1919, but they did this rather covertly).

Meier (he was ten years older than Fedotov) ultimately formed into a Christian philosopher. We have learned about his efforts only quite recently. And the reason for this being, that having been arrested and perishing in places not so very remote, Meier in some manner managed to see that his works left behind would be preserved, and the manuscript just a few years back finally saw the Divine light of day and was published in Paris in a single small booklet. And actually, this edition will appear here also for us.

During this time also at Peterburg was Sergei Bezobrazov, a young historian and friend of Fedotov, who had followed out a convoluted path from a misty sort of pantheistic religiosity towards Orthodoxy. Bezobrazov worked at the Peterburg library (now named for Saltykov-Schedrin) together with Anton Katashev (the former one-time Minister of Culture in the Provisional Government, and later a reknown church historian in the emigration), and Karashev led Bezobrazov to the threshold of the Orthodox Church, in the literal sense of the word. Bezobrazov afterwards emigrated and became a scholar, a researcher of the New Testament, and accepted the priestly dignity. He died in 1965. And to Bishop Kassian (Bezobrazov) belongs the redaction of a new translation of the whole New Testament corpus, which came out in London.

Bezobrazov had begun saying to Fedotov and Meier, that it was time to pick up and go, else all here would perish for naught. Meier replied: "No, I was born here. What purpose would there be in this? Stand fast, wheresoever you happen to be", -- such was the gist of his reply. The discussions were heated.

Georgii Petrovich was coming all closer and closer to Christianity. Basically speaking, materialism no longer tended to exist for him: this was a superficial doctrine, failing to reflect the primary thing, specifically, that which comprises the essential core of human life and history. He attempts to uncover Christian an historiography, a Christian historiosophy.

The beginning of his activity as a publicist is modest. In 1924 the publishing house "Brokhaus und Efron", then still existed, so to speak, at the sufferance of the victors (and true, not for long). From it appears the first book of Fedotov, concerning the reknown French thinker, Peter Abelard.

Peter Abelard lived during the XII Century. He had extraordinarily a tragic fate. He fell in love with his student Heloise, and fate separated them (I shall not go into this in detail), and it all ended very deplorably: Abelard and Heloise were forced to retire to monasteries. Abelard was the founder of Medieval Scholasticism (in the best sense of the word), and of rational methods of cognition. But it was not a mere matter of chance that Georgii Petrovich turned to Abelard, since for him reason always comprised a sharp and important Divine weapon.

Having made his split with Marxism, he remained a Democrat -- all his life. Occupied with science, he never renounced his faith. Having become a Christian, he never renounced the gift of reason. Striking a balance of harmony, combining in a single man faith, knowledge, goodness and an adamant firmness, a devotion to democratism on principle, an extraordinary intensity of love for the fatherland, yet with total a breadth of view and disdain for any sort of chauvinism -- all these are features, characteristic of Fedotov as a writer, a thinker, a publicist and historian.

During this time he writes a work about Dante, but it does not get it past the censor. And this serves as a signal for him: Fedotov understands, that either he has to compromise, or be silent. He prefers to leave. For his study on the Middle Ages he receives a commission to go to the West and he remains there. For a certain while, there is a wandering about, as with the majority of the emigrants, but ultimately he becomes close with a circle of remarkable people: the likes of Berdyaev and Mother Maria (Kuz'mina-Karavaeva, Skobtsova) -- a poetess, acquainted with Blok and acclaimed by him, a social activist also, in the past having actively participated in the work of the Socialist-Revolutionary Party, and deferring to no one. During this period she had already become a monastic, a nun. And as you know, Mother Maria perished in a German concentration camp shortly before the end of the Second World War. In France she is regarded as one of the greatest heroes of the Resistance. Here too they have written about her, and there was even a film. I have heard from people, who personally knew Mother Maria, that they were deeply distressed by this film. Well, I found it acceptable, since finally they acknowledged such a remarkable woman, and even managed a certain external semblance of appearance with the actress Kasatkina, judging by the photographs. But herein the profoundly religious, the spiritual intensity, which motivated this woman, was impossible to transmit. Mother Maria was, forgive me for this jargonistic term, an ideologue. She formed a definitive ideology, which she derived from the noted phrase of Dostoevsky in "The Brothers Karamazov" -- "a great obedience to the world": she became a nun, so as to serve people in the world. She was the advocate of an active, and visible Christianity, life-affirming, in the world, and heroic. She was such both before her monasticism, and in monasticism. She served people and she died giving her life for people -- for Christ! Fedotov was her close friend, along with Father Dmitrii Klepinin, who like her perished in a German concentration camp.

Berdyaev, Fundaminsky and Fedotov found themself in the middle between two camps. On the one side -- were the monarchists, nostalgic people, people, who were convinced, that in the former world everything was wonderful and that necessary only was a reanimating of the bygone order of things. On the other side -- were people, sympathetic with all the revolutionary changes and also feeling, that a new era had begun, making it necessary to be done with everything inherited from the old. Fedotov finds neither side acceptable. And he begins to publish a journal, "The New City".

"The New City" -- is a journal on the social ideal. Publishing therein were economists, politicians, philosophers, who wanted to provide intellectual stimulus for people, given to mental reflection (primarily for the emigrants, obviously). In it were printed very precise political prognoses (the journal essentially was filled with articles by Fedotov). I had the good fortune to read through a whole segment of this journal, which came out prior to the war, in Paris. Fedotov was saying, in addressing the monarchist camp: you do dream in vain about the overthrow of the Bolsheviks -- they already have long been overthrown! They no longer still rule -- it is Stalin that rules; and it is not by chance that he wages a struggle against the "Society of Old Bolsheviks" (there actually was such a Society, which was liquidated by Stalin). This was entirely innocent a society, but for Stalin they were unnecessary, since they tended to remind him, that he himself had arrived as it were after the fact. All those characteristics of Stalinism, which at present fill the publicist scene, as well as serious investigations, were noted by Fedotov at the very time, when it happened, but afar! I have read his 1936-1937 articles -- all the prognoses, all the description of events was completely accurate.

Fedotov was remarkably able to discern the most primary tendencies within history. But what made him remarkable as a thinker? Fedotov felt, that culture in general is either unnecessary and superfluous a thing, or else it possesses a sacred, a Divine significance and content. He became the first and foremost Russian theologian of culture. Being a Democrat and a man of absolute a national toleration, he nonetheless stressed, that a culture has to assume concrete national forms, that within each culture obtains its own individual features, and this is a matter of creativity. Each artist has to create his own, since he is an individuum. And Fedotov stressed, that a culture in its totality -- is likewise a sort of collective individuum.

As a basis for understanding, in what consists the meaning and particular uniqueness of Russia's cultural composite, he turns to the past and writes, perhaps, one of the chief books in his life, which he entitles "The Saints of Ancient Rus"". Working on it nudged him further into teaching at the Paris Theological Academy. He indicates in this book, that in having accepted from Byzantium the ascetic ideal, Russian Christianity begins to introduce into it a caritative element, an element of service, an element of mercy and compassion -- which in Byzantium was far less pronounced. Fedotov points out, that this occurred within Kievan Rus', in the era of Rublev and Epiphanii the Wise, during the time of the Renaissance; how the people in forming the monasteries, were at the same time suppliers of food, hospitality and enlightenment for the surrounding world.

In this book, "The Saints of Ancient Rus'", is shown the enormous cultural and economic work of the monasteries. But do not think, that this book -- is merely some sort of one-sided a panegyric of praise. Within it is a section on the tragedy of Russian sanctity. The tragedy consisted in this, that within the defining era, the XV-XVI Centuries, the churchly leadership, in striving towards an active social caritative (compassionate) activity, was striving simultaneously for the wealth to do its work. It would seem, that this is obvious. Saint Iosif Volotsky said: the monasteries need to have land, need to have peasants, in order to lift the level of the country, in order to contribute to its economic growth, in order to assist people in times of famine and hardship. The intent was fine, but you yourself can readily imagine, to what sort of abuses all this led to. And against this Josephite mindset spoke out a group of Trans-Volga startsi-elders.

Himself hailing from the Volga, Fedotov deeply esteemed them. At the head of the Trans-Volga elders, who were called "non-possessors", stood the Monk Nil Sorsky, who first of all came out against the execution of the heterodox (whereas Iosif [Voloysky] acknowledged the legitimacy of executing heretics), and secondly, Saint Nil Sorsky came out against the monastic land-holdings, against the riches which the Church possesses, in contrast to the simplicity of the times of the Gospel. He was thus such an opponent of all the ceremonial, the superfluous, the redundancy in the Church, that he even left very striking a final-testament: needless for me are any pompous funeral ceremonies, nothing, and even my body let it go to the beasts, cast it into the forest, for the hungry wolves to gnaw it bare -- to be of benefit to the utmost. Certainly, the monks did not do this, but with this he wanted to emphasise, the significance of everything earthly for him.

The Orthodox Church -- the Byzantine, the Bulgarian, the Serbian, and the Russian as one of the most immense of the Orthodox Churches -- frequently have been reproached for social passivity. And Fedotov herein decided to show, that this is inaccurate.

He then writes a brilliant work of research (a very well written book, it reads like a novel) -- "Saint Philip, Metropolitan of Moscow". In this book Fedotov says, that if the Church in the person of Metropolitan Aleksei, the spiritual father of Dmitrii Donskoy and friend of the Monk Sergei of Radonezh, assisted in the consolidation of the Moscow state and the power of the Moscow tsar, then, when this power rejected the Gospel commands in the person of Ivan the Terrible, the selfsame Church in the person of Metropolitan Philip began a struggle against tyranny. Since

Philip, the Metropolitan of Moscow, was for Fedotov -- a model of a resolute servant of the Church.

After this book, a whole series of articles appears, devoted to the problem of the origins of the Russian Intelligentsia. And with brilliant a literary mastery Fedotov showed, how in the era of Peter I within the bosom of a single people there came to be formed two peoples. They spoke different languages, and they in fact held different world-views, they dressed in different an attire, and they had different a psychology; they lived side by side like two totally alien tribes. And this abnormal situation led to a morbid complex of guilt in the educated class, the intelligentsia, which began to deify and idolise the people, feeling in regard to it a sense of guilt and thinking, that it can be possible to save it, by breaking all forth into the light, shattering all the structures. Fedotov in one of the articles even presents this like an unfolding drama, the first act of which happens at Kiev, the second -- at Moscow, the third -- at Peterburg etc; and it all ends up with a great wrecking of things: the Intelligentsia puts all its efforts into destroying the empire, and itself gets crushed under the debris.

What did Fedotov propose for this stormy period? Creativity and work. Building things up, -- he said, -- is a divine gift and a Divine summoning.

His objectivity is stunning. In one of his articles he wrote: yes, La Passionaria (Dolores Ibarruri) -- is a frightful woman, consumed with hate, but for me she is closer, than is Francisco Franco, who regards himself a Christian. When this article came out, it set off such a scandal within the emigration, that the professors were compelled to speak out in rebuke of him. But just like in the 1920's when Fedotov had refused to compromise, so again in the emigration he likewise would not consent to do so.

In considering the politics of the Soviet Union, he was always objective. And if some particular manipulations by Stalin seemed to him important and beneficial for Russia (on the international plane), then he wrote about them in positive a light. Fedotov said, that in doing this, Stalin was acting not merely out of his own interests, but in the interests of the state, to the benefit of the state. Again there spread an outcry, and it all ended with odious a scene -- there was a gathering of the Theological Academy (Fedotov at this time was in London), and at this gathering they compelled everyone to sign a petition stating, that this man was a "red", and towards him there should be no tolerance, he should publicly repent and recant -- in short, a micro "toe the party line" gathering. And then Berdyaev exploded with a thunderous article, "Does there Exist Freedom of Thought and Conscience in Orthodoxy?" The article was cutting to the extreme. He wrote it with anguish and disgust, since the judgement on Fedotov had been signed out of a cowardice even by such people, as Bulgakov (who certainly in his soul did not think this way, and understood, that Fedotov stood on solid a scale of objectivity, and to denounce him for this is impossible). Fedotov had to quit the Academy. Then the war broke out and it put everyone in their place.

With tremendous an effort, Fedotov managed to get out of German-occupied France. Mother Maria, his friend, was arrested, and sent off to a concentration camp. All over the place there are massive arrests. Father Dmitrii Klepinin, arrested on changes of forging documents for Jews trying to stay concealed in occupied France, likewise was thrown into a concentration camp and perished. After lengthy adventures, and thanks to the assistance of various committees, Fedotov ultimately winds up in America. And glory to God for this, since in Paris he had nothing more to do with those theologians.

He becomes a professor at a theological seminary (still now existing) named for Holy Prince Vladimir, where he works on his final book, "An History of Russian Religious Thought". Everything, worked out by him in his book on Metropolitan Philip and the Saints of Ancient Rus', went into this two-volume edition. And wow! This book was published only in English. I suggest, that Georgii Petrovich wrote it in Russian, and that actually this original manuscript exists and can be found, that it hopefully will be found (his relatives still live in America), and then thank God it will be published here in Russian for us.

Before his death Fedotov writes an article, sort of a final-testament, entitled "The Republic of Saint Sophia". Not declarations, not slogans, not sundry abstract philosophic arguments -- Fedotov is operating here using real history. He is writing about the democratic foundations of Russian culture, lodged within the Novgorod legacy. The Republic of Saint Sophia -- is Novgorod. And he ends this article before his death with an appeal for the necessity of a rebirth of this ancient spirit of Novgorod, where already there were elements of the people's representation, of elections, where even the Novgorod archbishop was elected; this reflected an ancient germination of democracy. And as Fedotov showed in his investigations, whatever the culture in the final end, it feeds like a tree off the sappings of its history.

And there is no basis necessarily to think, that the cultural tradition is rigidly dependent upon tyranny and totalitarianism. In it too there were other elements, capable of being reborn and coming to fruition.

In conclusion, so that you may have a certain feel for Fedotov's style, I want to read you a few lines of his, since I am not convinced, that his works will get published anytime soon.

I remember one story, which Fedotov told, explaining his position as regards creativity and culture. Many people, the thinking sort of Christians, have said: creativity and culture are unnecessary, because the only thing needful is to concern oneself with Divine matters. Fedotov offered the history of a certain Catholic saint: when still a seminarian, he was playing with a ball in the garden, and up to him came a certain monk who decided to vex him and said: "What would you be doing, if you knew for sure, that tomorrow would be the end of the world?" And the future saint answered: "I would continue playing ball".

What is the meaning behind this? If playing ball is a bad thing, then it would be necessary never to play it, irregardless of whether the world ends sooner or later; if however this has some sort of a significance before the Face of God, then it is needful always to play, whenever possible. And he transfers this over to culture. If culture -- be an offspring of Satan (and in this Fedotov certainly does not believe), then it is necessary to cast it aside, irregardless of whether tomorrow be the end of the world or it take a million years to come. If culture is a form of the creativity of the human spirit before the Face of God, then too it is needful to be concerned with it, and not merely be petrified with fright at the impending end. People have thus been frightening themself for centuries, not wanting to work, not wanting to create, and merely saying: why bother, since the world is going to end. And as a result they wind up in the position of those, who have squandered and wasted their gifts, their talents, in vain. And furthermore, in the Gospel Our Lord Jesus says, that the Judgement Day, when there will be demanded an accounting for those wasted talents, can happen at any moment.

Fedotov exhorts us and tells us, that freedom -- is like a small and delicate plant and that we ought neither to be surprised by this nor be so fearful over it, because just like a tiny and fragile bit of life first arose within the enormous world-edifice, and then overspread the entire planet, so also freedom at the very beginning was not a feature, present for all mankind. (And this corresponds precisely to reality. I shall not offer the facts for it, because obviously it has been so).

Fedotov writes: "Rousseau, essentially, wanted to say: man ought to be free, or that, man was created in order to be free. And in this is an eternal truth of Rousseau. But this is nowise the same thing, as saying: man was born free.

Freedom is a later and delicate blossom of culture. This nowise lessens its value. And it is not only because that which is most precious -- is the fragile and rare. Man becomes fully man only within the process of culture, and only in it, at its summits, can be found the expression of his loftiest strivings and possibilities. Only as regards these attainments can one judge concerning the nature and destiny of man".

Further on he writes: "Within the biological world there govern the iron laws of instinct, of the struggle of species and races, an endlessly repeated cycle of vital processes. There, where everything is conditioned by necessity, it is impossible to find any gaps or flaws, by which freedom might pierce through. And where organic life assumes social a character, it is thoroughly totalitarian. With the bees there is communism, with the ants there is slavery, in the beastly herd there is the absolute force of following the leader".

Everything that Fedotov writes, tends to precisely correspond to actuality. And he is suggesting, that social forms for us are but repetitions of the animal level of life. Freedom however -- is but the privilege of man. "Even in the world of culture, -- continues Fedotov, -- freedom appears as infrequent and late a guest. In our survey of tens or dozens of the higher civilisations, known to us, and which for the modern historian constitutes seemingly once a singular historical process, we tend to find in merely but one of them freedom in our sense of the word..."

I shall further elucidate. He speaks about how despotisms have existed in Iran, and on the banks of the Hwang Ho, the Yangtze, in Mesopotamia, in Iraq, in ancient Mexico, in Egypt -- everywhere there existed tyrannies, -- except in the small land of Greece, where the idea of democracy arose. As sort of historical a wonder.

"The person, -- he continues, -- is everywhere subordinated to the collective, which itself determines the forms and boundaries of its dominion. This dominion can be very harsh, as in Mexico or Assyria, or humane, as in Egypt or in China, but nowhere does it acknowledge the autonomy of existence of the person. Nowhere is there a special sacred sphere of interests, off limits for the state. The state itself is regarded as sacred, and the utmost absolute demands of the religion therein tend to coincide with the pretensions of state sovereignty.

Yes, freedom -- is the exception across the range of great cultures. But culture itself -- is the exception across the background of natural life. Man himself, his spiritual life -- is the strange exception amongst living beings. But indeed life itself, organic a phenomenon, -- is likewise the exception in the material world. We enter here into the sphere of the unseen, but there is much a basis to those theories, which consider that only planet Earth may have had created the favourable conditions for the arising of organic life (moreover, many of our erudite at present think thus). But what is the significance of the Earth within the Solar System, what is the significance of the Sun within the Milky Way, what is the significance of our "galaxy" within the Universe?

One of two things: either we remain stuck upon the outwardly pervasive "naturo-scientific" point of view, and we then arrive at pessimistic a conclusion: the Earth -- life -- man -- culture -- freedom -- are all so insignificant a thing, ultimately not worthwhile dwelling upon. Having arisen through the accidental chance play on one of the specks of the world edifice, they are doomed to disappear without a trace into the cosmic night.

Or we can invert the whole scale of valuations and proceed with a way out, not by the quantitative, but rather from the qualitative. And therein man, his spirit and his culture, become the crown and the purpose for the world creation. All the innumerable galaxies exist ultimately for this, to produce the miraculous wonder -- a free and reason-endowed corporeal being, predestined to a royal lordship over the Universe.

There remains unresolved -- on a practical level though not important -- the enigma of the significance of the small matters of great magnitude: why does almost all the valuably-great occur within the materially-small? A verymost interesting problem for philosophy...

Freedom has a share in the fate of everything lofty and of value in the world. The small and the politically splintered Greece gave to the world -- science, gave those forms of thought and artistic perception, which even amidst the awareness of the various limitations, nevertheless up to the present tend to define the world-view of hundreds of millions of people. The comparatively tiny Judea gave the world the greatest, or singularly-true religion -- there being not two, but one -- which is confessed by people on all the continents. A small island beyond the English Channel worked out a system of political institutions, which -- while being less universal, than Christendom or science, -- nonetheless holds sway in three portions of the world, and is now victoriously contending in combat with its mortal enemies", -- this was written towards the end of the war, when the Allies were struggling against Hitler.

"A limitation in origin still as such does not signify a limitation of action or significance. Being born at a certain spot upon the earthly sphere can be an invite to dominion over the world; and many remain always bound up within one definite cultural circle. But others -- and the supreme ones -- exist for everyone. All peoples are called to Christianity. Every man, to a greater or lesser degree, is capable of scientific thought. But not all acknowledge -- nor are obligated to admit -- the canons of Greek beauty. Are all peoples capable of admitting the value of freedom, and realising it? This is a question at present that is being decided in the world. not by theoretical considerations, but only by experience can it be decided".

And thus, Georgii Fedotov puts to every and all the various peoples, -- who of them is capable of freedom, and who but are to remain in slavery.

Mother Maria (Skobtsova)

Today we finish up with the series of lectures, which have been very important for all of us, in our having had the opportunity, the opportunity of presenting to many a first-time indeed happy, a first-time joyful acquaintance with the great, the truly great current of Russian Religious Philosophy spanning the end of the last century and into our own century. Why should we complete this cycle of lectures with the name of Mother Maria? She was not a professional philosopher. She was a person, who in our land gradually, imperceptibly began to gain fame after approximately fifty years; a person, about whom were written poetic verses, essays, historical accounts and even a novel; a film was made, certainly very heavily censured, but nonetheless there is something of the genuine Mother Maria in it.

This woman, hero of the Resistance, martyress, artist -- was a philosopher, but it was namely however in that profound sense of the word, in which as a genuine philosopher she was perceived as such by her contemporaries, by her friends. Berdyaev was her close and like-minded friend. Father Sergei Bulgakov highly esteemed her. She was personally connected with that Pleiad, which has come to be termed the Silver Age of Russian art, literature, philosophy and theology. But it was not only her personal connection, not only her organic involvement in this amazing, unrepeatable, beautiful onrush of spiritual culture that impels us today to speak about her within the context of our series of lectures, but also because she was a philosopher of action -- not an abstract theoretical contemplator, not a person, wanting to hide away in an ivory tower, not a person, as it were some mere guest upon the earth, indifferent, aspiring only to some sort of sphere of metaphysical speculations. Under the influence of the ideas of Vladimir Solov'ev, of Bulgakov, Berdyaev and others, she formed for herself a definite view of the world and history. And this became for her not some "ideal construct", not our so-called "in better years" saying, but rather it became pivotal to her life, and she realised all this -- each day, in an arduous struggle, in a cross-bearing sacrificial service, all the way to her death as a martyr.

Elizaveta Iur'evna Kuz'mina-Karavaeva (her maiden name was Pilenko) was born in 1891 at Riga. Her youth was spent near Anapa. She was born into highly intelligent a family with an interesting past. One of her ancestors, Delone [de Launay], was the last commander of the Bastille; afterwards he participated in the Napoleonic campaign, fell into captivity and remained in Russia[1] -- this from the family annals of the future Mother Maria. Her father was learned a man -- an agronomist, an horticulturalist, and later after her birth, he became Director of the Nikitsk Botanical Gardens that you all know of. The settlement, where they lived, was called Pilenko after their family name, and then was called Iurovka after her father's name. At present I want to sketch out a sort of general portrait of her for you.

She was the first woman student at large at the Peterburg Theological Academy. But her roots were not in churchliness, since her mother, who out-survived her, was not closely involved with the traditional churchly aspect. The old world for the future Mother Maria was personified by Konstantin Petrovich Pobedonostsev -- a figure all powerful at the end of the past century and beginning of our century as the Over-Prokurator of the Holy Synod. This was a man deep, multi-faceted, complex, contradictory, a militant conservative, but at the same time open to many currents. He was the publisher and translator of the Catholic book, "The Imitation of Christ", by Thomas a Kempis, although his politics in regards to various religious confessions was very harsh. Little Liza was fond of him, and all the old world for her was connected with the image of old Pobedonostsev.

Those of you, who have read Andrei Bely's "Peterburg", likely have to know, that the chief hero in it, Senator Obleukhov, to a certain degree is copied upon Pobedonostsev. His cold, insolent face you can see in the reknown picture by Repin, "Session of the State Council". Thus so,

---

[1] translator note: This is incorrect. The last commander of the Bastille, Bernard René Jourdan, marquis de Launay (1740-1789), was actually killed, indeed quite savagely torn to pieces, at the Storming of the Bastille. This embellished family tree myth may have been passed on to Fr Men' by way of the Russian dissident poet, Vadim Delone (or Delonne or Delaunay; 1947-1983), who was related to Mother Maria through a common ancestor Boris Delone (Delaunay 1890-1980; of ultimately Irish ancestry via France).

but for her he was not cold a figure, rather instead warm, he dallied at play with her, he brought her sweets, and such things remain in heart all one's life. The old world for her was not so terrible. But in 1907 Pobedonostsev dies, and the girl is influenced by other sources. On the one hand, she is a young woman of the aesthetic trend, with those who were then termed decadents. Today we tend to view the "Silver Age" with exhilaration, a certain delight, fully merited. Leafing through the pages of "The Golden Fleece", "Scales", "Works and Days", "Musaget" and other publications of the turn of the century, it is impossible not to feel the intellectual enchantment, the artistic medium of that period. But within it there was, certainly, much also that was doubtful, disputable, morally questionable, much that was decadent in the direct sense of the word. And then too on the other hand -- was the influence of those, who were suffering on behalf of the people. The people was something literally god-like for the Intelligentsia of the late XIX early XX Centuries. Under the image of the people was often conceived not the thinking portion of society, not its most active part, but namely rather the peasantry, often quite unfamiliar and unknown for the Intelligentsia, and poorly studied. And hence there was "the going to the people", hence the readiness to suffer for it. All this had occurred over the span of several generations, it came fully to life in the 60's of the XIX Century, and Elizaveta Iur'evna became involved in both these currents.

In her early years she met up with Blok. And certainly, he was an idol of the times for the youth back then. When she was fifteen, Nikolai Gumilev was enamoured with her. All this had as it were an effect on her, but already then she was unique a girl, unique a young woman, unique a person.

Here is an image of her, as sketched by Blok back then:

> When you stand upon my path,
> So vivacious, so beautiful,
> But so sternly pensive,
> About the sad you speak to all,
> About mortality you dwell to think,
> None do you deign to love,
> And scorn you your beauty --
> What for? Perchance do I offend you?...
> Speak not so much about the sad,

Think not so much on ends and reasons,
All this, while I dare think,
In that fifteen years you only be.
Yet rather I should want,
That you but simple a man could love
Who loves earth and heaven
Moreso, than reforming and unreforming
Lofty speeches about earth and heaven.
Then truly, I shall be glad for you,
Since -- only in loving
Has one the right to be deemed human.

The poet relates, as you might sense in these verses, that there was something unique about this strange girl. It would seem, that she is in a blossoming of her powers -- energetic, sharp-minded, merry -- yet at the same time with some burden set upon her heart. This was a compassion for the world. With her there was always an acute feeling of compassion for others, and it afterwards brought her to the revolutionaries: she became a member of the party of the SR's, the Socialist Revolutionaries. There was even an instance, when they entrusted her with a terrorist act, but she sensed, evidently, that this was impossible for her.

Together with the young people of the time she awaited and heralded the coming tempest. And the tempest indeed did come, and she participated in the tempest, but already at that moment she had come to sense, how terrible a thing is violence, and that from evil good is not to be made. She becomes an adjunct, or as they then expressed it, the comrade of the city head in Anapa, and later on simply the city head. A famous episode from this time was reported by the late Evgenii Bogat in his article on Mother Maria, a final and posthumous article published in "Iunost'" ["Youth"], -- some of you surely will have read it. When the anarchists descended upon Anapa, they wanted to be given the right to do whatsoever they wanted, and in general the right to rampage through the city. These were sailors who had come to her, and she made so bold an effect on them, that she quelled the anarchist mob. She saw to it, that in the city there was no pillaging, nor murder.

In 1920 she heads to the West. In Paris her Christian world-view gradually assumes a completed and total form. She relies upon the philosophy of Vladimir Solov'ev, upon the thought of Berdyaev, and becomes close with Konstantin Mochulsky. I think that but few of you know of this man. He was a writer, quite to be proud of, the author of noteworthy monograph studies on Solov'ev, Blok, Andrei Bely, Gogol and others. He likewise died an emigre. Mochulsky was a thinker and writer of very broad a scope, a man, totally foreign to any sort of fanaticism or narrowness, -- this is what also attracted Elizaveta Iur'evna to him.

Towards the end of the 1920's she splits up from her second husband. And their paths diverge. For a certain while he had been a member in the administration of the [Deniken White Guard] Dobrovol'chesky Army, and later on he worked as a taxi chauffeur.

And she lost at first one daughter; then her other daughter, an older one, Gayana, went off to the Soviet Union and there died. And within the spiritual and moral experience of the future Mother Maria there arises the feeling of universal motherhood -- she experienced it while sitting there at the bed of her dying daughter. For her the suffering of the world became something, that needs to be redeemed, and in which it is necessary to participate. I would say, that throughout the whole of the religious philosophy of the past hundred years, no one has so inwardly experienced the mystery of Golgotha, the mystery of the Garden of Gethsemane night, the mystery of Redemption, the mystery of shared suffering, as has Elizaveta Iur'evna. She gave an expression to this in verse:

> I did seek the mysterious sort
> Those, that midst the night remain the seeing,
> What in life the times and seasons hath suppressed,
> Whereof to rejoice whilst lamenting.
> I did seek the dreamers, the prophets,
> Always afoot the heavenly ladders
> Sighting signs of moments inaccessible,
> Singing us songs inaudible.
> And have found the poor, the dissolute, the orphaned,
> The drunken, the despondent, the unneeded,
> Gone wanton all the ways of the world,
> The homeless, the hungry and the breadless.

The philosophic and theological corpus of the works of Mother Maria is not especially large, but up til now it has not been fully collected together. It lies scattered through the rarest of emigre publications. There

appeared separately her booklet on Solov'ev, and another on Khomyakov --
one of the forefathers of the Russian Religious renaissance, and yet another
on Dostoevsky, whom she perceived as a verymost profound expresser of
the Christian understanding of existence and life. She had also a smallish
work, "The Sacred Earth". The theme is not fortuitous, not by chance. They
have always been telling us, that spirit is something sacred and holy, that
spirit is the bearer of the Divine and the great. But, as I have already
mentioned to you, within the creativity of Merezhkovsky and others was
posited questions about creativity, about nature, about the world, about
flesh, about earthly love -- about all that, which is to be done in the world.
And Merezhkovsky already back then had proposed suchlike a term:
"sacred flesh" -- that it likewise ought to be regarded as sacred. But with
him this was something seen dryly, merely schematically. Mother Maria
however rephrased this as "The Sacred Earth". She said: yes, life is a dirty
business, vile, repulsive, but to waste and throw it away, as people often
happen to do, in attempting to come to terms with the problem of
alienation, -- this is a false path. It is necessary to make holy, to cleanse, to
raise up that which is downcast, that which has been trampled into the dirt.
This theme of a sanctified earth, of sanctified life, becomes central for her.
She writes a work, "In Search of Synthesis". I think, that her ponderings
over churchly an effort had no little an influence upon this work. In it she
says, that Christianity has distorted the true models of life by its retreat
from it, in an extreme asceticism. And the anti-Christian movements have
been of a mind to instead create an utopia, which then would fully displace
the spiritual totally into the background. "The task facing the present day
and the days to come, -- she wrote, -- is the creation of a new utopia, but in
the best sense of the word, one which would unite in itself both heaven and
earth". She justifies this, based on Solov'ev, with the term "God-manhood".
Mankind is called to be God-manly, so that within it will be sanctified both
the flesh, and spirit. We are unperfected people, but we are not spirits
merely, we are connected by all sorts of threads with nature, which
likewise was created by God; granted it is a fallen nature, granted it is
distorted, but it was Divinely wrought -- it was created by God. Before
man, before his inner, his spiritual life stands the enormous task of the
sacralisation of existence. Moreover, a total asceticism is impossible for
the social order of things. She asserted, that social activity, the concern for
neighbour, is the greatest moral duty of mankind, of man, and of the
Church in this regard. She firmly asserted this based upon the Gospel. This

was the attempt at synthesis. And for this, in order to realise this in practice, in fact, she begins no longer still a Populist thing of going to the people, but rather a descent into the hell existing amongst the Russian emigration.

People, having lost everything, often -- the near and dear, almost always -- their property and means, bereft of native-land, of home, profession, many inwardly devastated, the tremendous majority impoverished, and left embittered -- this was very painful a situation to deal with. Elizaveta Iur'evna relates one instance. She had gone to some sort of a workers group among the emigres and began conducting a talk with them, and one of them gloomily said: "What good is it in giving us a talk, better if you should wash our floors". And she was not offended at hearing this, she understood suddenly the correctness of these words, and immediately she tied up something as an apron and began to scrub and clean the dirty hovel. And seeing this, the workers became rather embarrassed, and ashamed, and then they invited her to eat with them, and so she sat with them and she understood, that to be of service to people it is needful to do so, fully and to the very limit. She perceived, that only thus is it possible to live, that it is impossible to live only halfway, or a fourth, it is fully -- to the very end, to the very death in surrendering oneself.

And hence, the thoughts about becoming a monastic, a nun. Berdyaev, her friend, in his regarding her as very bright a woman within the emigration, reacted rather sceptically to this desire of hers. Still another of her friends was so upset over this, that he did not even come for her monastic tonsuring. Metropolitan Evlogii (Georgievsky), who headed the majority of the emigre parishes, had warm regard for her, and upon consideration he assented to her tonsure. He envisioned, that she might create a new monastic movement. In his memoirs afterwards he wrote, that the new movement had not been realised, but she did create the group, "Orthodox Action", which had its own followers and successors. The metropolitan with a certain irony said, that in her monastic activity she had still in her the mannerisms of a revolutionary woman, a real fighter -- and to him all this seemed strange. But her monastic tonsuring did happen. In 1932 it was impossible to find for her a proper monastic podryanik, the under-cassock garment, but they found a man's one, from some former monk, and with a chuckle she said, that these old clothes needed a devoting to the Church, given their sad history. And only later on was she able to get herself a genuine monastic apostol'nik, head-veil, and the rest.

And right from the very beginning, monasticism for her was not the typical withdrawal into a cell, behind a wall, not a departure from the world, but rather a striving to serve the world twice as much. All that which had formerly existed for her herself, one thing after another had passed out of her life. She had given lectures, she had traveled to the poor, she went to the sick, and when she became a nun, all her activity became concentrated on helping the needy. Mother Maria created a shelter for young women, for the needy, she created inexpensive places to get a meal. This is difficult for us to imagine at present, but this was back in the 1930's, and the emigres were actually bad off. Right early in the morning in her nun's veil she would be walking through the market-place, she would gather leftover cabbage leaves and sometimes for quite a while, over many a day, she prepared this for all the brethren.

Mother Maria was a person of many abilities, she was capable of all kinds of things with golden hands as it were -- she cooked, and she embroidered. She made for the church a beautiful embroidery, this was her final work in life -- in the concentration camp before her death she embroidered an icon, which she did not get to complete. She wrote, and she got published. I shall not speak in particular about her poetry, quite philosophical, often this is a poetry like unto that of Job.

Well, her basic concept is this, that the Christian -- is a person, embodying Christ within them, and that a person has to be totally devoted, -- and this is not a mere matter of words. When she accepted tonsure with the name Mary, she said: "Well, now the time for mere words is ended". It is interesting, that back during the revolutionary years there was discussion over the fact, that she had donated her property near Anapa to the people and they asked her: "why have you done this?" -- She answered: "Out of a noble gesture". But now she had no time left over for noble gestures, there was only work, incessant toil. And with what cheerfulness, with what energy, with what an alacrity of mind and absence of condescension she did all this! She would go to the prostitutes, to the poor, to people that were scorned. They were not strangers for her. And here is why in her verses, and in those philosophical works, which she published in various emigre journals, -- this was not some theoretical matter, this was not some up in the clouds contorted philosophy, but was rather the crystaline experience of soul of a self-denying person.

Yet honestly it must be said, that many Orthodox people looked at her with disbelief, with a smirk. Some former emigres have told me, that they regarded her as a crazy woman, an eccentric, and complaining, that she was disgracing her monastic habit in going to these here kind of people, that she was consorting with dubious and reprobate a sort of people. And well, they would say, here is one such example. A certain girl asked to try on her monastic attire, and she with a laugh gave it over, and both of them thought it cute in doing so. But everyone said: How can she do such a thing! Yes, the strait-laced had hard a time over her.

Her charitable establishment was at first situated at a certain Paris villa, and then at 77 Lourmel Street was founded the Centre for Spiritual and Material Aid. And it was characteristic of her, that she always attempted to help people both spiritually, and materially. One of our sharp-minded fellows has observed, that some Christians are always ready, when asked for bread, to give the Holy Scriptures instead. This was never the way with her. When someone asked for bread, she gave bread -- as much as she was able, it stands to reason, since she was not amply endowed with means: what she had she acquired by her own hard work. At the Centre there was a church, and serving there as priest was the learned monk Father Kyprian Kern, a rigid adherent of strict traditional rules, and he was at his wit's end, over what this woman was doing. It became quite tense between them. He considered it, that monasticism was a withdrawal from the world with a complete break off from the former and the present day life. She considered it, that there can be another view with monasticism. She does not deny the proper place for a traditional ascetic monasticism. But, having dwelt in the Baltic region, and having seen the local women's monasteries there, she said (in approximately the sense of her words): they have renounced both family and comfort, but still they have it so comfortable; they have arranged themself a nest, these monastic nuns, a wonderful, peaceful, beautiful sort of nest. Granted, that there, it is without husband and children, but it is a nest all the same. She admits, that in this there is its own meaning. The girls pray in these monasteries, they keep up the old traditions, and they work, in order to feed themself. This is all fine. But there has to be something else, something more. And then she writes a paradoxical work, to which she puts the provocative title, "A Justification of Phariseeism".

What was the gist of her thought on this? She pointed out, that in each historical era there has to be people, impotent creatively, but on whom is placed the task to preserve tradition in conservative a form. Then it all comes apart and changes, and the movement moves on. The ancient

Pharisees were suchlike a type of people. In our modern phraseology we customarily tend to regard the pharisee as identical with the hypocrite, as being phony etc. But historically in fact the Pharisees were pious people, they were traditionalists -- their task was to preserve tradition. But often such safeguarding tendencies lead to a tragic opposition to everything new. This even led to the result, that the Pharisees rose up in indignant revolt against the preachings of Jesus Christ. Against His preachings! -- still even before they were able to accuse Him, that He had proclaimed Himself the Messiah. Moreover in that He had never openly done so. They sensed the stirring of a new breeze in His words, and they said: let everything remain and stay the way it is.

In whatever the era, in whatever the land (moreover, in whatever the religion) there is, -- says Mother Maria, -- suchlike a safeguarding element. Can it be considered only negatively ? No. Within history the "Phariseeism" (thus she literally terms it) has its own role: it preserves that, which was acquired by the spiritual creativity of former times, in order to pass this on to later generations. In this is the merit, but in this is also the tragedy of Phariseeism. Well, you can easily imagine, that when she employed the word "Phariseeism", she was succinctly polemicising against those Orthodox traditionalists, who tended to condemn her open-ended understanding of Christianity.

But in a short while everything became easier, because Father Kiprian Kern got replaced (he indeed was a kinsman of Pushkin's mistress Anna Kern, and he was a scholar and writer, the author of a whole series of remarkable researches). In his place came then Father Dmitrii Klepinin, born in 1904, the son of an architect; his brother was the historian N. A. Klepinin, who perished here in 1939, and was likewise young, deciding to journey to the Soviet Union, in order as it were to open bridges between the emigres and the Soviet Russia. He came in 1937 (not the very best of times) and perished two years later. He is the author of a book on Aleksandr Nevsky, which should soon come out here.

Father Dmitrii Klepinin was a man of deep faith, of extraordinarily good an heart, firm convictions, and totally sharing in the views of Mother Maria. He assisted her with her efforts in "Orthodox Action", her endless concern for the suffering, he became her unnoticed helper, her spiritual guide and co-martyr, since he likewise perished in the same place that she did, -- the German concentration camp at Ravensbrueck. And here today, through an amazing coincidence of circumstances (so we are told) is present with us Anton Arjakovsky, by birth a grandson of Father Dmitrii Klepinin. At the finish of our discussion I think that he will perhaps be willing to say something about his grandfather.

They worked together also at that tragic moment in time, when there occurred the German occupation of France. Would they sit home, and stay in their tower safely barricaded away from it all? Never! Both Mother Maria and Father Dmitrii became active figures in the Resistance, and though having left Russia, neither he nor she ever lost their love for their fatherland. One time after the meal someone said, that with the German invasion there had perished so many thousands of Soviet soldiers, and one of those present gibed: "Still not enough of 'em". And to this Mother Maria retorted: "Get out of here, and you know where the Gestapo address is". She always believed in the victory of the Russian side. She indeed wrote, that the leader of the "Master Race" -- is paranoid a fellow, whose proper place is not at the head, but in the crazy house. And this, moreover, was not said in secret, this became a vital impulse to her work. Genuine work with the Resistance. And here the underground experience from the old times came in handy. She gathered military information, by night she listened to the radio (this was a crime), she helped those who were being hunted down by the Nazis, and in particular, hiding those who were Jewish, and to whom Father Dmitrii sometimes gave documents, certifying that they had been baptised and were not Jews etc. And in the final end this resulted in the arrest of both of them in 1943.

I shall not dwell on the details, in the movie this was all depicted quite clearly, although certainly also, with distortion. For example, the Gestapo officer Hoffmann, who arrested her, according to the reminiscences of her mother, said to her mother: "You will never see your daughter again. You have done a bad job in raising her. She is helping our enemies. She helps the Jews". And to this her mother replied: "She is a Christian, and for her there is neither Greek nor Jew. she helps everyone! And if you were in need, she then would also help you!" And Mother Maria smiled and said: "Yes likely, I would help". She had gotten the better of him. But in the film it gets all twisted around. She is made to say: "I would never help the likes of you". Well, you have to make allowances for our cinematography: it is not "a free bird", as everyone knows.

There are remarkable reminiscences collected about Mother Maria in the concentration camp. She even wound up in this setting prior to her arrest: back when at Paris they had rounded up hundreds of children from

Jewish families into the Velodrome Stadium, in order to truck them off to concentration camps, she managed to get in there and as best she could she attempted to help the people -- thousands of people, a single water-faucet for the whole place, and all them simply to the point of perishing from hunger, thirst and over-crowding spanning the course of several days. The sister of General de Gaulle remembers, that in these very hellish conditions Mother Maria surrounded herself with people and conversed and talked with them. These were appeals -- in the hellish conditions of the concentration camps to preserve a spiritual life, to preserve intellectual interests, to preserve love for one another. And that is how many remember her, those who were situated with her in those days. One of her fellow inmates remembers likewise, that they happened to be talking about something, and the SS woman came up and struck Mother Maria on the face, but she did not turn about and merely continued talking, as though this were but an annoying fly, -- and by this she wanted to show, that these people were not worth her notice.

Her son Yurii was also arrested with Father Dmitrii and Mother Maria -- all three perished: Father Dmitrii and Yurii from sickness and exhaustion, and Mother Maria would perhaps have died from exhaustion, but before the camp was liberated, as the war was entering its final days, they sent her off to the gas chamber. She was worn down with exhaustion to the last of her strength. There is many a legend preserved about this. One of them is provided in one of our first published accounts here about her: how she switched clothing with one of her fellow prisoners and went off to the gas chamber in place of that woman. This is a characteristic legend. It is not corroborated by the actual history, but still, she actually did go there for others. Which is all because, if she had chosen for herself the path of "a cell off in the woods", if her philosophy were a past-time of the mind or the feeding of an intellectual delight, she would not have wound up in the camp. But Mother Maria wanted to accomplish her philosophy of synthesis in practice, she wanted, that people should see, that the Cross of Christ -- is not simply something of symbolic a meaning, which we wear, but is rather a total commitment and a commitment even to the point of death.

We today have not, dear friends, touched upon for you even an hundredth part of that enormous and mysterious spiritual wealth, which comprised this person Mother Maria. Even if we had five evenings with you, the time would still be inadequate. But I do hope, that whoever of you, knowing little or even totally nothing about this amazing figure, will give it some thought today and attempt to find further materials about her.

With this we conclude the cycle of our lectures. And for me it is very important, that the final effect we have wrought with this portrait, is because, and I repeat this, -- Russian Religious Philosophy was never merely something for one's private chambers or study, detached from life, abstract. All its representatives were brave witnesses to Truth, confessors of the Gospel, they all in one way or another entered into the struggle with life, they all left the imprint, each in their own way, of their views not only on paper, but also in life. They were the saints of our culture, not formally canonised, but actually images, the which our present-day and future generations can take the measure to strive to equal.

To give of oneself to the very limit, the very end -- this is also an evangelic, a Gospel feat. Only by this is the world saved. Decades back, when Mother Maria was young, there was a different slogan: "down with everything!" -- it led to the collapse of spiritual and material values. When people however learn to give of themself, they fulfill the great command of Christ, and this command has to be extended both into material life, and into the life of society -- into everything, even into bread, which the earth gives birth to. Because the earth will cease to beget it then, when man becomes unworthy of it.

And thus, this religious philosophy, set upon the rock-solid foundation of Christian truths, sends out roots into the most existentially vital basics, through which is revealed to us the greatest mystery of life -- the mystery of Divine Love, which created the world, which not only created the world, but in turn draws it unto Itself. And it draws not some in-general sort of anonymous impersonal generations, but the rather -- draws each of us.

Mother Maria had reverence for the mystery of the human person, and in this she shared the convictions of her friends -- Nikolai Berdyaev, Father Sergei Bulgakov, Father Dmitrii Klepinin, Semeon Frank, Georgii Fedotov -- they were all representatives of Christian Personalism, which posits the person to be at those lofty heights, which the Creator Himself set for it.

(I thank you, very much so!).

Translator Comments

And with these final words, "I thank you, very much so" ("Spasibo bol'shoe" rendered literally), Fr. Aleksandr Men' concludes our present text, bidding us "farewell" and as it were taking polite leave from us. Now, however, it is with a chill sense of foreboding that we perceive that in merely one week later to the very day, -- our mortal life will in turn take leave of Fr. Men': he is brutally murdered on 9 September 1990, a crime never since solved nor perpetrator found. His funeral service occurs on 11 September 1990 -- the OS feastday of the "Beheading of St. John the Baptist" [NS 29 August], another in yet one of a series of inauspiciously tremulous 9/11's...

Soon it will be, 25 long years ago that this transpired. For us alive and mature then, at times it seems like just yesterday while at the same time it seems half a long lifetime ago -- one of the anomalies of consciousness peculiar to "existential time". And sobering indeed it is to realise, that perchance many a youthful reader of this book was then not yet even born.

Who was Fr. Aleksandr Men'? It is indeed impossible for this translator to begin to say, nor will he try recounting the details of Fr. Men's life. Such can be found both on the Internet, and in the some several books in English variously in or out of print. Fr. Men' was but one of a myriad number of significant figures immersed in the spiritual currents that survived both the "old regime" and the Soviet era. In our text, he at times alludes to the fact that these few whom he covers are but merely some of the so very many. And Fr. Men' himself is one of the so very many figures in the profound coursings of the currents of Russian religio-philosophic thought. A priest rather well known to the translator once said of Fr. Men': "He was a priest whom every conscientious priest should want to be!" Indeed, Fr. Men' was studiously learned, he wrote and worked extensively, adeptly within and up to the limit allowed by the strictures of the Soviet system. Not immersed in blind ritualism, but rather with a pervasive search for meaning he served as a sort of apostolic outreach to a broad array of Russians, intellectually and spiritually adrift, but serious in their searchings.

Our book, among its merits, provides a glimpse into Russia during its final years of the Soviet era, a sort of "period piece" vista. Our younger readers may be little familiar with the time, in that so much has happened since. It was the "Gorbachev era". It was a time of the magic words "perestroika" (restructuring) and "glasnost'" (openness, transparency). Communist politicians even sheepishly boasted of having been secretly baptised in infancy thru the conniving of their grandmothers. Unthinkable, totally unimaginable but even a few years before, Fr. Men' was able to teach and lecture openly (without the proverbial glance over his shoulder), and even to do so on Russian television! The Church -- that "forbidden fruit" frowned upon and mocked during the long years of the Soviet regime, was no longer viewed in negative and baneful a light; hence the newfound appeal of religion, formerly disdained. Long neglected churches in the following years were rebuilt and re-opened or many built anew. Typical it was for many "believers" now eagerly come to church, piously having lighted a candle and standing during the interminably long church services, to ask the fellow next to them, "What's going on?", and receive no coherent reply (i.e. "I don't know, either"). Since then, great progress, a great religious progress and renewal has occurred. And Fr. Men' is an evidence, that although religion was disabused in the long Soviet era, religion (at great price) in Soviet Russia was never dead.

Our text at several points alludes to the repatriating, the "returning home", of Soviet Russia's "forbidden authors". (Solzhenitsyn was one who managed to do so while still alive). The Lectures comprising our text represent an early moment of this process. The 1990's into the following decade saw a delightful deluge of these authors reprinted in Russia, filtering thru even into the West. This has since somewhat slowed into a trickle. There is so much that could be translated, alas, had one the needed several lifetimes to spare...

The general reader, "by chance" having stumbled onto this book, may be surprised that there is, and long has been, such a thing as -- "Russian Religious Philosophy". The word "philosophy" means, of course, the "love of wisdom", and hence of truth. In practical a sense, philosophy per se is rather moreso an avocation than pecuniary a vocation. Serious philosophy is ill-suited to the pragmatic needs of institutional religion and society, and is often viewed by these as some sort of a "doddering and muddled old uncle". Yet philosophy at depth attempts to deal with the "who/what/why" of existence, to grapple with the "accursed questions" in search for the meaning of life, which slumber beneathe the surface for every person, though also numbed by the narcotic escapes in the noise of modern life. There is a paradoxical and antinomic aspect to philosophy: it can assume a character metaphysical (i.e. "beyond the physical") even in instances where it denies the metaphysical, or religious a character even when it is irreligious (i.e. militant atheism). At its best, philosophy can be a value quest in utmost nobility of soul; at its worst, something trite.

In this regard, Fr. Men's efforts within these religio-philosophic lectures are nowise trite. On the contrary, his outreach is significant, his Russian audience (and subsequent readership) spanning the spectrum from the neophyte on the subject to the learned erudite, each intellectually enriched. Behind our translation is the desire to further expand this spectrum to the present reader, in English a text. And hopefully, to some degree our translation captures the cadence of the spoken lectures, later transcribed; the style flows readily, loquaciously, filled with a vitality of enthusiasm. One might suggest, that there is an aesthetic element to the proper cadence of speech, akin to music, underlying the art of rhetoric, or oratory. And Fr. Men' does so with the soul of an artist: drawn behind the some several figures whom he has chosen to emphasise in the foreground, is a vast panoramic sweep, epic like, of figures and movements that we strain closer to discern. There are, of course, innumerable tomes on the subject of Russian thought, among which our text may prove invaluable a collegiate "secondary source".

Our work may prove of value even to the academic specialist. Fr. Men' supplements his account with details obscured or missing from the rather moreso academic histories of Russian philosophy, whether by Nicholas Lossky, or Fr. Vasily Zenkovsky, or others of more recent vintage -- which often are out of print expensive and difficult to find. One might suggest that Fr. Men' brings his figures to life, clothes them with flesh and makes them human, uniquely so, against the backdrop of their times. But also like both N. Lossky and V. Zenkovsky, Fr. Men' was part of the "process", he was no mere "ivory tower" academic. Nor were those whom he chose to discuss in our text mere "ivory tower" academics. Rather, they were figures of enduring significance, quite learned, of cultural and creative depth, at times immersed in aspects of academia, at times on the fringes of academia, or even in exile from it (e.g. Vl. Solov'ev).

One essential element here regarding Fr. Men', is that of "appropinquity", of proximity or nearness to the situation. Here is one dramatically clear example, amidst some vexation for the translator. In his account on Fr. Pavel Florensky, Fr. Men' notes that the birthday of Fr. Florensky is NS 22 January (which is Fr. Men's own birthday). Some years back, in our translation, we inserted a "trans. note" suggesting that actually the correct day is NS 21 January, a minor error from Fr. Men' conflating the two days. Yet currently on the Internet we find both 22 January and 21 January as the NS day of birth for Fr. Florensky in 1882 -- both indeed based upon the OS day of 9 January. A real dilemma, -- which is correct? What the solution? Well, because of the speed of the 1917 Communist Revolution, the Russian Orthodox Church continues to follow the Old Style (Julian) Calendar, whereas Russian civil life switched over to the New Style (Gregorian) Calendar of the West. A difference of 13 days currently separates the two calendars, which is why the 25 December feast of the Nativity of Christ is celebrated on 7 January in Russia. Currently a 13 day difference, *when* did it increase from a 12 day difference? It was -- on *1 March 1900*! And thus, OS 9 January in 1882 was actually NS 21 January 1882... (This 13 day difference will change to 14 days difference on 1 March 2100, so that the feast of the Nativity in Russia will begin to occur on 8 January in the year 2101). But this is not the only confluence of fate between Fr. Florensky and Fr. Men'. In our text, Fr. Men' mentions how his own father recollected studying under Fr. Florensky in the Soviet late 1920's, this strange spectacle attired in cassock, in riasa. And Fr. Men's own mother points out to him, when he was of yet tender an age, the wife of Fr. Florensky saying, -- "that woman bears heavy a cross!". Nor does the confluence of fate end here. Both men, both priests, meet untimely an end, of violent death -- at the very same age of 55!

Congruent connecting threads of fate with other figures are hinted at variously within our text, refracted through the mind and soul of Fr. Men', situated within the "process" and the "currents".

In the soon 25 years since his death, the legacy of Fr. Men' has somewhat fragmented and become bereft of dynamic vitality. And those of us in our prime then have gotten older, slowed down. Books, both by and about Fr. Men' have appeared, briefly, and in limited circulation. Continuing the legacy in Moscow is the *Aleksandr Men' Fond*, which is headed by Fr. Men's brother, Pavel Men'. The Fond's website, "aleksandrmen.ru/fam/pan.html", contains an extensive wealth of Fr. Men' materials (almost entirely in Russian): vita accounts, photos, videos, textual transcriptions, and suchlike. At "aleksandrmen.ru" are links to brief multi-lingual pages, including English (n.b. link to the impressive Sergei Bessmertny *slaid-fil'm* on Fr. Men's life). Also in English language is "alexandermen.com" providing some links and commentary.

Regarding bibliographic source details, our present English text is a translation of transcribed Fr. Men' lectures (rather confusingly) found on the Fond website, and comprise part of a larger work, published in 1995, under the title "*Mirovaya dukhovnaya kul'tura*" [compiled by Aleksandr Belavin, pub. "Nizhegorodskaya yarmarka", 671 pages]. This work was divided into 5 sections: our "Russian Religious Philosophy" comprises the 4th section.

Independent of this larger text, in subsequent years this 4th section, "Russkaya religioznaya filosofiya", was published separately. In 2003 appeared a paperback Russian version, published by the "Church of holy unmercenaries Cosmas and Damian at Shubine" (where the Fond is situated), Moscow, 280 pages. And in year 2008 appeared hardback Russian version, publisher "Zhizn' s Bogom", Moscow, 416 pages.

Our present text is the 1st English translation. A translator, given free rein, chooses that which most strongly appeals and speaks to him. The Russian religious philosopher, N. A. Berdyaev, holds a dear place in the heart of this translator, and has done so for many a year. Already back in the year 2000 Fr. Men's "Berdyaev Lecture" was translated and posted about upon the Internet. Left in our present text is a relict "Translator Postscriptum" testifying to the joy of finding such kindred spirits...

It was some several years later that the rest of our present text was translated, typed, by 2009 in search of a publisher. And under peculiar an impetus. They say that Fr. Men' had some degree of perspicacity, insights. Some parishioner or other chanced to mention to the translator that there was this "mysterious Russian woman" in the vicinity who knew Fr. Men'. This "mysterious woman", by name Lidia Muranova, lived a mere 30 miles distant. Her modest home, scene of many a long discussion, typically Russian, more resembles the wing of a library than a domicile. Lidia was one of a loose network of those given blessing by Fr. Men' to relocate to America. And at one point, she had worked closely with Fr. Men', co-narrating with him several visually vivid slide-films (to find upon the Fond website, at top left click "*Видеотека*" and then at top right click "*слайд-фильмы*").

Our present text is dedicated to the memory of Fr. Men', and in its own small way seeks to contribute to his legacy. Along with this, it is also a tribute to the devotion of Lidia Muranova to his memory...

Already back in the year 2009 this translation was ready for a publisher, but to the dismay of the naive translator, no willing and viable publisher was found. And so it was wistfully postponed, another task "saved until someday retirement". Retirement occasionally demands its due. Fr. Men' once heralded the return of a repatriated Berdyaev to Russia. Now, in return, several recently just published books by Berdyaev, never previously translated, have paved the path for the publishing of our present Fr. Men' text. There is providential an urgency, indeed, when the impossible becomes possible, at particular a moment...

Lacrimae, the tears of lament, tearing at the very heart, the bittersweet regret over 25 bygone lost years of what might have been, had horrid the tragedy never occurred. Traumatic the moment: September 1990 and Fr. Aleksandr Men'! But this time should be not only a time of regrets, rather the contrary, it should stand as an enduring eulogy of praise. The Greek-based word "*eu-logos*" means to "*speak well*" of someone, to speak words of praise, traditionally by way of an oration (Latin "*oratio*", "*ora pro nobis*"), subtly perchance prayerful for the reposed. And indeed the eulogy of praise bestown by Fr. Alesandr for those others within our present book serves also in eloquent eulogy to him. Had the quirks of Providence not thwarted his plans for a worldly career, had he not hearkened to the subtle stirrings of his inmost soul, and following out the "breath of Spirit leading whence it will", our world, our intellectual questing for the meaning of existence, for truth -- would be all the worse off. Russian religious philosophy, so rich a world, waiting to be explored...

Fr. Men' begins our book speaking of "Predecessors", and now too, he himself has joined, has merged into that profoundly deep and enduring current of Russian religious philosophy. "their memory is from generation unto generation (*pamyat' v rod i rod*")... This book is dedicated, thus,--

In "*25th Year Memory of Legacy to Fr. Aleksandr Men'*"
May the Lord God grant unto Archpriest Aleksandr Men', --
Memory Eternal! Вечная Память!

Fr. Stephen Janos
19 June 2015

frsj Publications

1.) **N. A. BERDYAEV** *"The Philosophy of Inequality"*
1st English Translation of Berdyaev's 1918/1923 book,
"Filosofia neravenstva" (Kl. № 20).
(ISBN-13: 9780996399203 / ISBN-10: 0996399208)
406 pages (6/4/15)

2.) **N. A. BERDYAEV** *"The Spiritual Crisis of the Intelligentsia"*
1st English Translation of Berdyaev's 1910 book,
"Dukhovnyi krizis intelligentsii" (Kl. № 4).
(ISBN-13: 9780996399210 / ISBN-10: 0996399216)
346 pages (6/19/15)

3.) **FR. ALEKSANDR MEN'** *"Russian Religious Philosophy: 1989-1990 Lectures"* -- 1st English Translation
Published in 25th Year Commemoration of Fr Men' Memory
(ISBN-13: 9780996399227 / ISBN-10: 0996399224)
(ISBN-13: 9780996399265 / ISBN-10: 0996399267) *Paperback*
214 pages (7/14/15)

4.) **E. SKOBTSOVA (MOTHER MARIA)**
"The Crucible of Doubts: Khomyakov, Dostoevsky, Solov'ev, In Search of Synthesis -- Four 1929 Works".
(ISBN-13: 9780996399234 / ISBN-10: 0996399232)
166 pages (5/20/16) 1st English Translation

5.) **N. A. BERDYAEV** *"The Fate of Russia"*
1st English Translation of Berdyaev's 1918 book,
"Sud'ba Rossii". (Kl. № 15).
(ISBN-13: 9780996399241 / ISBN-10: 0996399240)
250 pages (10/1/16)

6.) N. A. BERDYAEV *"Aleksei Stepanovich Khomyakov"*
1st English Translation of Berdyaev's 1912 book,
"Алексей Степанович Хомяков" (Kl. № 6).
(ISBN-13: 9780996399258 / ISBN-10: 0996399259)
224 Pages (5/8/17)

*   *   *

Forthcoming Works in Preparation:

N. A. BERDYAEV *"Astride the Abyss of War and Revolutions:*
Articles 1914-1922" -- 1st English Translation of a collection
of 98 articles penned by Berdyaev covering the period of
WWI & Russian 1917 Revolutions

N. A. BERDYAEV *"Sub Specie Aeternitatis:*
Essays Philosophic, Social and Literary (1900-1906)".
1st English Translation of Berdyaev's 1907 book,
"Sub specie aeternitatis. Опыты философские, социальные
и литературные (1900-1906 гг.)". (Kl. № 3).

N. A. BERDYAEV *"The Philosophy of Freedom"*
1st English Translation of Berdyaev's 1911 book,
"Filosofiia svobody" (Kl. № 5).

CPSIA information can be obtained
at www.ICGtesting.com
Printed in the USA
BVHW041300090519
547852BV00016B/128/P